Understanding the Occult

Understanding the Occult

Fragmentation and Repair of the Self

VOLNEY P. GAY

FORTRESS PRESS   Minneapolis

Library of Congress Cataloging-in-Publication Data

Gay, Volney Patrick.
  Understanding the occult.

  Bibliography: p.
  Includes index.
    1. Occultism—History. 2. Occultism—Psychological aspects. 3. Occultism—Religious aspects. I. Title.
  BF1411.G37 1989   133   88–45238
  ISBN 0–8006–2307–X

3447K88   Printed in the United States of America   1–2307

For my colleagues
at the
St. Louis Psychoanalytic Institute

Contents

Preface

THE OCCULT

Occult beliefs and occult wishes permeate human life. News magazines report fantastic stories, with color pictures, of Hollywood stars who describe spirit possession. Famous and unknown people have occult experiences, and noble and ignoble people entertain occult beliefs.

An instance of a noble person entertaining occult beliefs occurs in John Ford's 1939 film about Abraham Lincoln, *Young Mr. Lincoln.* Henry Fonda portrays the young Abraham, before he achieved recognition and well before he assumed the mantle of the Great Emancipator and our greatest president. In many scenes Ford portrays Lincoln in a dual fashion: he is the poor boy made good, who, from his own perspective at that time, has an uncertain future, and he is the president who will hold together an entire nation. From our perspective, he is a man with a certain destiny. When we look back to Lincoln's early life, we wish to find signs that will predict that certain destiny.

The director does not disappoint this wish, but neither does he pander to it. Fonda portrays the young Lincoln as confused, at times, about his own talents and his mission. This Abe Lincoln is no Napoleon in love with himself and his sense of history. Yet neither do we wish to see Lincoln just happen upon a career and from there just happen into the presidency. To rescue Lincoln from seeming either grandiose or bumbling, the film introduces a lovely young woman, Ann Rutledge. Ann sees in Lincoln aspects of greatness that she champions even against his own doubts and hesitations. John Ford frames the relationship between Ann and Lincoln in archetypal motifs, particularly those of the American frontier and nature. In an early scene, Ann and Lincoln walk side by side, a fence between them and us, the viewers. Behind them we see a rushing springtime river. Spring buds frame their heads. Ann encourages Lincoln to think about himself as bound for something great; she does not pretend to know what that is, but her deepest feelings are for this man and his future in the law. Soon, from the viewer's point of view, Ann dies and we see Lincoln walk exactly the same pathway alone. The same river, fence, and trees frame the scene, but this time it is late winter. Ice chokes back the flowing water, the ground is frozen, and no birds sing. Lincoln stoops down and addresses himself to Ann's grave: he must decide whether to stay in the little village of New Salem or go on to Springfield, and, as we know, the monumental tasks that lie beyond Springfield.

This sets the stage for a minor occult event. In this period of doubt, having lost the woman who had helped him funnel his ambitions, Lincoln reverts for a moment to magical thinking. He says to Ann that he will stand a stick up and let it fall; if it falls toward the little town he will stay there, but if it falls toward her he will interpret that to mean it points toward the law and Springfield. Lincoln stands the stick up, lets it fall, and reports to Ann that it fell toward her; that is, toward the law and his destiny.

If John Ford had stopped the scene at this point, it would have comprised a typical instance of occult events: a person seeks an extraordinary sign about events that cannot be known, in this case, the future. News magazine accounts of occult events and most champions of the occult would require us to end the story here, for it leaves the entire event mysterious. It lets us imagine that, yes, there were divine forces at play in selecting the young man from Illinois to lead this nation, and that these forces had already arranged his great mission. The occult mood, begun when Lincoln addressed the grave of his absent loved one, precisely the one who had helped him maintain a sense of his greatness, would be perpetuated.[1]

Yet this solution would detract from Lincoln's great humanness. It would cast him in the light of Napoleon or even Hitler: leaders who felt themselves absolutely justified by divine powers and therefore not beholden to mere mortals. This would not fit the Lincoln John Ford wished to portray; nor would it match the wonderful self-awareness and wit we associate with Lincoln. Therefore, Ford has the young man ponder the stick and say to Ann that perhaps he had pushed it a little that way.

I am a professor of religious studies and psychiatry. For a long time I have tried to puzzle out the occult mood. Examined under the light of scientific procedure, occult moments appear irrational, for they are always contrary to what science tells us is true. Science says, for example, that human beings cannot receive thoughts transmitted by persons long dead, nor can dreams foretell the future, nor can random events, like a stick falling one way or another, predict human actions. Yet, on examining my own experience, that of my patients, and that of many other persons who report similar events, I recognize that this psychiatric response is not adequate, for it focuses on "beliefs" as if these were basic elements in a person's life. But as a psychoanalyst and an adult human being, I realize that beliefs are not always basic elements in one's life. Few people deduce their beliefs any more than they deduce which language they speak or to which country they pledge their allegiance. On the contrary, I wish to show that the occult mood and occult beliefs occur *in response* to events in one's life. In other words, occult beliefs are not deduced opinions about one's world. Rather, occult beliefs are the products of previous experiences; they are the effects of earlier causes; they are the visible outcomes of invisible processes.

FRAGMENTATION AND REPAIR
OF THE SELF

In this book I offer a causal explanation for occult beliefs. I try to show what events in a person's life typically precede the occult moment, and why the occult moment is so important to that person's sense of herself or himself. I do not attempt to judge the truth of occult beliefs; I try to show when they arise and what work they perform.

To anticipate the following book, consider, again, young Mr. Lincoln at Ann's grave. Through her death he has lost a person who provided him a loving sense of his future when he could not do that for himself. In the face of that loss he reverted to magic, hoping to find personal powers to comfort him and guide him away from grandiosity and toward his proper place. At the same time, we, the film viewers, share Lincoln's sense of urgency, for we also wish to have settled this man's great destiny. This short scene illustrates the three ingredients that make up the occult mood. First, an intense relationship is formed, in which one person "holds" another person together. This relationship is typically one in which a mothering figure nurtures the other just as Ann nurtured Lincoln. Second, that relationship is severed, through death or through a falling-out. Because one has lost the very person who protected one against disorganization, one is distraught, just as Lincoln was distraught by Ann's death. In severe cases this psychological disorganization is termed fragmentation of the self. Third, the occult event occurs in response to that disorganization. The occult event repairs, momentarily, the fragmented self. In this book I examine these ingredients in detail and attempt to show how they appear again and again in the lives of the great and the unknown.

Acknowledgments

Researching and writing this book was aided through the office of the Dean of the Vanderbilt Graduate School (Professor Russell G. Hamilton), the Vanderbilt University Research Council, the Dean of the College of Arts and Science (Professor Jacque Voegeli), and the Chair of Religious Studies (Professor Daniel Patte). I thank them all.

Passages from *Memories, Dreams, Reflections* by C. G. Jung, edited by Aniela Jaffe, translated by Richard and Clara Winston, copyright © by Random House, Inc., in 1961, 1962, 1963. Reprinted by permission of Pantheon Books, a Division of Random House, Inc.

Portions of my article, "Augustine: The Reader as Selfobject," in the *Journal for the Scientific Study of Religion,* March, 1986.

Passages from *The Life and Work of Sigmund Freud,* Vols. I, II, III by Ernest Jones. Copyright © by Ernest Jones in 1953, 1955, 1957.

Poem, "Constancy in Change," by J. W. Goethe, translated by J. F. Nim. In *Goethe: Selected Poems,* edited by C. Middleton. Copyright © by Shurhkamp/Insel Publishers.

Introduction
Three Stories of the Occult

It may be helpful to tell, briefly, three stories about occult events. The first two occurred to people I knew, at least indirectly. The third is from the life of Sir Arthur Conan Doyle, author of the Sherlock Holmes mysteries. First, I recount the stories. Then, I discuss why they are worthy of attention. Last, I summarize this book.

EVIL FORCES INVADE A
WEST COAST CITY

A long time ago, when I was much younger and living in a small city on the west coast, evil forces attacked my great-aunt and her son, my cousin. At least that is what I learned by listening intently as the grownups discussed the case. My cousin, then in his early twenties, had left our little city to find his fortune in a much larger city a thousand miles away. There, in California, he took up with a woman older than himself who claimed to be both an artist and a witch. During the day she painted and sculpted; during the night she invoked evil spirits. She became well-known in both fields. A few months after he had fallen under this woman's spell, my cousin began to have second thoughts about the wisdom of his choice. For one thing, she would fly into intense rages when she suspected that he had found any other woman attractive. For another, she demanded more and more assurance of his absolute devotion to her. My cousin felt less and less in love. He began to call my aunt long distance. In these telephone consultations he tried to figure out how he could break free of his witch-girlfriend. My aunt recounted these phone calls to the grownups assembled in her living room. She described my cousin's struggles to rid himself of his artistic witch-girlfriend. Apparently the artistic witch would have none of it. She wanted my cousin to remain under her spell. She pursued him everywhere he went, bothered his friends, and made him miserable.

Finally, in desperation, my cousin beseeched his mother. She understood instantly that her son was caught in this woman's spell. Drawing upon years of occult reading, and with some consultation with other devotees of these arts, my aunt made a final diagnosis: her son was bewitched. She called him back to our little city.

He returned home, exhausted yet also, it seemed to me, thrilled by the occult adventure he had been through. His mother and her colleagues were relieved to have retrieved him from the clutches of witchcraft. But within a few days my cousin began to feel morose and sleepless. He had also lost some of his things in the move home. His mother and her colleagues explained what had happened. First, my cousin had been seduced by this artist's black magic. Second, she needed him for her dark practices. There was some hint that these included certain sexual acts that could not be described within the hearing of a young boy. Third, this witch had followed my cousin to his hometown using some complicated kind of soul travel. Other people said that the spate of bad luck that had surrounded my cousin probably was due to the influence of evil forces who associated themselves with the witch-artist.

In fact, the adults around me began to attribute all of my cousin's problems, his sleeplessness, the lost articles, and his "nervousness" to the work of this witch. No odd sound, no ache or pain or irritability, no small coincidences appeared in my great-aunt's or cousin's life that were not ascribed to the dark influence of this witch-artist. And, on the other side, when my cousin's luck turned better, or he felt more like his old self, these improvements were attributed to the positive effect of my aunt's spiritual interventions.

All the members of my cousin's immediate family joined my aunt in her efforts to protect her son. They organized vigils through the evening. Usually one of the adult men volunteered to guard my aunt's house through the night. Somebody felt that it would be a good idea to be armed during these vigils, and so each of my numerous uncles and older male cousins took his turn of armed duty. The women made a pot of strong coffee, and each man did his best to protect my aunt's house by peering out into the night, his hand never too far away from a loaded revolver.

Luckily, it was midsummer, and the dark lasted only seven or so hours. When daylight broke the vigil was over and everyone felt relieved that another night had passed without catastrophe. Of course, there was a host of minor incidents to report: a dog had barked exactly at midnight; a candle flame had flickered for no apparent reason; a cold wind, whose origin was impossible to explain, had come round the sentry's shoulders and made him shudder. Some of the guards described a strange light that washed across the trees and then disappeared.

Even those of us on the periphery of the family recognized how dramatic these nocturnal defenses were. None of us, at least none of the children, were bothered by the stories we heard about the strange doings in my aunt's house that summer. On the contrary, having been raised on science fiction, ghost stories, and fairy tales, the maneuvers my aunt put into place seemed reasonable. At least they seemed appropriate, given our education via movies and television. When my aunt chanted prayers, both Christian and Buddhist, and when she circled the house with lit candles, we all felt that these were suitable efforts to ward off evil spirits.

We had seen similar provisions made against evil, and we could affirm the need to wear a cross when confronted by wolfmen, vampires, and similar creatures who loved the dark. We knew that Count Dracula cast no reflection in mirrors. We also knew that these were stories, make-believe and probably not true—in the ordinary sense of that term. We did not know, or could not perceive, how much anguish my cousin actually suffered. We saw the elaborate plans and spiritual defense put into place as exciting, if eccentric, summer activity.

Looking back, I see that my cousin was tremendously upset. He was suffering something that disordered his life and frightened him as much as if his doctor had told him he had cancer. My cousin improved slowly. At the end of the summer he felt better and got out of bed more and more. And in the middle of fall he picked himself up and left his mother's house again. He found a job in the midwest and left our little city.

Defining the Occult

The dictionary tells us that the term *the occult* comes from the Latin word *occulere*, which means "to hide." In its earliest English usage *occult* referred to things hidden from view or concealed from sight; an underground river that connects two bodies of water is occult. A more poetic usage appears in astronomy: occult refers there to the "concealment of one heavenly body by another passing between it and the observer, as of a star or planet by the moon." As early as the sixteenth century *occult* also meant privy or secret; that which should be divulged only to the initiates. At the same time *occult* connoted those things beyond ordinary understanding. The *Oxford English Dictionary (OED)* quotes a text from 1665, "Some secret Art of the Soul, which to us is utterly occult, and without the ken of our Intellects."[1]

Within the same epoch, the middle of the seventeenth century, occult beliefs and practices were ascribed to persons who claimed the ability to ascertain these secrets and to solve these mysteries through the operation of what the *OED* terms "reputed sciences," like astrology, alchemy, theosophy, and the like. To this list of ancient occult beliefs we may add contemporary "reputed sciences": parapsychology, the study of UFOs, spiritism, astral projection, the study of Atlantis, and many others.

These definitions of the term *occult* capture an essential feature of occult beliefs that persists into our time.[2] This is that occult beliefs and practices have the trappings or the appearance of science. Occult believers and proponents of occult teachings always claim that their studies are a form of science and that under the proper conditions their occult beliefs can be validated in the same way that other scientific claims are validated.

This general characteristic of occult beliefs gives them a special attraction to persons who wish to bridge the gap that seems to separate traditional religion from traditional science. For occult claims are about topics that traditional religious authorities consider to be matters of faith understood as inexplicable by ordinary means, for example, life after death. By definition, matters of faith do not require and are not open to validation by ordinary scientific means. Occultists, in contrast, always seek to find ways to substantiate their claims using the scientific equipment available to them. In the Middle Ages this equipment was primarily made up of chemical apparatus used to study minerals and other substances. We find, therefore, that the chief occult practice of the period was alchemy, as it was in China, India, Greece, and other cultures that operated at levels of technology similar to those of medieval Europe.

As soon as new technological procedures emerged, occultists added them to their repertoire and pressed them into the task of validating occult beliefs. In the seventeenth and eighteenth centuries, for example, occult philosophers explained their spiritualist beliefs using the terms and machinery of the newly discovered electrical apparatus. In the nineteenth century, the newly discovered processes of photography and telegraphy were added to the occult workshop: occult doctrines about mental telepathy, for example, are easily redescribed as a kind of spiritual telegraphy using spiritual substances to transmit messages from one electrical device, a brain, to another. In our century parapsychologists have used computers to validate their statistical claims about processes like ESP (extrasensory perception) whose existence can be established only if one can rule out chance occurrences. Therefore, champions of ESP must show that, statistically speaking, it is highly unlikely that an individual could simply guess a string of correct answers about materials hidden from view.

If one rules out mere chance as the explanation for correct guesses about cards that are hidden, that are "occult," one can claim that there must be some unknown ability, namely, ESP, that accounts for such success. In a similar way, many contemporary occult treatises use concepts from modern physical theory, especially quantum mechanics, that seem to contradict the commonsense world of ordinary life. Since some quantum theories seem to contradict the rules of space, time, and causality that have always stymied occult research, quantum concepts appear ready-made for the task of justifying occult beliefs.

As we will see throughout this book, occult believers always wish to rule out chance as an explanation for mysterious connections between, say, one's feeling of dread and the subsequent appearance of an earthquake. The idea that such events might be connected to one another solely by chance disturbs occult believers. It requires them to give up the hope that there is a hidden link that connects their inner world of profound wishes with the external world. To refer back to our original definition of the occult, we can say that occult believers wish to find the hidden underground river that connects events in their mental world, their internal world of desires, wishes, and fears, with the external world, the world of separation from loved ones, of loss, and of death. This profound wish and need to find these hidden links between one's inner life and the outer world draws people to the occult.

These dictionary definitions of the term *occult* parallel the way I use the term in this book. I use the term to refer to all those beliefs and practices in which people claim an extraordinary capacity to know what they cannot know.[3] If someone predicts accurately the name of the winner of the Kentucky Derby ten years into the future, for example, we would consider that an instance of occult knowledge. If the same person predicts the first full moon in December, ten years from now, we would not consider that an instance of occult knowledge because everyone can look up such information. Such knowledge is not hidden, impossible, and unavailable to ordinary means of gathering accurate information.

A VISIT FROM A
HEAVENLY HOST

I forgot that summer of spiritual contests, went to school, graduated, married, and taught religion and psychology in Canada. My aunt's story returned to me when I heard another occult story from a male graduate student. While I did not know him well, he wanted to tell somebody about his experience, and my training in psychoanalysis and religious studies appealed to him. He was obviously distraught and burst into long sobs as he recounted his story. On the surface, his story seemed unlike my cousin's. But on reflection, it struck me that there were common themes linking the two together. First, though, his story needs to be told.

He had been raised in an intensely religious family in a small city in northern Ontario. His family's church was very proud of its rigorous moral standards. In a small town noted for its prudent and conservative citizenry, my student's church stood out as by far the most demanding upon its members. Naturally, movies and dancing were forbidden, and soda pop, popular music, contemporary clothing, and dating were held to be the work of the devil. Within this small church my student's parents played a role second only to the preacher's in importance. His parents, especially his father, could always be relied upon to contribute more than a fair share of their meager income to the church.

In addition, his father was renowned for the wrath that he loosed upon church members who had erred, especially upon younger members who seemed capable of sexual sins. If pride were not a sin, one could say that my student's father was intensely proud of his labor on behalf of the church and of his role as champion of its moral teachings. My student, who was the youngest of a large family, felt called upon to reflect his father's public teachings. He dedicated himself to that task. No child won more points in Sunday school, knew more Bible verses, or prayed more fervently for moral direction than did my student. When it came time for him to make a public declaration of his relationship to Jesus, my student did his best to shoulder the great task that lay ahead of him: to dedicate himself to spiritual perfection. His denomination was the purest in the town; his church was the purest of all the churches in the denomination; and his father was the purest man—next to the preacher—in the church. My student would be like a lamp to the other children in the church, and to those who wallowed in sin outside the church community he would appear untouchable and uncriticizable.

When he chose a wife from among the young women who attended his family's church, the young man dedicated himself to fulfilling his new role as husband and head of a new family. Because he was the last child to leave her house, his mother suffered a great deal, for now the baby of the family had left her. To decrease her pain and provide her the company she wanted, my student offered to build his house next to his parents' house. That way, grandma and grandpa would be able to see their youngest grandchildren, and my student's young wife would have the guidance of an older, experienced woman to help raise the many children for which everyone wished. In addition, my student's wife would not be alone for the four- or five-week stretches of time during which her husband did missionary work in the far north. At least twice a year my student volunteered a month of labor to help a group of Indians repair their homes. Driving there, working, and returning required some thirty or more days of hard labor. These sacrifices were expected of all church members, and that my student did more than the average only reflected the intensity of his fervor.

Some years passed in this way. My student worked at menial jobs, raised a family, worked for his church, and performed his missionary duties with zeal. He had never been happier. This all changed when he returned home from a missionary trip a day earlier than planned. Wanting to surprise his wife, he drove home without phoning and entered his house late in the evening. He heard sounds in his bedroom. Looking in, he saw his father struggling into his overalls. His naked wife shrieked and then cowered in the bed, her long hair covering her chest. The older man said nothing. He finished dressing, stood up, and, looking straight ahead, left the little house. My student was dumbfounded. He could not make his voice heard. He came close to fainting. Finally, his wife spoke. Her affair with her father-in-law had begun years earlier, when my student was away on his trips to the Indian village. My student's wife said there was some question as to the paternity of the children. Probably they were fathered by her husband, but one or two of them might be children of her father-in-law.

After this initial outburst and confession that evening she said nothing. Indeed, no one said anything to anyone after that moment of discovery. Work, family prayer, church attendance, and the like continued as if nothing had occurred. My student described his deep psychological torment and sudden sense of abandonment. He felt that he could not talk to his preacher, for that would shame his father. In the same way, he could not talk to his mother for the whole story would break her heart. When my student attempted to pray for guidance, he found that prayer failed to help him as well.

Finally, after many weeks of immense confusion, my student shuddered at the thought of staying with his wife and living next door to his father. He abandoned his family. He headed south to a large city in Ontario near the American border. Almost by accident, he enrolled in night courses in a public university. There he rekindled an old enthusiasm for reading. Used to hard work, he applied himself wholeheartedly to this new task. The fury with which he approached it also helped him deal with the immense loneliness he suffered. He could not tolerate being in his father's presence, yet he missed his own children desperately. In the process of getting a divorce he had seen his children not more than once a month. No one in his town knew why he left so suddenly and abandoned his beautiful family. His name was vilified, and the many intense friendships he had formed over a lifetime of church membership disappeared when his immoral actions became public.

He advanced quickly in night school, earned a bachelor's degree in twenty months, and entered graduate school. His instructors, and even the deans, recognized his talents and encouraged him with scholarships and awards that made it possible for him to concentrate on his academic work. Yet during the weekends, especially on Sundays, he found himself on the verge of suicidal depression. His friends were with their own families; the libraries were closed; and he found the idea of church impossible to contemplate. Yet neither could he break his lifelong habit of devoting Sunday to spiritual labor of some sort. He tried fulfilling that demand by schoolwork. But that did not always work.

Eventually he discovered alcohol, a substance that was entirely new to him. When Sunday rolled around again and he felt himself sliding once more into depression, he drank and continued to drink until he no longer felt anything. Drinking got him through his Sunday ordeal, and by Monday he could return to his beloved school, meet his friends, and overcome his depression. He felt that he could tell no one about his drinking.

As he entered his second year of graduate study, an associate dean of the graduate department befriended him. The dean, a man some twenty years older than my student, admired the younger man's intensity and seemingly endless love of learning. Initially, the younger man felt completely unworthy of any attention from a man as illustrious as the dean. In fact, he often blushed when he mentioned the older man's compliments. So while my student labored to write the best paper possible and strove mightily to earn the highest marks, he was surprised when he did well, and he choked with gratitude when he was rewarded. After an initial phase of awkwardness and embarrassment on my student's part, the two men became friends as well as colleagues. As this transformation occurred, the younger man no longer felt the need to drink on weekends. Often he spent Sundays with the dean and the dean's wife, staying with them in their cottage on a nearby lake. He treasured these get-togethers and often organized his entire week around them: Sunday became the highlight of his week, not its termination. On those Sundays when he was alone, not visiting the dean and the dean's wife, my student felt at peace and not depressed.

Next to the early years of his marriage, these months were the happiest moments of my student's life. He had discovered that he had an excellent mind and that his ability to work hard made it seem that he would have a life far beyond the narrow existence he had envisioned while living in the north in his little town. At the same time, he came to take for granted that his relationship with the dean was something he had earned and could rely upon.

He was stunned, therefore, when the dean mentioned that he had decided to take a job in one of the western provinces. The new job paid a lot more money than his current job, and his wife was from that part of Canada too. So, there was really no reason not to take this opportunity and leave for the far western province. The older man had been friendly to the young man and suggested that if he were ever in that part of the country, some four thousand miles away, he should drop by. The dean added, as an afterthought, that during the summer he and his wife would be in Europe, so such a reunion would have to occur, if ever, the following year. With that and a handshake, he left.

The younger man also took his leave and made his way home. Although he felt dizzy and sick to his stomach, he wanted a drink. The couple of beers he had in his apartment were not enough, and on Sunday evening in Ontario he could not buy a drink. At the same time he began thinking again about suicide. The old feelings of worthlessness and an odd mix of rage and sadness set in. He slept poorly that night. The next morning, just as he awakened and stumbled into his living room, he had a vision.

The vision was that of an old, white-bearded man who seemed to hover somewhere just beyond the apartment walls. The old man spoke in a foreign language, but my student could understand it through some miracle of translation. The white-headed old man said that he lived in heaven, a place he then described as much like earth but far more beautiful, with peace abounding. He also made it clear that he, the heavenly resident, understood how things could get so bad on earth that some people might choose to end their lives rather than continue to suffer. This meant that suicide was not, in fact, a sin, as some churches taught, and that people who committed suicide were free to join him in heaven. This vision lasted some eight or ten minutes and then faded away.

During his talk with the heavenly visitor, my student felt immensely relieved. The old man's declarations about heaven were especially comforting, for it meant that the worst thought he had ever considered, killing himself, did not remove him from the rolls of those who had earned a place in heaven. Following his vision, the young man felt much less unhappy. As he told me the story, he did not doubt that he had seen and heard the heavenly visitor, yet he also felt uneasy.

When he came to see me, a few days had passed, and he felt that the entire experience was mysterious. If it had occurred while he was still a member of his father's church, he would have known what it meant and how to respond to it. But now, he had a college education behind him, and he had rejected his father's church and its explanations of such events. The vision seemed perplexing. Did it mean he was crazy? Was this a blessing, as he would have considered it at one time, or was it a symptom of a mental breakdown? Should he go home and submit himself to his father's church? Should he take himself to a mental hospital? Both options seemed terrible to him. Fortunately, he also had access to an excellent student health facility and there received competent help.

CONAN DOYLE AND THE OCCULT

We have heard two stories about occult experiences that occurred to ordinary people: one group in the Pacific northwest; the other in a city in Canada. It might seem that such events can occur only in such circumstances and not to persons of high education and social achievements, but this is not true. Our third account is of Sir Arthur Conan Doyle, the great English novelist.

Conan Doyle, the creator of Sherlock Holmes, was a man of uncommon achievements and uncommon intellect. Trained as a physician, he fabricated two immortal characters, Dr. Watson and the uncanny Holmes. The latter gentleman entrances us most. To the most horrible crimes, with the least obvious clues, done under the most obscure circumstances, Holmes brings a rigorous sense of scientific thinking. The stranger the crime, the more interesting to our hero and the more tightly knit his solution. Speaking for commoners like ourselves, Dr. Watson explains that one cannot understand why a redheaded man is paid to copy out the *Encyclopedia Britannica*. To this puzzle Holmes brings a brilliant scientific solution. In this case, it distracted the red-headed man from a robbery occurring right under his nose.

Yet Conan Doyle himself presents a mystery that even the great detective Holmes could not solve. The genius who created Sherlock Holmes was convinced that dead people spoke to him, in public and in private, that certain mediums could make spirits take on earthly appearance, and that one could photograph fairies and similar miniature folk.

Conan Doyle had begun collecting descriptions of occult happenings early in his life. It was only in his middle age that he believed them. A striking instance is his support of the validity of "spirit photography." For a small cost a photographer would take one's picture and, through certain processes, reveal the normally invisible spirits who hovered around one.

In 1922, Conan Doyle published *The Coming of the Fairies.* He reproduced photographs of little dancing figures cavorting in front of a surprised child. Critics noted that the fairies resembled those seen in a well-known advertisement and that the photographs were composed of two distinct pictures. Conan Doyle persisted in his assertions. He wrote six more works defending spiritualism and advancing its aims.

He returned to the theme of fairy photography four years later when he published, in 1926, his two-volume *The History of Spiritualism.* There Conan Doyle describes how the Psychological Society lined its walls with more than three hundred "chosen spirit photographs taken by Boursnell."[4] Spirit photographs, similar to photographs of fairies, were renditions of an ordinary mortal and the spirits who surrounded him. The spirit photographer would sit you down, adjust the camera, snap your picture, and then later show you a photograph that showed you sitting there *plus* the images of illustrious spirits who, it appeared, hovered around you. Young artists, for example, might discover that the spirits of Michelangelo and Leonardo da Vinci hovered near them, helping them. Young soldiers might discover that the spirits of Napoleon, Julius Caesar, and other great generals stood near them, supporting them with real but invisible good will. Spirit photography vindicated spiritualists who believed that the dead on the Other Side might communicate with those remaining yet on This Side. Spirit photography promised, then, to demonstrate scientifically the validity of these deep yearnings for contact with departed loved ones and for guidance from the illustrious names of the past, both recent and distant. If one could photograph spirits, surely one might hope to talk with them as well.

Conan Doyle considered the evidence for and against such photographs and concluded: "Whatever the eventual explanation, the only hypothesis which at present covers the facts is that of a wise invisible

Intelligence, presiding over the operation and working in his fashion."[5] Skeptics will note how easy it is to fake such photographs. With the advent of more sophisticated equipment and foolproof tests for chicanery, the whole enterprise of spirit photography dried up.[6]

Like the great storyteller that he was, Conan Doyle wrote accounts of voice mediums, telepathy, and other events that are fascinating and well-written. Yet they are unbelievable. They exemplify the mystery I described above: How could the creator of Sherlock Holmes reject every rationalist principle for which the great detective stood? How would the sleuth of Baker Street react to spiritualist claims that, for example, it was a disembodied hand that plunged the knife into the victim's heart?

Physical Mediums

To illustrate the depth of Conan Doyle's convictions, I summarize his account of the ectoplasmic larynx. The story unfolds midst his description of "Physical Mediums." These are men and women who claim that they can make spiritual entities materialize, at least in the deepest trance during a "sitting." A traditional feature of such sittings is the production of spirit voices, which convey all manner of information, including detailed renditions of existence Across the Pale, that is, on the Other Side. One can well imagine the excitement of a recently widowed woman, for example, who hears her husband's voice telling her that he is safe and secure in a world much like her own. Aside from those cases where the medium's voice provides the vehicle for the spirits, the problem arises of accounting for the spirits' ability to speak. With this problem in mind, Conan Doyle advises us that the spirits most likely fashion a human larynx out of ectoplasm. With this instrument they can respond to the feverish questions from the astounded members of the séance.

What is this ecotoplasm? Spiritualists claim that it is the visible manifestation of the spirits as they emerge from the body or mouth of the medium. Descriptions vary, but Conan Doyle says it is a milky white, sticky substance, cloudy in its form, that takes shape as the medium enters deeper into the trance. As with other such manifestations, the quality of the event depends upon the audience. While this is curious physiology, it is reasonable psychology. Conan Doyle quotes an article in *The Spiritualist:* "Worldly and suspicious people get the feebler manifestations; the spirits then have often a pale ghastly [sic] look, as usual when the power is weak."[7] In other words, skeptics poison the whole tone of intimate relationships between sitters, spirits, and medium.

The ectoplasm is entirely flexible and under the guidance of the spirits. They can fashion from it whatever they wish (rather like an infinitely talented sculptor who need only think the object's shape for it to appear). By definition, then, spirits could easily fashion a human larynx. With that in hand they could then produce human language.

This explanation raises a great many problems. It seems plausible to suppose that sounds might be produced by a synthetic larynx. But this synthetic organ would require synthetic lungs, synthetic nerves, and a synthetic brain to direct the flow of air, not to mention form articulate letters. Spiritualists respond that the spirits themselves provide these latter capacities. Yet if spirits can manage all that, why bother to fashion an ectoplasmic portion of the apparatus? Conan Doyle adds that this theory has been attested to by the spirits themselves and so, we assume, has increased veracity.

How can numerous charlatans fool persons as intelligent and educated as Conan Doyle? In contrast to Conan Doyle, the great Houdini, who became a close friend to Conan Doyle and his second wife, mounted a personal campaign to debunk what he felt were false and harmful spiritualist claims.

Charles Higham reports that Houdini forced himself to attend a séance with Jean Doyle and Sir Arthur where Jean, acting as the medium, wrote out messages from Houdini's dead mother. Houdini never doubted the Doyles's immense sincerity and goodwill. Yet he noted to himself that the well-formed English messages derived from Jean's automatic writings could not be valid since "my sainted Mother could not write English and spoke broken English."[8] Houdini waited a decent length of time before he contradicted Sir Arthur, who by that time was routinely denounced by the liberal press for his forays into Spiritualism.

THE MYSTERY OF OCCULT BELIEF: THREE CLUES

No one of sound mind accused Conan Doyle of fraud or even evangelism for the Spiritualist's cause. Yet most people were mystified by the depth of his devotion to such outlandish claims. Certainly part of that devotion stemmed from his ferocious capacity to declare his beliefs and follow through in the face of the sternest criticisms. He championed the rights of the unjustly accused, even when he found them personally reprehensible.

The mystery lies in the unspoken needs that could have driven him to put aside his critical intelligence and take up such implausible beliefs.

How could so fine a mind submit itself to the predictable abuse from both the charlatans who perpetrated the séances, and the numerous skeptics who had no difficulty in piercing the pretentious veils that surround occult claims? Although he was immensely respected as the author of Sherlock Holmes, Conan Doyle was not spared numerous rebuttals and denunciations by skeptics of all persuasions. Yet each of us, at some time, has felt the need to believe in the occult. The mystery is why we, too, need such beliefs, and when do they appear so attractive.

This book attempts to solve this central mystery. Let us reflect upon the three accounts given above of occult events. What pattern emerges from them? I believe that we can find three clues to the mystery of occult belief.

The first clue is the emotional intensity with which Conan Doyle and others seek out occult knowledge. As a rough gauge of that emotion, we note the power that we would need to exert in an ordinary debate with Conan Doyle—not to mention Sherlock Holmes—if we wished to convince him of the existence, say, of supernatural agents responsible for a crime. Who of us would dare? Yet Conan Doyle effectively did the same thing to himself. It follows that the emotional issues that the occult addresses are equal in power to, or even stronger than, the rational abilities of the occult devotee. What emotional needs or yearnings could yield such power?

These considerations give form to our first clue. Our clue is that the factors impelling occult belief and underlying occult experience are based on profound and archaic feelings. These feelings must precede and underlie the feelings and intellectual skills that develop over time as an infant matures into a child and as a child matures into an adult.

Our second clue to the mystery of occult belief appears in Conan Doyle's account of ectoplasm. He quotes at length from a former skeptic, a Mr. E. A. Brackett. Mr. Brackett had begun as a skeptic, but he changed his attitude toward the occult and then saw new realities:

> The key that unlocks the glories of another life is pure affection, simple and confiding as that which prompts the child to throw its arms around its mother's neck. To those who pride themselves upon their intellectual attainments, this may seem to be a surrender of the exercise of what they call the higher faculties. So far from this being the case, I can truly say that until I adopted this course, sincerely and without reservation, I learned nothing about these things. Instead of clouding my reason and judgment, it opened my mind to a clearer and more intelligent perception of what was passing before me. That spirit of gentleness, of loving kindness, which more than anything else crowns with eternal beauty the teachings of the Christ, should find its full expression in our association with these beings.[9]

Our second clue is the immense feeling of loving, maternal affection so well illustrated in this quotation. Mr. Brackett describes a sense of freedom from rational, skeptical aloofness. When he surrendered these adult intellectual modes, he could rush back into his mother's arms. The second clue then suggests that occult experience replicates an aspect of the child's positive experience of being mothered, of being held and loved with "pure affection." We recall that my cousin felt the need to return to his mother for support against the "bad" witch-mother his girlfriend seemed to be. In a similar way, my student saw his vision after he had felt abandoned by the loving, kindly, and idealized dean who seemed unaware of how much the young man had come to depend upon their relationship. The "mothering" Mr. Brackett describes might better be described as "parenting," since the dean was not in fact my student's mother.

The third clue to the mystery of occult beliefs comes from a consideration of the occult mood. The occult is the hidden. The term itself comes from the Latin, meaning to shut off or to close. The occult, then, is something shut off, something hidden from ordinary sight and, by extension, ordinary reasoning. The occult mood is a complex feeling anyone can enter, given the proper circumstances. It is strikingly similar to homesickness and nostalgia in the peculiar force and suddenness with which it can overcome us.

That mood is easy to describe, but hard to explain. No matter how reasonable one is in ordinary circumstances, finding oneself alone, on an old highway, late at night, in a strange country, with the wind picking up, makes for a different mood. If we add to this scene that one has just returned from a funeral of a friend our age who died suddenly of an inexplicable and unseen disease—and we are driving his car—our mood shifts even further. Who knows what dangers lurk in such circumstances?

Expert storytellers and film directors employ their art to effect precisely such shifts in mood. The dreamlike stupor that Hitchcock's movies can induce, for example, is a vital part of their power. When Norman Bates prepares to strike again, we seem to feel the ineluctable force of his impulses. At the same time, Hitchcock preys on our childhood fears of the dark and especially the basement when he has the hero drawn, almost against his better judgment, into the rooms below, where he sees the ultimate horror.

In daylight, after a good sleep and adequate breakfast, such possibilities evaporate like fog on a fall morning. Then most of us disdain such beliefs or assign them quickly to the strain of the moment, since we are reasonable and mature adults. But is it just the change in scenery that makes the difference to us? If so, we are confessing that our moods are produced by our environment, and not by ourselves.

Our third clue to the mystery of occult experience is the wish implied in this claim. That wish is that we want our moods to be the products of events *outside* ourselves, rather than the products of events *inside* ourselves. The third clue, then, is that occult events occur when we have internal experiences that we want to experience as if they were due to external causes.

To put this another way, when my cousin fled home to his mother, and when my student had his vision, we must assume that those external events occurred as projections of internal processes taking place within the personalities of both young men.

There must be something "inside" us that intervenes between our experience of a mood, say, the blues, and the external world. For some people a rainy afternoon is a fine time for a cup of tea, music, and reading. For other people it is a supposed cause of depression and loneliness. Like nostalgia, the occult mood is called forth by certain events that elicit within us memories and fantasies tied to deep and often unconscious feelings. Those are the ultimate source of our mood. They are tied, with numerous threads and hidden passages, to our deepest hopes.

What do these three clues add up to? First, occult experience is far more powerful than mere reason. It seems to proceed from levels of human experience preceding the acquisition of the rational thought that governs supposedly adult behavior. Second, occult experience is tied to very early experience of surrender to a mothering person. That sense of surrender is pleasing, or can be pleasing. It can also be frightening, because it may be tied to another fear that one can never retreat from the infinite mother's embrace. Third, occult experience is tied to a deep sense of oneself, a "self-state." In this self-state an internal process is experienced as if it were an external event.

SUMMARY:
THE BOOK IN BRIEF

I have recounted three stories. The first two are about ordinary people; the third is about Conan Doyle's adamant belief in occult teachings. While the fame of the participants varies, I suggest that the pattern underlying these accounts does not. In this book I intend to examine these kinds of experience. I wish to see if we can discover in them a pattern of events that leads up to the occult moment. This pattern of loss followed by anxiety followed by an occult moment is most evident in the first two stories about the witch and the heavenly visitor. It is not as clear in the accounts of Conan Doyle's occult beliefs and actions. Ideally, we should be able to locate an exact sequence of loss and anxiety in Conan Doyle's life that parallels those we saw in the first two stories. I have not been able to locate that pattern. Yet I included these accounts of Conan Doyle because I wish to indicate that occult experience and occult beliefs are not signs of a weak personality. The mystery of why Conan Doyle became so adamant in his championing of occult claims remains unsolved.

I do not intend to judge the truth of these three accounts. All ordinary evidence suggests that my great-aunt was wrong in her ascription of evil powers to the woman from California. Should a camera have filmed my student's every move on the morning he saw the heavenly visitor, that camera would have recorded only the actions of a solitary and distraught man. During Conan Doyle's lifetime many people pleaded with him not to expose himself to the fraud that was practiced constantly by the mediums who affixed themselves to him. As we have seen, the great Houdini tried to rescue his friend from the humiliating attacks that were made against the famous creator of Sherlock Holmes.

Most likely, many, if not all, of the occult events described in this book are not subject to validation by ordinary means. However, my focus is not upon the most fantastic part of these stories. Rather, I wish to focus upon the sequence of events in each person's life, especially the sequence of emotional losses that precede the occult moment.

To carry out that examination, I employ a set of clinical theorems developed by an American psychoanalyst, Heinz Kohut.[10] Kohut developed these theorems out of his work with a certain type of patient, persons who manifest a so-called narcissistic personality disturbance. I believe that Kohut's theory is one way to explain occult experience. I believe that with his theory we can explain the three clues elucidated above; for Kohut gives us a way to understand why an archaic experience in the preverbal period of mother and infant relationship can produce a self that is prone to disruption. When the child fails to experience the child's mother as fundamentally supportive, on the child's side, the child fails to develop a self that can absorb easily the ups and downs of ordinary life. When this child confronts painful losses, as my student did when his dean abandoned him, the child faces a kind of terror that Kohut terms "fragmentation anxiety." In the face of this kind of anxiety, that one's actual self is falling into fragments, the person creates an external experience—the occult moment—which provides a momentary sense of self-repair and self-coherence.

In our original definition of the term *the occult*, we saw that it refers to powers or things that are hidden from view. Underground streams that link one body of water to another are occult. By using Kohut's clinical discoveries about fragmenting experiences, I believe that we can find a precise psychological analogy to this image of hidden connection. I believe that occult experience occurs when people feel suddenly that a hidden, yet vital, connection between themselves and other people is broken. The stream of affection and help that they gained from these other people is dried up. Consequently, the vital tasks—to maintain a sense of self and self-boundaries—which these people performed for them are no longer performed. When these tasks are not performed, the boundaries of the self weaken and the internal experience Kohut terms "fragmentation anxiety" becomes more and more likely. A person vulnerable to occult experience is one who is searching for a way to find again a road back to relationship, back to a sense of union, and back to a feeling of connectedness with others. This feeling of connectedness with a benign, caring other overcomes the horrible experience of fragmentation. This is the story I wish to tell in this book. First, I explain Kohut's basic insights and show why they help us understand occult experience. Second, I apply these insights to the life stories of great Western personalities: Sigmund Freud, Carl Jung, Goethe, and others. I believe that we can see in these life stories a way to validate Kohut's clinical discoveries.

1
Occult Experience in Everyday Life

Conversely, anyone who has completely and finally rid himself of animistic beliefs will be insensible to . . . the uncanny.
—Sigmund Freud, "The Uncanny"

Most educated people consider occult experience rare. They agree with Freud. When he matured into a reasonable man, Freud says, he gave up believing in such things. Using his term, the *uncanny*, we may summarize his opinion by saying that persons who continue to experience and believe in uncanny or occult events have not surmounted their infantile past. They show a deficit in their ability to examine the validity of their fantasies against what they know to be true, that is, they have a deficit in "reality testing."[1] Occult events occur to eccentric people, or in eccentric places. People who live alone in the Arizona desert may be visited by Martians. People who live alone in old houses in New England may be visited by ghosts. The ghosts in the film *Ghostbusters* are occult and so is the ugly little space creature in *E.T.* Such occult events seem confined to the movies or the front

19

pages of grocery-store tabloids. The occult is not, apparently, part of everyday life. Some people may seek fortunetellers, consult astrologers, and believe other such nonsense, but the well-educated and mentally healthy do not. Some authorities claim that about half of all adult Americans read their horoscopes religiously. Yet one can still assert that occult experiences happen to the less educated among us; in other words, occult beliefs are different from occult experiences.

I do not share Freud's opinion. First, it is elitist. People who advance it tend to disdain those lesser than themselves. Second, it is false. I find that most people have had some kind of occult experience. Even persons of great intellect, like Freud himself, report occult experiences.

In fact, Freud had many occult experiences, and he entertained many occult beliefs. Ernest Jones, Freud's great biographer and friend, describes this aspect of Freud's life in detail. Jones was offended by the strength of Freud's fascination for the occult. Freud was convinced that there was a kernel of truth in doctrines about telepathy. He regaled Jones with stories of uncanny events with his patients, "especially after midnight."[2] Although he was always wrong, Freud never gave up his long-standing belief that he could predict the year of his own death, that thought transmission could occur over long distances, and that dreams might foretell the future. (The story of Freud's occult experiences and his occult beliefs is a long and interesting one, and we will examine it in chap. 4.) According to Jones, Freud restrained from publishing his actual beliefs about occult claims for fear of harming the scientific status of his science, psychoanalysis. But in private conversations, especially as the evening progressed, Freud spoke more freely and pronounced with deep conviction that "there was more on heaven and earth" than Jones's English mind could allow. I suggest that neither Freud himself nor Jones treated Freud's occultism with empathy.

Credulity and enthusiasm are not empathic responses to occult claims. If an analyst shares a patient's phobia about speaking in public, for example, that is sympathy, not empathy. Jones's disdain for occult beliefs and occult believers is entirely unempathic. Freud's lapses into occult beliefs shamed Jones, who makes it clear that he shares Freud's self-evaluation when Freud describes an uncanny event: "On encountering the sister of a dead patient, whom she closely resembled, he was so taken aback that for a moment he said to himself: 'So after all it is true that the dead may return.' This was instantly followed by *a feeling of shame at his momentary weakness.*"[3]

Freud and Jones condemn occult experience as shameful, as something to be shaken off, rejected, and overcome. Strong, mature, and worthy persons do not believe such things. If they do, they struggle to overcome their weakness. The intensity of Jones's attacks on occult belief contrasts sharply with the empathic neutrality he and other analysts of his time manifested toward sexual perversions. Why is this? How could men as learned and sophisticated as Freud and Jones condemn one part of human experience, occult beliefs, yet treat with equanimity another part, sexual perversions?

Part of Freud's greatness lies in his willingness to examine the inner meaning of human experience that had been despised by official culture: dreams, neurotic symptoms, sexual perversions, and psychotic fantasies. Yet he was not willing to use his great diagnostic and empathic capacities to investigate religion, which is more respectable than the occult. Even in his works on religion Freud is never very far from moralizing against it. As he says in a late essay, psychoanalysis has but one great enemy, religion.

Freud's official and public response to the occult is on the side of repression, not empathic understanding. His and Jones's harsh evaluations prevent a full psychoanalytic investigation of occult experience. To condemn this form of human experience as morally suspect is to reject out of hand the possibility of understanding it with the tools of psychoanalytic empathy.

I do not share Freud's dismissal of occult beliefs and experience. On the contrary, I believe recent advances in psychoanalytic science, especially those associated with the work of Heinz Kohut, permit us to reclaim this portion of human experience. I think that everyone has had occult experience. We recall the odd pleasure we get when a friend calls us precisely at the moment that very friend was on our mind. Many mothers will swear that they knew something bad had happened to their child before they received the phone call describing the skiing accident in detail. These are all instances of occult experience.

Occultists have created hundreds of technical terms to describe incidents like these. Knowing the intentions of another person far removed from us is an example of telepathy. The ability to know events that transpire at great distances is called traveling clairvoyance. A grander example of traveling clairvoyance is a famous story about the Swedish scientist and mystic, Emanuel Swedenborg. While at a dinner party with sixteen other people, Swedenborg envisioned accurately a great fire sweeping through Stockholm, some three hundred miles away.

We leave these accounts of daily life and consider the claims of mystics and other religious authorities. It may seem that we are no longer talking about the occult and ordinary life, yet I think we are. The only difference between the stories told in my great-aunt's living room and the stories recounted in books by Arthur Conan Doyle is the fame of the parties involved. The ideas that underlie these experiences seem identical. A continuum stretches between events reported in tabloid headlines and the most sublime events recorded by saints, philosophers, and poets.

I wish to show that each of these occult moments is the product of an underlying cause. This cause—a rupture in a personal relationship—gives rise to occult experience in all its forms. I will suggest that this process occurred in the lives of Saint Augustine and Sigmund Freud, just as it did in the life of my great-aunt. I will suggest that there is an underlying pattern in all instances of occult experience. While the pattern may be more evident in some cases than in others, I suggest that it is invariable.

To use an analogy, the occult sequence is fixed like any other sequence of causal events in human experience. When it occurs to famous or powerful or particularly creative people, it becomes significant. In this sense the occult sequence I wish to illuminate is something like a marriage ceremony. When the Prince of Wales marries, it is international news. When ordinary people marry, no reporters appear to document the proceedings. The national television networks do not preempt their soap operas to televise live coverage of the exchange of vows uniting an unknown man with an unknown woman. But the two wedding ceremonies, one conducted in St. Paul's Cathedral, the other in a local Baptist church, are the same.

I suggest that occult experiences occur in a similar way in most people's lives, regardless of the intensity of the experience. In this book, I suggest that we can discover a pattern that runs throughout occult experience. That pattern consists of a sequence of actions, thoughts, and ideas that occur one after the other. Like the pattern or rules that govern a marriage ceremony, the pattern of the occult sequence is fixed.

Of course, there is one large difference between a marriage ceremony and an occult experience. The pattern of statements and vows that makes up the marriage ceremony is based on law and custom. It could be changed—with a great deal of effort. The pattern of feelings and ideas that makes up the occult sequence is based on psychological laws. I doubt that those underlying laws could be changed. Certainly, no state legislature would be powerful enough to alter the way in which persons experience occult moments.

What is the sequence? And if it is so fixed, why are there so many different claims about the occult? In other words, why did someone as brilliant as Swedenborg create his stupendously complex theology if the actual processes that produced his experience are simple? Referring back to Freud, how could a man of his genius fail to see the contradiction in his own statements about the occult? What makes us think that we can advance beyond either Freud or Swedenborg in our attempt to understand the occult?

AN EMPATHIC APPROACH
TO THE OCCULT?
KOHUT'S PSYCHOANALYTIC REVOLUTION

Psychoanalytic science has advanced since Freud's time. These advances permit us to see what Freud could not. I believe that the work of the late Chicago analyst Heinz Kohut gives us a new set of psychoanalytic theorems about an entire domain of human experience that was not available to Freud. This new domain of experience can be characterized in different ways. Within the technical literature of contemporary psychoanalysis Kohut's work is referred to as self-psychology.

This school of contemporary psychoanalysis began with special focus on the "narcissistic disorders." People who manifest narcissistic disorders are prone to profound experiences of shame and humiliation. Yet, paradoxically, at other times these same people feel profoundly superior to others, blessed with powers and abilities far beyond the norm. Unfortunately, neither extreme state is a happy one. To feel like a miserable fool is painful. But to feel as if one is bursting with great ideas, floating far above the heads of mere mortals, is equally miserable.

In both modes persons with a so-called narcissistic personality disturbance suffer an intense feeling of dislocation of themselves. It is not difficult to feel sorry for people who feel badly about themselves. We can tolerate their attacks on their selves and offer our condolences and good cheer. It is a lot harder to be nice to someone in love with himself. Terms applied to persons on the upswing of the narcissistic pendulum are moralizing and condemning. Such persons are called fatheaded, narcissistic, conceited, self-centered, and inflated. They are also full of hot air, gas, bunk, and vaingloriousness.

These are all terms of abuse, and fairly mild ones at that when compared to the more colorful slang terms heaped upon anyone who shows too much concern about his or her self-esteem. Obviously, none of these terms occurs within official psychoanalytic reflections on narcissism. Yet even within those official statements, including Freud's earliest remarks on narcissism, one finds a similar moralizing tone used against the narcissistically vulnerable person.

Traditional psychoanalytic theorists treated issues of self-esteem as relatively minor portions of human suffering. Freud himself wrote an important essay on self-esteem.[4] Yet in it he implied that narcissistic yearnings diminished to the degree that one matured and sought out love relationships with others. In a simplified sense, Freud says that narcissism grows at the expense of love of others (or "object love"). Freud concludes that mature people will show little narcissism. Very self-centered (narcissistic) people should show very little object love.

As a senior analyst, Kohut had occasion to treat select groups of patients. He treated people who had had a previous analysis, people who were in training to become psychoanalysts themselves, and the children of psychoanalysts. If Freud were correct that mature people should show very little narcissism, then these three groups of well-trained and well-raised people should show a predominance of "object love." Most of them should have grown beyond early forms of narcissism.

Kohut found that such was not the case. Contrary to the received wisdom, even these mature and talented patients manifested deep problems with their self-esteem. For example, a well-respected psychiatrist describes himself as hollow, unable to enjoy his family, and unsure of his worth as a therapist. To highlight only one portion of a very rich discussion, Kohut points out the striking incongruity between this man's actual self-regard (his emptiness) and his public image as a happy, talented, and productive professional. Kohut believed that persons like this man had had incomplete analyses. Many of them had been helped by their previous treatment, yet therapists had overlooked systematically the core issue of self-esteem. According to traditional rules these talented and mature persons had had a full analysis. Yet their own sense of themselves and their self-worth remained untouched by their therapeutic encounter. Because these narcissistic dimensions of their personality remained unanalyzed, their problems with self-esteem remained unsolved.

Kohut criticized a whole epoch of psychoanalytic theory and psychoanalytic training. Alongside the many advances made possible by workers like Heinz Hartmann and others, Kohut says, are the overlooked portions of human experience labeled "narcissistic." Kohut criticized himself as well. He was no outsider to the American establishment. Kohut served as president of the American Psychoanalytic Association at one time, and as vice president of the International Psycho-Analytic Association at another time. When he criticized traditional psychoanalytic practice and traditional psychoanalytic theory, he did so as an insider and former advocate.

A TEST CASE:
THE TWO ANALYSES OF MR. Z

In his famous paper, "The Two Analyses of Mr. Z,"[5] Kohut describes a patient whom he treated twice. He conducted the first analysis while still a member of the establishment who viewed narcissism as an infantile and incomplete form of love. The first analysis lasted about four years. The second analysis began about five years after the termination of the first analysis. It too lasted for about four years. Between the two analyses Kohut had developed his basic insights about narcissistic pathologies. He conducted the second analysis of Mr. Z after he had rejected the traditional view with all its moralizing undertones. The two analyses serve as test cases, the new theory versus the old, using the same patient and same analyst.

The difference between the two analyses of Mr. Z is immense. Mr. Z was an unmarried graduate student in his mid-twenties when he first consulted Kohut. His complaints were vague: a sense of loneliness, disinterest in his life, and slight physical discomforts. More striking was his emotional life: he had no significant interest in women, and his most important companion was another unmarried young man. The two young men often spent evenings together with Mr. Z's mother, attending artistic events or going to movies. Kohut learned much later that it was the loss of his ongoing contact with this friend that precipitated Mr. Z's decision to seek psychotherapy. His friend had not included Mr. Z in a new relationship with a woman, and he had much less time for Mr. Z now that he was devoting most of it to his female friend. The loss of this male friend had upset Mr. Z's threesome, and as a result Mr. Z sought out Kohut. It is not possible to summarize a case history that is already highly condensed, but it will help to quote Kohut's description of key moments in the therapy. The first summarizes a major event in Mr. Z's life when he was three and a half years old:

> Mr. Z's father became seriously ill and was hospitalized for several months. The father's illness by itself would undoubtedly have been upsetting. What was of even greater importance, however, was that during the hospitalization the father fell in love with a nurse who took care of him, and after his recovery he decided not to return home but to live with the nurse. During the time of this relationship, which lasted about a year and a half, the father seems only rarely to have visited his family.[6]

Kohut's understanding of this long break in Mr. Z's relationship with his father and its meaning for the young boy changed dramatically. In the first analysis Kohut focused his attention upon Mr. Z's sense of entitlement, which dominated a good part of his relationship with Kohut. Kohut explained outbursts of "infantile" demands and consequent rage when these demands were frustrated as the product of Mr. Z's mother. She had overindulged him during her husband's absence. Since Mr. Z was an only child, and since his father had betrayed Mr. Z's mother, Mr. Z became the center of his mother's life.

Kohut explained Mr. Z's adult "narcissistic delusions" as the consequence of a basic imbalance in Mr. Z's childhood, "the absence of a father who would have been an oedipal rival."[7] In other words, because Mr. Z's father failed to parent his boy from the ages of three and a half to five, the boy had no strong male figure who could help control him, especially one who could stand realistically against the boy as an unbeatable rival for his mother's attention and favors. Because Mr. Z's father had absented himself from the family during this time, the young boy had, in effect, won a victory by default. The competitive and hostile urges that appear especially in boys of this age remained unchecked.

Kohut interpreted Mr. Z's "arrogant feelings of entitlement" as throwbacks to his infantile experience with his mother. Kohut therefore spent a good deal of effort confronting Mr. Z with the "delusional" nature of his narcissistic demands. Kohut did far more than this, of course, and it would be a mistake to trivialize the rigor of Kohut's work in either of the two analyses of Mr. Z. But it is helpful to note the dramatic shift in Kohut's attitude toward his patient's "narcissistic" demands.

In the first analysis Kohut tolerated Mr. Z's complaints. But he eventually demanded that his patient desist: "I consistently, and with increasing firmness, rejected the reactivation of his narcissistic attitudes, expectations and demands. . . . "[8] In the second analysis, some five and a half years later, Kohut encountered precisely the same set of attitudes, demands, and expectations. But he no longer criticized his patient for them, nor did he attempt to "educate" Mr. Z out of these infantile modes. Rather, thanks to his explorations and studies of that epoch, Kohut could approach his patient's total material empathically—that is, psychoanalytically—and not with barely hidden condemnations. In his major papers of that time, Kohut elaborated his basic understanding that all children need parents who will reflect and honor their need to be esteemed intrinsically in themselves.[9] This may seem like a truism, but it has profound implications in Mr. Z's story.

Reconsidering His Mother's Illness

In his first analysis, Mr. Z had reported that his mother had inspected his feces every day from earliest age to about six. Having heard this story, Kohut used it against the patient to explain why he had remained so "narcissistic" about his adult productions: "I can still remember *the slightly ironical tone of my voice,* meant to assist him in overcoming his childish grandiosity. . . . "[10] The ironical and moralistic tone of this statement contrasts dramatically with the tone of Kohut's second analysis, after he discovered the role of empathy. Mr. Z recounted the same stories, but this time Kohut understood far better how sick Mr. Z's mother had been. (In the interval between the two analyses she had a severe psychiatric illness.) "[H]er preoccupation with his faeces stopped, apparently abruptly, when he was about six years old; she then became obsessed with his skin as she had been with his bowels before. Every Saturday afternoon—the procedure became an unalterable ritual, just as the faeces-inspection had been—she examined his face in minutest detail, in particular—and increasingly as he moved toward adolescence—with regard to any developing blackheads she could detect."[11]

Mr. Z dreaded these examinations, especially as they turned into detailed ritual attacks upon himself. In the first part of the ritual Mr. Z's mother examined his face and described "disapprovingly in great detail what she saw." In the second part she used her fingernails to dig out any blackhead so discovered. Kohut asks himself an excellent question about the mother's manifestly psychopathological behaviors: How did he overlook them? How did he ignore the depth of Mr. Z's mother's sickness? How did he ignore the depth of Mr. Z's suffering at her hands throughout these tortuous rituals?

Kohut's answer is persuasive. He had no theory of mother-child interaction that would permit him to see the way Mr. Z's mother *needed* her son to be the sick, flawed object—full of blackheads or feces—that she could examine and "improve" by her compulsive actions. Mr. Z's mother obeyed her own compulsion to rescue her own vulnerable and "flawed" self, which was indeed constantly threatened by disintegration, by identifying herself with her son and, more exactly, his face. Mr. Z's mother elaborated upon a universal parental theme—pride in one's child—and, because of the depth of her fragmentation anxiety, created out of it a rationale for the complete domination of her son.

A later event lets us gauge the depth of her domination of her son and Mr. Z's despair that he could ever break free of it. He was deeply pleased when he learned as a young man that she was in fact mentally ill and had been diagnosed as such; "he now, potentially at least, had witnesses"[12] that his mother had been wrong in the way she treated him.

Thanks to the development of his insights into the universal features of narcissistic needs, and the concept of "selfobject," Kohut could reassess Mr. Z's mother and offer a diagnosis. He does this in "The Two Analyses of Mr. Z": "She was, in essence, a 'borderline case.' The psychotic core, the central pre-psychological chaos of her personality, the central hollowness of her self was covered over by a rigidly maintained hold on and control over her selfobjects whom she needed in order to shore up her self."[13]

Kohut invented the term *selfobject* to describe a certain kind of relationship. In such relationships one person uses another person to perform psychological functions that the first person cannot perform for herself or himself. In normal families, parents typically perform selfobject functions for their children when their children need that extra bit of help. When a five-year-old is afraid of thunder, for example, the child's parents comfort the child and soothe the child's fears. Eventually the child becomes able to soothe herself or himself, even in the absence of the child's parents. If all goes well, children whose parents have served such selfobject roles will themselves become capable of soothing others. Hence, there is a natural progress from the child's state of requiring a great deal of selfobject relatedness from the child's environment, to performing those functions for the child's self, to becoming a selfobject for others.

With regard to Mr. Z's mother, we can underline a crucial aspect of the concept. Human beings do not "grow out of" the need for selfobjects at any time in the life cycle. The need and search for selfobjects, whether persons, causes, or ideals, persists as long as the human self persists. What changes is the degree to which we can find persons, causes, or ideals that are suitable. Kohut does not condemn Mr. Z's mother for using her child in the way she did—as a selfobject she could examine in detail on Saturdays. Her tragedy was her inability to find adults or adult causes that would perform that function for her. In the absence of appropriate persons she drafted her son into that role. At the same time, given the depth of her own narcissistic wounds, we can guess that her own life story is one of profound deficits and narcissistic wounds.

As do all children, Mr. Z needed his mother to be on his side, to love and affirm him. If those infinite goods had a certain cost to them, namely, to take part in the bizarre rituals she demanded of him, that was a small price to pay for survival. Unfortunately, while Mr. Z could help sustain his mother through serving her selfobject needs, she could not do the same consistently for him.

It appears that even as a boy Mr. Z recognized, at moments, the depth of his mother's illness. But he could not sustain these insights. First, he was a boy and not an adult with an adult's psychological strengths. Second, and perhaps more important, she was his mother. In many ways she was, therefore, his world, especially when he was very young and living alone with her. Adults may forget how absolute is a parent's power. An adult analogy might be from a Bogart film, *The Caine Mutiny.* The film portrays the despair a crazy captain can engender in his crew, who eventually mutiny rather than suffer under his paranoid accusations. To live with a crazy parent is far more dangerous and despairing than serving a demented captain. The lowly sailor, no matter how harassed, can hope to escape. A young child, certainly a three- or four-year-old, has no such hopes and no capacity to entertain them.

Masturbation as Retreat and Restitution

Instead, the young child often does what Mr. Z did as a young boy: he turned to his own body for as much comfort as possible. We recall that Mr. Z had no siblings, and his father was absent during the crucial years between three and a half and five. As a consequence, Mr. Z, like many other children in similar circumstances, turned to masturbation. In "endlessly prolonged masturbatory activities"[14] the young boy attempted to define himself to himself.

Unlike ordinary masturbation, which is impulsive and driven like other appetites, the young Mr. Z's actions were continuous. In ordinary masturbation the urges that impel it disappear upon orgasm. But in the compulsive form the urges that underlie the need to stroke and fondle one's body are not cyclical, like sexuality or hunger. Rather, they are continuous, since the need to feel oneself to be a separate self—independent, strong, and not sick—is also continuous.

In the first analysis Kohut had explained the young boy's masturbation as "drive gratification."[15] In the second he explained the intensity and compulsiveness of these acts as desperate attempts by the young boy to avoid the black mood of his depressed mother. According to the concepts developed in this chapter, the young Mr. Z needed to escape the entanglement of his mother's use of him as her selfobject. Masturbation was an attempt to "provide for himself a feeling of aliveness, manifestations of that surviving remnant of the vitality of a rudimentary self which was now finally in the process of firm delimitation."[16]

Obviously, Kohut is not saying that the young boy *thought* about any of these issues, at least in the way that we think about them. The young boy did not choose masturbation. He discovered it and with that discovery found a temporary haven from his own and his mother's depression. At the same time there were moments when he recognized that his mother was odd. For example, few of his friends wished to visit him in his house when his mother was around. But these momentary insights were far too dangerous to maintain in consciousness. Even during his second analysis, as an adult, Mr. Z struggled to forget what he knew to be true. His awareness of his mother's pathology could not be "maintained without a great deal of emotional toil."[17] Each time he got close to this insight he suffered a "nameless fear" which Kohut terms "disintegration anxiety." Elsewhere he terms the same fear "fragmentation anxiety."

Again, it is important to note that selfobject relationships are *relationships*. The young boy's panic and his attempts to control it by masturbating and at times smelling and tasting his feces should be seen in the context of his mother's panic and her attempts to control her panic: "The pathogenic parent, the father or the mother who enslaves the child because of his or her own need for a selfobject, completely disregards the child's sexual activity as long as it is part of the child's depression about the unbreakable merger."[18]

In the first analysis, following traditional psychoanalytic norms, Kohut focused his attention upon his patient's pathology, almost excluding the context in which that pathology developed. The focus upon Mr. Z's internal life was, in part, responsible for Kohut's overlooking the severe pathology in Mr. Z's mother.

In the second analysis Kohut was far more willing to take Mr. Z's point of view. In other words, Kohut was able to empathize with the young boy's total experience of himself (the intrapsychic world) and his milieu (the external world). The boy's experience of himself included the profound panic his mother engendered. His sometimes frantic masturbation relieved him temporarily. The boy's experience of his mother included a sense of doom, of unending entanglement with a person whose very face sometimes seemed to disappear.

It would be a mistake to assume that Kohut's ability to empathize with his patient far better in the second analysis means that Kohut had become morally better. Empathy is not a moral capacity as such. Rather, Kohut was able to comprehend his patient better in the second analysis, and forgo the hostile irony of the first analysis, because he understood the meaning of Mr. Z's "delusional" demands. Empathy, in this sense and as I expand upon it below, is based on accurate perception of the meaning of another's experience.

AN EMPATHIC APPROACH TO
OCCULT EXPERIENCE

We began this chapter with an account of Freud's ambivalent feelings about occult belief and occult experience. I suggested that Freud's shameful response to his own intense fascination with the occult was not an empathic one. On the contrary, both Freud and his biographer, Ernest Jones, treated these parts of Freud's emotional life with disdain and irony. The presence of such moralizing signals the absence of psychoanalytic understanding. This moralizing against narcissistic yearnings parallels the moralizing against occult beliefs evident in Jones's official denunciation, even when occult beliefs appeared in the life of Jones's idealized master, Freud himself.

Kohut's work has been subject to a vast amount of commentary. Since the publication of "Forms and Transformations of Narcissism" in 1966,[19] numerous psychoanalytic authorities have debated the merits of his work. In this essay, I use three of Kohut's major concepts as plausible guides toward a clinical understanding of occult experience. Those three concepts are (1) the central role empathy plays in psychoanalytic investigations, (2) the meaning of fragmentation anxiety, and (3) the universal need for the kind of relationship Kohut terms "selfobject." We have considered each concept in our account of the two analyses of Mr. Z. I discuss each of these concepts in more detail below.

Empathy Defines Psychoanalytic Method

In ordinary language empathy refers to the capacity to be in tune emotionally with another person. Kohut did not originate psychoanalytic interest in empathy. Long before, Freud and other psychoanalysts had realized that they could not reach their patients without some degree of emotional attunement. There is much evidence that Freud, for example, treated his patients with a great deal of friendly affection, far more, in fact, than the stereotyped portraits would suggest. Yet until the publication of Kohut's paper "Introspection, Empathy, and Psychoanalysis" in 1959,[20] few analysts had investigated empathy systematically. Since I rely upon portions of that paper throughout this book, I will summarize portions of it that I find pertinent to an empathic account of occult experience.

Kohut's subtitle is important to our concern: "An examination of the relationship between a mode of observation and theory." He stresses the issue of mode of observation because he wants to define psychoanalysis by *its modes of investigation, not by its doctrines.* "The limits of psychoanalysis are given by the limits of potential introspection and empathy."[21]

Psychoanalysts may agree that concepts like "oedipus complex" describe the basic conflicts of their patients—in this century. It is conceivable that even that basic conflict, between a child's innate drive to express sexuality and prohibitions upon that drive, might alter as fundamental patterns of parenting change. Should this happen, even the most traditional of psychoanalysts would have to admit that the doctrine of the oedipus complex would be valid no longer. Would that also mean that psychoanalytic science would be no longer valid? Would one have to close up all the institutes, for example, and send patients to the behaviorists?

These drastic actions would be necessary only if one defined psychoanalysis by a set of beliefs or doctrines, rather as one might define a religious sect. Kohut maintains that doctrinal definitions harm psychoanalysis. No other science defines itself by adherence to a single set of doctrines, the truth of which is held to be immutable. Physicists, for example, have not defined their science by a fixed set of beliefs about Newtonian theory. One might say that the hallmark of a bona fide science is its capacity to replace partial truths with larger, more encompassing theorems. With that notion of science in mind, Kohut defines psychoanalysis as a mode of inquiry into human mental life based on the scientific use of introspection and empathy.[22]

As long as human beings have an inner world of private experience, accessible only through introspection, psychoanalytic science will be possible. But to say that there will always be the possibility of a psychoanalytic science is not to guarantee its existence. Before Freud's great discoveries there was no lack of introspection and forms of empathy. What distinguishes psychoanalytic, that is, scientific, forms of empathy from similar investigations by poets and philosophers?

Kohut's answer is persuasive: With the aid of the technical rules of free association and resistance analysis psychoanalysts discovered a "hitherto unknown kind of inner experience," the unconscious.[23] This is an elegant definition. But it makes sense only if one understands these two technical rules. Let us examine them more closely.

Free Association and Resistance Analysis

The rule of free association states that a patient is to report everything that crosses his or her mind as he or she lies upon the couch. This may seem trivial or at least easy. It is neither. For the demand or request for free association asks the patient to give up the subtle and automatic responses we all use to censor our thoughts and feelings to ourselves, even as they occur.

One cannot be a patient or therapist for long before discovering that a moment of true free association is difficult to come by. A huge number of problems emerge. One's thoughts seem too unimportant, too trivial, too silly, or too obscene to report outright. In addition, the numerous itches, strains, muscle tension, half-formed sensations, visualizations, half-remembered songs, and the like that filter through one's mind are difficult to sort and verbalize instantaneously. If this were not sufficient aggravation, there also are apt to be moments when the mind is blank, nothing comes, and a heavy silence ensues.

The request for free association burdens the patient. But it yields something that would otherwise remain obscure. For by "failing" to obey the rule the patient and analyst discover exactly what the patient *cannot* talk about. Similarly, a physiologist using a treadmill assesses a patient's ability to use oxygen and locates that point where the stress and strains are too severe. At this point the physiologist notes the upper limits of the patient's current cardiovascular functioning. At the analogous point with an analytic patient the analyst notes the point of resistance. The demand for free association makes possible the analysis of resistance because resistance is, generally, the inability to associate freely. The term has a larger and more extended meaning in the clinical literature. But resistance owes its basic meaning to Freud's discovery that his patients often found themselves unable to complete their stories. Even highly motivated and candid patients reached a point in their narrations when they manifested resistances to the task of free association.

True to his genius, Freud valued these moments of resistance. Rather than discard them as signs of failure on the patient's part, Freud valued them as diagnostic indicators. They marked the point at which Freud could begin to explore their causes. Rather than agree with the patient that nothing came to mind, or agree with the rationalist who found no obvious pattern in such difficulties, Freud investigated resistances. In fact, as Kohut suggests, "resistance analysis," the investigation of those moments when patients cannot say what is on their mind (or when they "forget" their therapy hour, decide to move to Brazil, etc.), constitutes psychoanalytic technique.

Freud made his investigations scientific when he sought the causes of resistances. The technical term *the unconscious* is one way to name the source of such resistances. Unlike his great predecessors, the poets and philosophers who had also advanced notions of an "unconscious," Freud used the concept of the unconscious to explain observable behavior. When a patient who normally speaks quite easily suddenly falls silent, for example, we suspect the presence of resistances to free association. These resistances emanate from unconscious conflicts.

It is not difficult to find precursors to many of Freud's ideas, taken one by one as if they were metaphysical speculations. It is far more difficult to locate thinkers before Freud who investigated systematically the *causes* of slips of the tongue, dreams, errors, forgetting, and symptoms, that is, the detritus of mental life.

Because he used the concept of the unconscious as a clinical postulate, Freud was able to ask what other investigators could not: Why did you forget? Why is there nothing on your mind? What is the meaning of your error, slip, or symptom? That is, what motive or set of motives could account for your actions? To use one of Freud's favorite metaphors, what set of ideas is missing (is unconscious) which, if found, would make this irrational action or idea understandable?

These questions, new techniques, and the use of empathic immersion in his own life and the lives of his patients allowed Freud to discover unknown inner experiences. This seems paradoxical. For if *inner experience* refers to something that occurs within a person, it seems wrong to say that it could remain unknown. But the paradox is only apparent. It is puzzling only if one agrees with the unstated assumption that people know what they think. In other words, Freud's claims about unconscious thought are paradoxical only if one defines *thought* entirely in conscious terms. According to this definition there could be no unconscious thoughts and therefore nothing called "the unconscious." Yet we realize that we never are aware of all our possible thoughts. The remaining thoughts are unconscious. To this truism Freud added the revolutionary insight that there can be a barrier between one's conscious thoughts and whole regions of one's unconscious thoughts. This barrier he sometimes termed the *repression barrier.* The repression barrier demarks the *system conscious* and the *system unconscious,* to use terms from Freud's middle period.

The whole of Freud's science turns upon this issue. It is often put in the form of a creed: Can one believe in the unconscious? There are numerous defenses of this creed and even more numerous attacks upon it. Kohut's solution to this form of the debate was, as noted above, to focus upon the operation of empathy. He chose to define it as vicarious introspection. If we consider what this succinct formula means, we may grasp better Kohut's intentions.

Empathy as Vicarious Introspection

Vicarious introspection means that one person, the therapist, tries to comprehend how another person, the patient, might introspect his or her inner world. I stress the fact that the therapist *tries* to comprehend because empathic listening is not mind reading. The analyst does not pretend to share the patient's actual experience. Empathy is not the product of mental merger. Unlike Mr. Spock on the starship Enterprise, the empathic analyst does not perform a "Vulcan Mind Meld" and so actually share the patient's inner experience. True, the analyst may recall having had feelings identical to those that the patient reports, but that is a moment of sympathetic resonance. The same thing occurs on stringed musical instruments when one set of strings begins to vibrate in response to the vibration of other strings. True, the analyst may call upon his or her own set of memories and feelings to find likely models of the patient's experience. But this is only one method among many that might be used to find an accurate rendition of a patient's internal experience.

Vicarious introspection means that the analyst attempts to comprehend the patient's internal terrain as seen by the patient. To use more technical terms, the analyst attempts to comprehend—vicariously—what the patient's ego experiences upon surveying its environment. What makes up this environment, which Kohut terms the "inner world"?[24] To answer this question, we may recall some of the things that one can introspect, such as:

1. thoughts
2. feelings or emotions
3. sensory perceptions
4. fantasies
5. general mood states

There might be better ways to inventory the contents of the inner world. Yet even this short list suggests the richness of that realm and so the riches that introspection can yield.

Thought. Most adults realize that they can examine their thought processes and discover, through introspection, that they are thinking ideas that are not congruent with polite society. Not only can one think obscene thoughts, but one can think about three obscene things at once and with equal pleasure, even if each is impossible in the external world.

As Kohut and Freud before him noted, poets and philosophers have explored these aspects of human experience since time immemorial. *The Egyptian Book of the Dead,* for example, contains marvelous bits of introspection. There the dead king is taught to reflect upon his life, especially upon his inner life, and to examine his conduct as he prepares for final judgment. Closer to our own time, Socrates is a Western ideal of the examined life. Part of his greatness lies in his identity as a man who deepened the human capacity for introspection. The fact that persons like Socrates have been able to advance this capacity suggests how rich the inner world is. The fact that Socrates enjoys tremendous prestige in our culture suggests how much we value such explorations. At the same time, we can gauge the complexity of introspective thought by noting that whole generations of scholars may devote themselves to the task of elucidating the work of a single great philosopher. Few philosophers, for example, would claim to have mastered every aspect of Hegel's introspective masterpiece, *The Phenomenology of the Spirit.*

Feelings. The complexity of sensations that make up human experience seems infinitely variable. Yet when compared to the variety and subtlety of human feelings, sensations seem relatively straightforward. Culture reserves a high place for men and women who can explore human feeling and convey their discoveries to others. Artists and poets who achieve such status remain idealized long after their deaths. The poems of John Keats, for example, remain vital and important to us two hundred years after he wrote them. Keats responded to the political issues of his day. His themes and concerns were standard for poets of his generation, yet his poetry has far outlived his time. Just why this is so is not an easy question to answer.

It is not accidental that persons who can give a plausible answer to that kind of question themselves become renowned. Great critics like T. S. Eliot, Ezra Pound, and Northrop Frye become significant figures in contemporary culture because they can extend our understanding of how artists like Keats are able to explore our common inner world. In a similar way clichés about Freud's place in Western thought are accurate: No one can think about human inner experience without reflecting upon Freud's discoveries.

Sensory Perceptions.   Under the heading of sensory perceptions we can list numerous forms of sensation. One can introspect the experience of vision and compare it to hearing or touch. When I see something far away from me at night that total experience differs dramatically from seeing the same object from the same spot during the day. If you stand on a high hill, for example, and watch jet airliners land at an airport at night, the vapor trails that were present during the day and that sharpen one's sense of movement are gone. In their place are dozens of lights, some colored, some not, some flashing, some not, some brilliant, and others faint. One still has a sense of speed and motion, but the movement of lights through dark space is entirely unlike the sense of speed engendered by the jet exhaust. There are other differences between the two sets of sensations.

Novelists, for example, are sensitive to the immense range of sensation available to us and describe these differences in great and fascinating detail.

The variety and subtlety of sensations, the feelings with which they are associated, and their intensity vary dramatically. The capacity to comprehend sensations varies also. Great critics of music, for example, are able to describe in detail the difference between a German and an American orchestra playing Bach. Great art critics can describe similar nuances between brush strokes in the early Cezanne paintings compared to his later works. Some wine connoisseurs can distinguish between two seemingly identical bottles of Burgundy—and identify the vintner, the year, and the slope of ground from which the grapes came. Expert barbecue tasters can distinguish between what nonexperts might feel are equally pungent barbecue sauces. One learns, for example, that one sauce needs more red peppers while the other sauce needs a little more bourbon. Travelogues, true romances, and "on location" stories are worth reading if they can enlarge our capacity to register distinct sensory perceptions. Film directors, choreographers, architects, and other artists become important to us to the degree that they can enlarge our range of sensory perception. With these new sensory perceptions comes a new range of pleasures. The pleasure of a grand vista, for example, makes it well worth the outrageous price one must pay to eat dinner in restaurants situated at the top of tall buildings.

Fantasies. Within the inner world also lie fantasies. Perhaps the most accessible fantasy is the daydream. Anyone who has listened to a boring speaker can attest to the deep pleasures of summoning up a favorite daydream. With little effort one can imagine oneself in Tahiti, for example, swimming in the warm waves, while one's body remains rooted in a folding chair in a stuffy lecture hall. One can introspect daydreams easily. Unlike night dreams, which tend to be "given" to us, daydreams submit to our direction. We can alter the scene, the action, the actors, and their dress on a whim. In the twinkling of an eye we can replace one fantasy with another.

An additional virtue of fantasies is their privacy. We do not have to reveal them. No one else can examine them or alter them without our permission. It is difficult to overestimate the pleasures of fantasies. It is also difficult to estimate the variety and type of fantasies available to the truly creative daydreamer.

Fantasies may be private, but they can be public. Science fiction is purely fantastic, as are most popular novels and drama. Yet we can know people well enough that we can "empathize" with them and intuit some aspects of their fantasy. Within the analytic relationship one may often comprehend a patient's fantasy *before* it emerges fully into consciousness. We can suppose, for example, that a young patient, raised by his loving grandfather after both his parents died, will respond to his female silver-haired analyst with dozens of fantasies. Among them will be, probably, the fantasy that the analyst will come to see her patient's intrinsic merits and adopt him, just as his loving grandfather had in the past. Naturally, the complexity of such fantasies and their availability to consciousness varies over time and between patients.

General Mood States. General mood states like boredom, agitation, or anxiety are also products of the internal world. They vary in intensity, range, and complexity, as do fantasies. One person may experience a

fleeting sense of dread, for example, when he sees a letter from the IRS
in his mailbox. Another person may respond to the same stimulus with a
much more severe and prolonged sense that the worst has come to pass,
that there is no hope. "Dark moods" are not rare. They appear in everyone's life and, luckily, seem to disappear on their own. "Happy moods"
occur also. Unfortunately, they also tend to disappear on their own. Literary artists as well as visual artists have examined in depth the range of
such moods for thousands of years. Homer captures a wonderful aspect
of Penelope's unhappiness, yet also her charm, when he describes her
long wait for her husband and her consternation upon hearing that
he, Odysseus, might be alive: "Presently Penelope from her chamber/
stepped in her thoughtful beauty" (19, 27–28). About two thousand
years later, in Renaissance England, Shakespeare created his great dramas, especially *Hamlet,* in which the character's mood, his inmost being, is laid bare and examined in detail. The great monologue that
begins, "To be or not to be" (III, i), describes Hamlet's interior life, that
is, his moods, and makes them accessible. Some four hundred years after his creation Hamlet continues to be loved in large part because
Shakespeare fabricated a living character whose moods and interior life
seem fully real.

In the late nineteenth century, the English novelist Thomas Hardy
wrote masterful accounts of the moods of his doomed heroes and hero-
ines. It is not possible to briefly render Hardy's genius, just as one
cannot do justice to Beethoven with a xylophone. But one can evoke
the basic theme. In *Jude the Obscure,* for example, Hardy describes a
young man's ardent love for a young woman, newly married, who
loathes her husband and his sexual use of her. The young man, Jude,
tries to comfort the woman, Sue, and says he wants her to be happy.
Sue responds, "I can't be! So few could enter my feelings—they would
say 'twas my fanciful fastidiousness, or something of that sort, and condemn me."[25] She goes on to explain how she made the mistake of marrying the wrong man and then complains that the law and ordinary
customs make it impossible to correct her mistake. But might not
other, more empathic people, understand? "When people of a later age
look back upon the barbarous customs and superstitions of the times
that we have the unhappiness to live in, what *will* they say!"

Kohut defined empathy as vicarious introspection. We have considered some of the types of internal experience that are available to our
own introspection. Following Kohut's definition, we can say that these
experiences, like feelings and mood states, are precisely the interior experiences available to vicarious introspection, that is, to empathic understanding. What I can introspect in myself, another person with sufficient

empathy should be able to comprehend. The important qualifier in this claim is "with sufficient empathy." The capacity to empathize with another person depends upon our training, experience, and native abilities. Just how these factors work together to produce a talented psychotherapist or someone with empathic abilities is mysterious.

Empathy is a mysterious skill, but not a magical one. It can be taught and improved upon by rigorous training; however, limitations to one's empathic ability are not due solely to ignorance. We are also reluctant to empathize with someone whose difficulties match our own. To be empathic is to comprehend painful feelings as well as pleasurable feelings. To be empathic toward another person is to comprehend states that are painful and disruptive, that is, potentially fragmenting. If that pain is too close to us and remains overwhelming, we cannot empathize with another who shares it. Among forms of psychic pain that are especially disruptive is fragmentation anxiety. We have seen a description of this kind of anxiety in Kohut's discussion of Mr. Z. We will consider this form of pain in more detail below.

FRAGMENTATION ANXIETY: CAUSE AND EFFECT

Some people who suffer intense wounds to their self-esteem experience themselves as if they were "falling apart" or fragmenting into separate pieces. Kohut discovered this sequence of cause and effect when he treated patients whom some clinicians felt were untreatable. These patients, who manifest a so-called narcissistic personality disturbance, cannot maintain a consistent sense that they are worthy and coherent. Instead, the person vulnerable to narcissistic disturbance shows great swings between opposite poles. Sometimes such a person feels extraordinarily proud of his or her absolute superiority to mere mortals, but at other times, he or she feels like nothing.

A graduate student in history, for example, sometimes feels stupid and inane, incapable of finishing the simplest assignment. Yet at other times the student feels equal to the greatest historians. Kohut puzzled over the problem of explaining how a talented person like this could manifest these opposed states of self-esteem. Of equal importance, Kohut noted that these states of experience, or "self-states," are painful. The first state, in which the young person feels worthless, is one of deep shame and embarrassment. The second state is the opposite. But it, too, is painful and carries its own special form of suffering.

Ordinary language has described a portion of this narcissistic experience when persons in such inflated states are said to be full of themselves, stuffy, bigheaded, or puffed up. To outsiders this behavior appears grandiose. The terms used to describe narcissism are critical and moralizing. People who act grandiosely have to be cut down to size, have their balloons busted, or, minimally, get their heads shrunk. Yet to the young historian, even during moments when he or she believes that his or her mind is one with the geniuses of the profession, these experiences are disrupting. He or she recognizes that something is out of kilter, and feels out of balance and incoherent. This narcissistic disability is as painful and disorganizing as that manifest in the other state, when he or she feels worthless and stupid.

Narcissistic Sufferings

Kohut and others have studied such patients in detail. They have elaborated rich and extensive theories of how such narcissistic disturbances arise in the course of child development, and I refer to some of these fascinating studies when they pertain to our concerns. However, my basic concern is to use Kohut's clinical discoveries about the ups and downs of narcissistic moods, so I will not attempt to justify every aspect of Kohut's reasoning.

I focus upon Kohut's discoveries about the sequences of experience that lead up to an event he terms "fragmentation." I believe that Kohut's basic discoveries about the traumatic events that precede narcissistic suffering, particularly fragmentation anxiety, parallel the processes that lead up to occult experience. Kohut discovered that any narcissistic wound, being slighted by a colleague, for example, elicited a subsequent feeling of fragmentation. As we will see below, fragmentation refers to the patient's subjective experience of feeling as if he or she were falling into separate fragments. The term *fragmentation* refers also to the patient's behavior: his or her thinking becomes disjointed; even posture and gait seem incoherent and disconnected. Kohut discovered that these internal experiences and external behavior occurred as the result of faults in a significant relationship. Discovery of this causal link between fault in relationship and fragmentation response is one aspect of Kohut's scientific achievement.

Kohut made this discovery because he treated manifestations of fragmentation anxiety empathically, not sympathetically. As described above, the difference between empathy and sympathy is fundamental. Empathy is an effort on the analyst's part to comprehend the chain of intrapsychic events that eventuates in the observed behavior. Sympathy is an emotional response in which the analyst shares the patient's manifest feelings. In the extreme case, sympathy is a kind of complete emotional identification.

A standard example of extreme sympathy occurs when, for instance, adolescent girls identify themselves completely with one member of the group who is overcome with emotion. As she screams and faints, having just received a rejection from her boyfriend, her classmates respond to her crisis with their own symptoms, screams, and fainting. As they are falling to the floor in their own distress, these young girls cannot help their classmate. In other words, sympathetic responses are usually not very helpful. Or to use yet another example, when we submit ourselves to the dentist's drill, we want the dentist to be empathic with our suffering, but not sympathetic. We want the dentist to know that the whirring of the drill, the horrible sensations in the nerve endings, the smell of burned tooth, and so forth, are unpleasant and make us wince with pain and disgust. We do not want the dentist to wince with pain and disgust. We want efficient, effective care. We do not want the dentist to share our pain. We want the dentist to recognize our pain and discomfort (and anxiety) and to finish as quickly as possible, or at least let us spit sooner rather than later.

Indications of Narcissistic Disturbance

Following a narcissistic loss, a patient may feel as if his or her body were falling apart, legs dissolving as he or she lies on the couch. Such reports might be signs of severe mental illness involving an irrevocable destruction of reality testing and the sense of self, that is, a form of psychosis. Yet when the analyst discovers that these feelings emerged immediately following, for instance, the announcement of a vacation break, we may suppose that these two events are causally related. To verify this supposition we record that these severe moments of fragmentation disappear when the analyst links them to the break in the treatment sequence.[26]

In Kohut's terms, the analyst looks for moments in the patient-therapist relationship when the patient experiences the analyst as uninvolved and unempathic. We stress the patient's point of view, and not that of some ideal observer who knows how adults should act, because the analyst cannot predict how the patient will construe every aspect of their relationship. A patient may request a change of hour or plan to miss a session of treatment, for example, and yet feel (unconsciously) enraged that the analyst is not present just when the patient requires help, namely, during the break that the patient has arranged. From a moralistic point of view, the patient's rage is wrong and unjustified. From an empathic, analytic point of view these rageful responses, like fragmentation experiences, must be understood as signs of the patient's profound narcissistic suffering.

To return to the occult, I suggest that we can identify causal sequences similar to those Kohut describes in his clinical essays. Does this mean that everyone who has an occult moment is as sick as Kohut's patients? No. Kohut helps us see that in addition to the severe forms of fragmentation he observed in his sickest patients, numerous instances occur in daily life. The momentary discomfort we may feel if a friend fails to greet us is a form of fragmentation.[27] In Kohut's language, when we feel our self unrecognized by people who are important to us, we experience a narcissistic wound and suffer a brief bout of fragmentation. In other words, we feel, if only for an instant, less sure of ourselves. We may fumble with our keys, forget what we were thinking, or falter in our prepared speech. (In a telling criticism of traditional analytic practice, Kohut notes that the time-honored task of analyzing a patient's parapraxes and slips may be harmful, not therapeutic. It often increases the patient's sense of fragmentation. To focus upon a patient's errors compounds the patient's suffering and obscures further the narcissistic wound that precipitated the original parapraxes.)[28]

The ordinary wounds to self-esteem that occur with regularity may appear to be minor events. They pass quickly. Most people would not recall them a day or two later. They are one pole of a continuum that extends all the way to major narcissistic wounds from which few people could escape unmarked.

Among the latter are the events that occur when infants are raised by disturbed parents who cannot comprehend their children's internal needs. A daughter raised by a psychotically depressed mother, for example, could not feel beautiful and worthy of a sexual life if her mother had failed to value and appreciate her daughter's maturation. Should this young woman then meet a man who found her sexually attractive, she would have a hard time comprehending his interest in her and her own excitement. (She might retreat from all sexual contact, or she might take the opposite tack and plunge into hurtful, masochistic relationships.)

Kohut became sensitive to fragmentation experiences when he worked with narcissistically vulnerable patients. They responded to lapses in his empathic understanding with acute pain. Some flew into uncontrollable rages, others threatened suicide, others felt depersonalized, like robots or some other inhuman machine. Why? Why would being a few minutes late, for example, precipitate an angry denunciation from a patient who was often late? Kohut's answer, in a simplified form, is that the analyst's tardiness makes the patient feel rejected once more by a person whose care and constancy he or she requires if he or she is to avoid feeling the terrors of fragmentation. Not everyone responds to the analyst's tardiness in this way. But not everyone has been raised in a home where basic needs to feel worthy of being understood were frustrated.

Kohut addressed this kind of problem over the twenty years he developed his work. His posthumous text *How Does Analysis Cure?*[29] is a detailed discussion of such unexpected reactions. I recommend this book to those who have not yet read Kohut.

THE CONCEPT OF SELFOBJECT
AND ITS MEANING

We used the term *selfobject* when we summarized Kohut's paper "The Two Analyses of Mr. Z." There the term referred to the ways in which Mr. Z's mother used her son to make her feel better about herself. This may seem vaguely understandable since even popular language speaks about parents who "use" their children for their own ends. The core meaning of the concept of selfobject, however, is not a moralistic one. Rather, the core meaning depends upon a view of how infants develop into children and children develop into adults. In more technical terms, Kohut's concept of selfobject is developmental (or genetic).

The developmental point of view is a way of understanding an adult's experience and behavior in light of that adult's developmental history. In one sense this is a truism. Obviously, how a person grew up and passed through the great epochs of human development influences current behavior. One does not need psychoanalysis to make this point. But in another sense the developmental point of view is far from obvious. In the technical theory Kohut advanced and in the work of similar psychoanalytic thinkers, the developmental point of view contains an exact set of claims about the source of particular difficulties.

When Kohut says that Mr. Z's mother failed to support her son's needs for adequate parenting between the ages of three and five, he means that the boy was passing through a period of growth in which he needed to have his urges toward self-definition satisfied.

Like other psychoanalysts working with very sick patients, Kohut feels that one can match the degree and type of illness in the adult with the period and severity of trauma the patient experienced as a child. Kohut claims that Mr. Z was damaged by his mother but not as badly as he might have been, for there was evidence that she had loved her son and felt secure in her mothering of him up to the time that her husband abandoned the family. In other words, Mr. Z's experience of "good enough" parenting from infancy up to the age of three or so immunized him against very severe psychopathology.

To put this into a general formula: Mr. Z had acquired sufficient sense of himself as a coherent entity and sufficient trust in his ability to find love in his world that he did not have to retreat into psychotic belief states when he was under stress. Mr. Z was able to do this because he had the minimal psychological equipment required for this type of learning and because his mother could provide a sufficiently empathic environment for him.

This minimally empathic environment can be defined in different ways. In Kohut's language, Mr. Z's mother was able to provide the holding and containing properties for her son when he was not capable of doing that. In more ordinary language, Mr. Z's mother could remain calm and loving toward her son when, faced by some physical or psychological distress, he felt on the verge of panic. She could instill hope in her boy that "this too shall pass." The frequent soothing gestures that good parents make automatically toward their distressed children are examples of selfobject functioning. When such parents perceive that their children are unhappy (afraid, terrified, angry, confused, etc.), they find ways to communicate to the child their adult sense that "relief is in sight." Good enough parents can offer their children solace. Parents can affirm that yes, this is an unhappy moment, but it will not last. As we will see in the following chapters, the need to find solace and hope appears throughout human lives. When that need is not met, adults, too, seek out someone or something that will make hope possible. These are the occasions upon which occult experiences are likely to occur.

The Capacity for Hope

The word *hope* is not a technical term. It comes from ordinary language and folk religion. But it reflects a vital aspect of the concept of selfobject and selfobject functioning. These technical terms refer to the parent's ability to convey to an infant or child that this intensely unhappy moment will not persist into the indefinite future. Hope is a feeling and belief that there *will be* a time when one can feel better than one does now. The good-enough father and good-enough mother can perform this selfobject function for the child because they can provide their child their own ego capacity to have hope.

Ego functions is a technical term. It names a set of capacities that include the ability to recognize the flow of time, tolerate physical distress, recognize the difference between dreaming and waking states, remember accurately, think rationally about a problem, employ abstract categories, secure and maintain friendships, and retain a consistent sense of self. During moments of stress or physical illness, or after a severe loss, one may not show the same level of ego functioning as usual. A large amount of alcohol dissolves many persons' ego function of social inhibitions. For persons with weak egos, alcohol may dissolve their tenuous grasp on moral or legal norms as well. There is no fixed, set number of ego functions. Because the concept pertains to the numerous dimensions of human psychological experience, there are as many sets of ego functions as there are theoreticians. Naturally, there are obvious functions that all serious persons would include in such sets. The capacity to learn, for example, is an ego function of primary importance. Without it, no human being could hope to advance. The capacity to learn, in turn, depends upon an accurate memory, so memory too can be counted as an ego function.

A complete list of ego functions, with a full and complete explanation for each function, would require a volume devoted to human personality theory. However, we can describe selfobject functioning as those moments in which another person performs an ego function for us. In this sense, then, when a friend supplies us with a fact we have forgotten, that friend has acted as a selfobject—for an instant. When we later console another friend who has lost a promotion, an election, an ideal, or a loved one, we are acting as selfobjects.

We have discussed selfobject functioning so far mainly in terms of painful experiences: loss, hurt, hopelessness, and the like. Yet selfobject functioning appears in pleasurable interactions as well. Adults may enjoy a child's intense silliness for a time. But at a certain point the adult tires of the repetition and suggests, sometimes firmly, that the game is over: "It is generally assumed that the repetitiveness of these games is a large factor in the adult's loss of interest. Our observations suggest that the high intensity of the child's excitement and joy is another factor."[30] In these instances the adult wants to modulate the child's exuberance and so seeks to decrease the intense excitement that the child may in fact be enjoying. Virginia Demos says that the effect these parent-child interactions have upon the child depends upon the parent's ability to calm the child down without shaming the child for the intensity of pleasure experienced. If the parent, a father, for example, criticizes his daughter for her silliness and intense pleasure in a game, the child may well understand his harsh tones as a condemnation of her sense of pleasure. Using Kohut's technical language, we can say that the father acts as an inhibiting, nonempathic selfobject. In more ordinary terms, he teaches his daughter that excitement and pleasure in moments of "wild abandon" will lead to shame and "vague discontent." If this kind of selfobject exchange comes to dominate the father's response to his daughter, the young girl will learn to question whether she dare enjoy herself, since "wild abandon" is "wrong," that is, only brings anger and depression.

The case history of Mr. Z describes an extreme instance in which his mother not only failed to provide positive selfobject functioning; she used her son as *her selfobject* and projected into him her own profound fragmentation anxieties. But not all instances of such a reversal between parent and child, where the parent uses the child to shore up a weak self, are as pathological as the relationship between Mr. Z and his mother.

The term *selfobject* is a neutral concept. We can apply it to a wide range of experiences and types of relationships. A fine example occurs at the end of the classic film, *Casablanca*. Rick (Humphrey Bogart) has fallen back in love with Ilsa (Ingrid Bergman), a former girlfriend. She has married a noble Frenchman whose role in the French Resistance makes him a target for German assassination. She too, however, falls in love and finds it impossible to stay away from Rick. What should she do? Should she follow her heart and remain with her true love, or serve the greater good and remain with her husband? She cannot decide and so tells Rick, roughly, "You must do the thinking for both of us!" Bogart accepts this demand for selfobject functioning. Naturally, he does the right thing.

Based on early and continuous assurances, the child acquires a sense of internal coherence not fully dependent upon the actual presence of the mother (or mothering person). In Kohut's language, when this occurs we can say that the child has formed a strong sense of self and is not liable to severe fragmentation anxiety. Consequently, we conclude that the child will not require, later in life, everyone in the child's environment to fulfill selfobject functions. The opposite holds true for persons with severe narcissistic impairments. We conclude that something went awry in the process of the consolidation of their sense of self. Consequently, they are vulnerable to fragmentation. Because fragmentation is so painful, they feel the need to find new persons to fulfill selfobject functions for them. Persons who suffer this degree of narcissistic vulnerability become patients who form selfobject transferences with their analysts. Kohut investigated this transference in his first monograph.[31]

SUMMARY:
KOHUT'S CLAIMS

We may summarize Kohut's basic claims. Impairments in early relationships between the child and selfobjects, for example, the mother, produce a child whose sense of self-coherence and self-worth is fragile. Even ordinary blows to self-esteem, so-called "narcissistic blows," are severely threatening to the fragile structure of self-regard. We note that "narcissistic blows" include anything that imbalances the self. Therefore, good news, an unexpected compliment, a sudden run of good luck, and similar positive events can be just as disorganizing as criticisms and rejections. Both kinds of experience threaten the hard-won stability of self. Adults with a history like Mr. Z's are much more vulnerable to suffering fragmentation anxiety. Because such anxiety is painful, people naturally seek ways to avoid fragmenting experiences. When persons who are so vulnerable suffer unavoidable injury, a narcissistic blow, they must repair themselves and their sense of intactness.

There are many ways to retrieve a sense of intactness. One is to engage in sexual actions that provide a temporary sense that one's body matches an internal fantasy of sexual power. Some narcissistically vulnerable persons, for example, may find that they have an immense need for homosexual contact. For a man, the fantasy that drives this hunger may include a belief that by incorporating another "large" man's penis into his own body he can unite his fragile and broken self with the idealized strength of his homosexual partner. For a woman, the urge to find a homosexual partner may be the enactment of a fantasy that by uniting herself sexually with another woman she may experience herself as male and her partner as female. The two women in this instance are not driven to homosexual embrace because of an upsurge in homosexual libido. Rather, it seems more likely that the unconscious fantasy enacted in the homosexual encounter is that of a male whose penis symbolizes a state of intactness, that is, not castrated, not fragmented. In this case homosexual contact appears compulsive because the anxiety against which it is a defense, fragmentation, is acute and terrible.

Another way to avoid fragmentation anxiety is to retreat into a cold, grandiose sense of oneself as untouched and untouchable by the fools who fail to comprehend one's superiority. Another way is to become adept at helping people when they, the other, seem vulnerable and needy. This gives one a role of superiority and makes it less likely that the other will see one's vulnerability. Kohut notes that this latter solution occurs frequently in the lives of persons who become talented psychotherapists. Such therapists often grew up with a parent whose depression or other impairment made the parent unable to reflect the child's narcissistic needs. The child becomes attuned to subtle clues in the parent's demeanor and, in a reversal of roles, provides selfobject functions for the parent. We saw this reversal of roles in Mr. Z's story. In this way such children repair their parents' narcissistic wounds. One unconscious motive for doing so is to make the parent strong enough to give back to the child what the child needs and cannot manufacture out of thin air: a sense of acceptance by an idealized other.

2
Inside the Occult Experience

QUEEN. To whom do you speak this?
HAMLET. Do you see nothing there?
QUEEN. Nothing at all; yet all that is I see.
HAMLET. Nor did you nothing here?
—William Shakespeare, *Hamlet*

Let us, furthermore, bear in mind the great practical importance of distinguishing perceptions from ideas, however intensely recalled. Our whole relation to the external world, to reality, depends on our ability to do so.
—Sigmund Freud, "A Metapsychological Supplement to the Theory of Dreams"

Was it a vision, or a waking dream?
Fled is that music—Do I wake or sleep?
—John Keats, *Ode to a Nightingale*

In this chapter, we develop a framework to apply to the stories in the following chapters of occult moments in the lives of Saint Augustine (354–430), Sigmund Freud (1856–1938), Carl Jung

(1875–1961), and other writers, including Johann Wolfgang Goethe (1749–1832), the greatest German poet.

Some might object that any framework is just another mold into which I force genuine and unique experiences. My framework might be a procrustean bed. Like that evil character out of Greek myth, I may chop off stories that do not fit my preconceptions and stretch others that fall short. This is an ever-present danger to anyone who wishes to explain experiences as varied and complex as occult moments.

Similar dangers confront critics and psychologists who advance theories about artistic creation. But it is instructive to go wrong. Therefore, I advance the following ideas about a template. Another more fitting metaphor might be that of a tidal pool, which is a small version of the much larger ocean. It is not a perfect model of the ocean, but it is available for study and so affords us landlubbers opportunities we might not otherwise have. To extend this metaphor one step further, one might say that occult experience is the tidal pool and religious experience the ocean. This chapter is one person's view of that tidal pool and the life forms which live there.

The framework I construct in this chapter uses a certain class of ideas to categorize a certain class of experiences. We have already developed some of the ideas: internal world, selfobject, empathy, and fragmentation anxiety. I add to these two new ideas: reality testing and repression. These are the rungs of a metaphorical ladder whose sides are the long chronological sequence of internal and external events that constitute the occult sequence. This sequence begins with the formation of the selfobject relationship, and continues through the breach in that relationship up to the moment when that breach is healed.

THE REALITY OF THE UNSEEN:
INSIDE THE MIND,
OUTSIDE THE MIND

This chapter began with three quotations, each addressing a single problem: How can one judge the truth of occult claims?

The first quotation is a dialogue between young Prince Hamlet and his mother, the queen. Hamlet's murdered father has commanded him to revenge the father's death. Hamlet begins to confront his mother with her guilt when the ghost appears and commands him to stop. Hamlet recoils in horror at this latest visitation. But the queen sees nothing and therefore chides her son for his inability to distinguish his madness from ordinary reality. To put the queen's thoughts into Freudian language, she believes that Hamlet is mentally deranged. The prince has lost the ordinary ability to distinguish between his wishes (for his father to return to the living) and his perceptions.

The quotation from Freud is from his discussion of dreams and the interesting fact that even the most mature persons experience the nonsense of dream thoughts as if they were real. As they dream, even intelligent persons show major lapses in their ability to test reality. Freud says the "institution" of reality testing develops slowly from infancy (when wishing dominates perception) to adulthood (when, as with the queen, perception dominates wishing). Reality testing is the ability to distinguish wishes from perceptions. Like other institutions built up slowly, reality testing is always vulnerable to collapse, to "regression."

Reality testing is an ego ability or an ego achievement. Freud defines it in the same way the queen does: What is *inside* a person's mind is fantasy; what is *outside* a person's mind is reality. Reality testing, then, is the ability to distinguish "between what is internal and what is external."[1] This ability develops slowly as the infant learns, after many failures, that its innate response to pain, wishing it away, does not work. Initially, Freud assumed that all infants attempt to satisfy their needs for food, warmth, affection, and such by calling upon their memory-image of the person who had pleased them in the past. To use Freud's terms, the infant spontaneously calls up the mnemonic image of the need-satisfying object and hopes that the evocation is equivalent to its actual appearance.

A hungry infant, for example, driven by its appetites, will spontaneously call up an image of the nursing breast, the bottle, or whatever object has satisfied it in the past. At this first moment in very young infants, there is no difference between the two images—one based on perception of the real mother, and the other called up from memory. Freud says that these two images are equivalent and in themselves offer the infant no way to distinguish one from the other.

The quotation from John Keats raises a question that troubles everyone caught in a twilight state between unconsciousness, in which dreams dominate, and consciousness, where dreams fade away. The question is, When I am asleep and dream and my dreams seem real, how can I distinguish one state from the other? To put this another way, when I wake and realize that what I thought was real was only a dream, I affirm that *this* state, ordinary consciousness, is "real."

How can we distinguish mere dreaming from the accurate perception of reality? How do infants develop into children who can distinguish mere wishes from actual perceptions? Clearly, children need some way to test and validate the source of their perceptions.

Freud says that they can do this by using their ability to move their muscles voluntarily. For by moving themselves, even slightly, infants can alter their perceptions of external objects. "A perception which is made to disappear by an action is recognized as external, as reality; where such an action makes no difference, the perception originates within the subject's own body—it is not real."[2]

During a dream, for example, one cannot walk around a group of trees that appears in the dream. We may believe that the trees are real. But we can also note, upon reflection, that dream images are not identical to ordinary perceptions because we cannot alter their appearance by altering our stance. Dream trees may cast shadows, but those shadows do not obey the laws of refraction, reflection, and geometry that govern real shadows from real trees.

Movie versions of dreams typically use mirrors to distort the visual images that appear on the screen. But even these distorted images are much more concrete, and much richer, than the two-dimensional images that occur in dreams. Yet the film images themselves are two-dimensional, not three-dimensional. We can distinguish them from an actual perception by using the numerous clues of depth, range, and alterations induced by our own movements.

One's ability to distinguish the internal world (thoughts, feelings, fantasies, wishes, sensations) from the external world (perceptions) depends upon control of one's musculature. If we were to lose control over our motility, our ability to test reality would decrease. In extreme cases, like paralysis or sleep, our capacity to distinguish fantasy from perception diminishes to the point that we mistake ideas derived from the inside and experience them as if they arrived from the outside.

The idea that reality testing depends upon the conscious control of musculature gives Freud a way to explain why dreams tend to be hallucinatory, that is, reality testing diminishes. During sleep one rarely has conscious control over one's musculature. One cannot will one's body to act in a certain way. Therefore, one cannot use the ordinary method to distinguish a set of ideas (or wishes or images) from a set of perceptions. On the contrary, dream ideas and thoughts become dream perceptions. On waking we may quickly realize that there are no monsters under the bed, but during the dream we had no such assurance. During the nightmare the monster seemed real and our terror was real, too.

Are Other Minds Like My Mind?

Freud's discussion of the concept of reality testing is far more complex than my summary. Yet we can see one problem that the theory raises for a psychoanalytic understanding of occult experience: If there is an absolute boundary between my internal world and the external world, how can I know that my internal world is like that of other people? I can listen carefully as they describe their experiences and their dreams, for example. I can report my own experiences and so compare my direct knowledge of my internal world with their reports of their internal worlds. But I can never enjoy their internal experience. I cannot cross the boundary that separates my internal world from the internal worlds of other people.

This may not seem to be an overwhelming problem. Most people are not bothered by what seems to be a logical quibble fit only for philosophers. But it is a problem for anyone, like Hamlet or Keats, who has struggled to understand the source of a vision, feeling, or insight. In its philosophic form, this problem is referred to as the problem of other minds. In its more poignant everyday form this problem is expressed by a young girl who once asked, "When I see green and others see green do they see the same green?" This was no random thought. It arose when she felt completely isolated from her family and her schoolmates. Understandably, as an adult this young girl became fascinated by technical issues in the philosophy of mind. She studied the history of philosophy, where she traced the logical issues surrounding the problem of other minds and located its historical sources. In this way she made significant discoveries in intellectual history, and she gained a significant degree of mastery over her internal anxiety about her own sense of self: She was not radically unlike other people.

The academic question, Are there other minds like my own? becomes a vital question for children. Are there other minds like my own who will comprehend me? To answer this second question in the negative, to say that there are no other minds capable of comprehending one's interior state, is to say that there are no empathic persons. For empathic persons can, for a moment, perceive accurately the nature of one's interior life, the landscape of one's internal world. As we have seen in our discussion of Mr. Z and his profound suffering, a child who lacks a minimally empathic parent lacks access to the most secure defense against fragmentation anxiety. That defense is the child's capacity to find adults who can perform ego functions, like the maintenance of self-esteem, that the child cannot perform alone. In other words, the best defense against fragmentation anxiety is the presence of suitable adults who can form selfobject links to the child.

The Reality of Hamlet and
the Reality of Ghosts

Hamlet's question to his mother was, essentially, Do you see what I see? We recall that Hamlet had recently lost his father through a violent crime, had seen his mother remarry in haste, and was forced to see his rightful place, the throne of Denmark, usurped by his uncle, whom his father's ghost had declared to be an incestuous murderer. Hamlet's mother, the queen, took Freud's side in the matter and argued that because she saw nothing in the spot toward which her son gestured, Hamlet was mad. Hamlet's vision must have been an internal event, projected out into the Danish night. Shakespeare, however, did not side with the queen in this matter. He had already indicated that Hamlet's faithful and eminently reasonable colleague Horatio had seen the ghost. Indeed, Horatio had tried to speak to the ghost and attempted to strike him with his pike. So the ghost was perfectly real—that is, valid—within the drama as well as within Hamlet's tormented mind.

There might be a better way of saying this. For to say the ghost is real "within" Hamlet's mind is to use Freud's radical dichotomy between inside (the inner world) and outside (the external world). We might better say that Hamlet's "mind" is not coextensive with his brain, or for that matter, any part of his solid flesh. We might, in other words, distinguish Hamlet's brain, a biological entity encased within his skull, from Hamlet's mind. Hamlet's mind is that rich set of ideas and capacities that exist *between* the prince, his friends, his family, and his kingdom. As the anthropologist Gregory Bateson suggests, the concepts and ideas evoked by the notion of mind are far more extensive and complex than those evoked by brain. One can speak at length about the mind of Socrates, for example, and dispute with others the correct interpretation of Socrates' intentions. One cannot speak about Socrates' brain, since that mass of flesh and tissue dissolved into dust long ago.

Hamlet's mind exists. It is a real entity. The ghost of Hamlet's father exists, too. It also is a real entity. We can understand both entities, describe them, and respond to them even if they are not ordinary three-dimensional objects, existing in ordinary space and time. In a similar way we can speak seriously about Hamlet's character, Hamlet's mind, and Hamlet's fate, even though we refer to a fictional entity, entirely the product of Shakespeare's mind. We can do so because Shakespeare's mind, Hamlet's mind, and our own minds are not defined or limited by our brains. Of course, we cannot point to Hamlet's mind in the same way we can point to ordinary objects, like books and coffee tables. Neither can we point to Hamlet himself, except as an idea shared by most persons educated in Western culture.

Yet we do not want to conclude that Hamlet is not real. On the contrary, he is intensely real. In fact, it is far easier to love Hamlet than it is to love most ordinary mortals. Hamlet influences us, stays with us, and will outlast us. Like the concept of mind, or the concept of selfobject, the idea of Hamlet as a character occupies a realm distinct from that of ordinary objects and ordinary persons. Yet minds, Hamlet, and selfobject relationships are all real, not mere fantasies like bad dreams or phantasms like imagined ghosts in haunted castles. Selfobject relationships are real, even if they are not measured by objective instruments. Socrates' mind and Hamlet's character are real also, even if one cannot use objective instruments to dissect them. I stress the similarities between these three entities—Hamlet, selfobject relationships, and Socrates—because they are also similar to occult events. Occult events do take place: that is, people attest to them, find them valuable, and respond to them. Yet we cannot treat this kind of real object (an occult experience) empathically if we expect to examine it using objective instruments. Some believers in occult sciences may object to this claim. Such believers might feel that I have trivialized their scientific claims. I do not wish to dispute the objective accuracy of all occult claims. I suggest that we can understand occult experience better if we treat it as an entity similar to selfobject relationships, Hamlet's character, or Socrates' mind.

To advance an empathic account of occult experience we must aim to elucidate, using external language, features of a purely internal experience. We must cross the conceptual boundary that separates other minds from our own. To cross that boundary we must explore the occult mood.

EMPATHY AND THE
OCCULT MOOD

In the Introduction to this book, we considered three stories of occult experience, two from the lives of ordinary people, the third from the life of Arthur Conan Doyle. We developed three clues to the mystery of occult belief: (1) it involves archaic feelings derived from very early experiences as a child, (2) those feelings center upon the experience of a mother's affection, and (3) these feelings together constitute a mood. This occult mood is similar to nostalgia. Both moods are oriented toward one's past. Unlike nostalgia, however, the occult mood is a self-state in which one looks to the *outside* rather than to the *inside*. In nostalgia one savors one's own feelings about one's past. Nostalgia can be bittersweet, but it is always linked to a recognition that these are *our* memories, *our* feelings, and *our* past. That is not true of the occult mood. As we have seen, an important dimension of occult experience is the feeling that the occult event occurs outside our memories and feelings.

In chapter 1 I outlined the ways in which the contemporary school of psychoanalytic thought of Heinz Kohut might help us employ these clues to solve the mystery of occult belief: How can fully rational and educated persons believe what is obviously unsupportable and outlandish?

In the first part of chapter 1 I used concepts from Kohut's psychology to explore occult experience, suggesting that Kohut's insights about fragmentation anxiety seemed to fit well the pattern of events that occur just before an occult experience. I did not suggest that everyone who has an occult experience is sick. There is no evidence, for example, that my graduate student was mentally impaired in any way. Nor is there any evidence that Conan Doyle was neurotic or emotionally impaired in the least. On the contrary, Conan Doyle's life is an exemplar of personal fortitude. I did suggest that there is a similarity in pattern between the events that produce fragmentation anxiety in persons with severe narcissistic vulnerability and the events that produce occult experience.

In the second part of chapter 1, I developed key concepts in Kohut's psychology that can help us explain the pattern of events that lead to occult experience. Those concepts are: (1) the universal human need to feel special and at the center of one's world (narcissism), (2) the need for a special empathic bond between parent and child (the selfobject relationship), (3) the terror that losing this bond arouses (fragmentation anxiety), and (4) the therapeutic event that can heal fragmentation anxiety (the empathic response).

In the last part of chapter 1, I discussed Kohut's definition of empathy as vicarious introspection. I distinguished empathy from sympathy. As a form of *introspection* empathy requires one to examine internal experience. To be empathic is to explore another person's internal world from the vantage point of that person's ego, to comprehend the likely feelings, thoughts, ideas, fantasies, moods, and other events that make up mental life. To be sympathetic is to share those experiences.

As we will see below, this is a key difference between an occult view of the occult and a psychoanalytic view of the occult. Those who hold an occult view of the occult want sympathetic hearings. Even Conan Doyle felt that he had to convince as many people as possible of the truth of spiritualism. Conan Doyle sacrificed a great deal of time and even a portion of his health to testify to the wisdom uncovered by the spiritualists and other occult experts who attached themselves to him. A psychoanalytic view of the occult is an empathic view, neither sympathetic to occult claims nor disdainful of them. Even well-trained therapists like Ernest Jones and Sigmund Freud, however, lapse into moralizing attacks against occult believers. It is more difficult to be empathic toward the person who has occult experience.

Sympathetic versus Empathic Views
of Occult Experience

I have contrasted sympathetic responses to the occult with empathic responses to occult claims for two reasons. First, it is easy to confuse empathy with being nice to someone. Empathy is the capacity to take another person's interior life seriously, but it is not a moral characteristic. A clever car salesperson may recognize, via vicarious introspection, that you are ashamed of the wreck you drive. When you stop the junker in front of the showroom and the engine continues to burp and the rusted-out tailpipe rattles against the dented fender, a keen observer may sense your dark mood. A good salesperson, one who pushes a lot of cars, can use his or her empathic grasp of your internal state to advantage. So-called charismatic leaders, too, have an innate skill to comprehend empathically their followers' fragmented states. The charismatic promise of peace and love declared in airports by adamant followers of one guru or another often seems to express a deeper hope of self-unification. Empathy may be the crucial mode without which children cannot grow and patients cannot improve, but not all empathic persons are loving or therapeutic. *Empathy* is a technical term for a certain kind of insight into another person's interior life.

A second reason to distinguish empathy from sympathy is that an empathic point of view is comprehensive, while a sympathetic point of view is not. To give an empathic account of an occult experience, for example, one must try to comprehend the entire sequence of events that led to the occult moment. Included in this chain of events are feelings and thoughts that may well be unconscious to the occult actor. But a sympathetic account of the same chain of events focuses only upon the actor's conscious, manifest feelings and thoughts.

For most actors in occult dramas, and for most onlookers to those dramas, the most exciting part of the occult event is the moment when the impossible is made possible. This fantastic moment becomes the center of excitement. For this reason film versions of occult events use elaborate special effects. Directors spare no effort to show us the fantastic moment when the ghost appears, the vision makes itself manifest, or the devil invades a young girl's body. A sympathetic response to occult experience is a response to these fantastic elements.

In contrast, an empathic response to an occult experience is much less dramatic than a sympathetic one. The lack of drama in an empathic response, however, is balanced by a far greater appreciation of the richness of the person's inner life *preceding* the occult moment. As I suggested above and in the Introduction, to treat occult moments as clinical phenomena one must examine the actions and feelings that led to the dramatic moment. To make this distinction between a sympathetic and an empathic account clearer, it may help to schematize how each point of view could be applied to the stories of my cousin and my student, which I related in the Introduction.

The conversations that fascinated my aunt's relatives, sitting in her living room, centered upon the possibility of witchcraft. Did witchcraft operate at long distances? Should one burn candles during the day as well as the evening to ward off evil forces? Who else in the family had close encounters with witches? My relatives sympathized with my cousin's own understanding of his experience. It may seem that my cousin believed everything he told his relatives about the witch. It may also seem that he wanted to convince them of the truth of these stories and receive from them sympathetic responses.

In part this is true. Certainly none of the adults in my cousin's family objected to his and his mother's version of the story about the artist-witch in California. But it is false to say that my cousin had no conflicts over his story. For one thing, he altered his accounts of the witchcraft, depending upon the time of evening he recounted the story and upon the mood of his listeners. Sometimes my cousin said that the artist-witch could fly. At other times, he changed this to a recollection that she said she could fly.

An unkind critic might say that this shift in stories proves that the entire account of witchcraft was a fabrication, pure and simple. I do not believe that; rather, I believe that my cousin's shift between one set of stories and another proves that he did not know what he believed. His beliefs and convictions fluctuated, just as other people's beliefs fluctuate according to their state of consciousness. My cousin's occult experience and occult beliefs were products of a divided consciousness.

There might be better terms than "divided consciousness." But it does seem descriptively accurate. My cousin's mind was in conflict, and my student's mind was in conflict when he saw the heavenly visitor. Such divisions in consciousness are not rare. Everyone can report instances of similar twilight states. For some people, the first moments after waking in the morning are a mix of dreamlike stupor and ordinary consciousness. For other people an intense emotional response to nature, for example, at the end of a perfect summer day, at sunset, evokes an odd mix of perception, memory, and waking dream.

Déjà vu is a common instance of this mixed experience. Most people can recall a moment of *déjà vu:* when one is certain that one has already experienced, in the past, precisely what one knows to be a new experience. In extreme instances *déjà vu* carries with it a sense of conviction that one has lived before, as another person, and "been here" in that previous life. Many standard occult beliefs about reincarnation, the transmission of thoughts, the "double" to oneself that lives on the opposite side of the world, and similar teachings explain *déjà vu* experience. These occult teachings, in other words, provide folk theory for the source of what is undeniable experience.

Experiences like *déjà vu* and similar states of mixed consciousness tend to be brief and to evaporate upon examination. Yet they are real. They happen and then fade away. Folk psychologists have always offered explanations for such moments of mixed consciousness. These folk explanations usually affirm an occult belief. For example, a standard theory of *déjà vu* is that one actually did live in a previous life, and the uncanny sense of having been here before is actually an accurate memory drawn from one's previous life. Many people accept these occult explanations. Other people reject them. Yet no one can deny that such mixed states of consciousness occur. When they do occur, we must agree with Keats. We are not sure if we sleep and so dream this moment, or are awake and so perceive something that is usually hidden from view. I think that one finds a similar mixed mood in occult experience. There appear to be moments, in other words, when persons transfixed by an occult experience may also recognize, dimly perhaps, that they wanted the occult event to occur just as it did.

My student recognized, dimly perhaps, that he wanted the events to occur as they did. To use the terms developed in chapter 1, through introspection the young man perceived that he had considered a number of alternatives to end his suffering. His first thought had been to get drunk, as he had before. Drinking helped dull all his feelings, especially his loneliness. If he drank enough, he would eventually pass out and then feel nothing. But he could not find enough alcohol. In desperation he sought other ways to undo his terrible sense of fragmentation. For a moment he considered suicide. Given his religious training, the idea of heavenly beings, whom one could join at some moment after death, was appealing. Because he lost, once again, the love of an idealized man, my student sought to find the love of a being who could not abandon him.

An Empathic View of Evil Forces

We can reformulate my cousin's story and my student's story into one-line summaries. The following diagrams sketch out the sequence of loss of selfobject relationship, fragmentation anxiety, and the need for repair in each story:

COUSIN

left home (= lost his mother as selfobject)

fragmentation anxiety

need to repair the self (to prevent fragmentation)

the occult event

We can refine this sequence by using the concept of selfobject developed in chapter 1:

Loss of selfobject

suffering

need to repair

occult event

We can summarize my student's story as well:

STUDENT

the dean left (= lost the dean's selfobject aid)

fragmentation anxiety

need to repair the self (to undo fragmentation)

the occult event

These one-line summaries of the two occult events are brief. My student might agree with my summary. But it does not capture the richness of his story, just as my first does not capture the richness of my cousin's story. These one-line summaries are not complete explorations of the occult moment. They are simply schemata, recipes, or flow charts of the events that I believe underlie any occult moment.

Granted that these are schematic, a deeper problem remains. If my schemata are accurate, the actual source of the occult event is within the personality, within the inner world, not in the external world. If this is true, why is this fact not accessible to the occult actor? Why would most such persons find my suggestions unbelievable? One can find occult devotees who are hostile to any attempt to comprehend their claims. But one can also find persons like my student and Conan Doyle whose sincerity cannot be doubted. These persons also find the explanation I offer impossible.

TWO FORMS OF UNKNOWING:
THE REPRESSED AND
THE INEXPRESSIBLE

Occult actors seem not to recognize the truth of my one-line summaries. How should we understand the differences between us? Are they correct? Am I correct? Must one of us be wrong? I can imagine three answers.

A first answer is to claim that the occult events occurred exactly as reported by the people involved. This is the sympathetic response to occult stories. There are many eminent persons who have accepted this answer. Conan Doyle and, as we will see, Carl Jung, the founder of analytical psychology, both advanced this sympathetic response.

A second answer is Freudian. It explains that the occult actor's inability to agree with a psychoanalytic interpretation is a product of repression. According to this view, occult actors have repressed into their unconscious ideas and feelings about the event that were at one time conscious. When my student, for example, said that it seemed as if the heavenly visitor were hovering above him, he must have repressed his usual abilities to recognize the difference between dream and reality, between wishful thinking and perception.

A third answer to the question as to why my accounts of occult experience differ from those of occult actors is that the occult moment is not a product of repression alone. This is the answer I propose to develop in this chapter. I will suggest that both the first response, the sympathetic answer, and the second response, the Freudian one, are partially correct. The sympathetic response captures a crucial part of the conscious experience in occult moments. The Freudian response points to a set of psychological mechanisms that seem responsible for the mixed consciousness that also occurs in occult moments.

We have considered the sympathetic response to occult claims above. We will consider it again when we study a case history concerning an occult moment considered genuine by the therapist. At this time it will pay to consider how the second and third answers differ from one another. To make that difference clear, we must consider what Freud meant by the term *repression*. We can then compare that concept with the answer I propose.

My answer is that the core element in occult experience is inexpressible, not because it is repressed, but because it pertains to a relationship (the self-selfobject tie) that is *not* intrapsychic. I suggest that honest people cannot help but experience occult experiences as pertaining to the external world. They *must* reject standard psychoanalytic interpretations of their experiences. They *must* claim that the event was real, that it occurred in the real world, and that they are not merely imagining it.

Occult actors must claim these things if they are honest, for from their point of view the occult moment occurred exactly as they report it. They are not pretending, not dreaming, and not hallucinating. I agree with them. I believe that we can understand why they are right.

To use Freud's language, I wish to show how occult experience is not merely the product of repression. That is, I will use Kohut's work to offer an alternative account of occult experience. This alternative account agrees with Freud's general theorem about such experience: that it arises in response to a need. My account disagrees with Freud's specific theorem that occult experiences are the products of repression. To understand these differences it will help briefly to consider the central concept of repression.

Repression and the Inner World

Sigmund Freud was born in 1856 and educated in the rigors of late-nineteenth-century science in Vienna. Freud inherited that epoch's grand scientific hope that the social sciences would soon match the advances made in the natural and biological sciences. It is difficult for us, living at the end of the twentieth century, to feel the excitement generated by the bold scientists of Freud's century. Yet even a brief survey of the first half of the nineteenth century reveals profound discoveries in physics, chemistry, biological sciences, neurology, geology, and, of course, Charles Darwin's great achievements in natural history.

These great discoveries share a heroic quality of scale. For example, by the middle of the century a number of physicists had formulated the essential features of the Second Law of Thermodynamics. Briefly stated, this law holds that in any closed system energy may be neither created nor destroyed, but only transformed. This law or principle is to hold for all cases, in all systems, in all known or knowable universes. With the Second Law in hand, one can rule out a great many claims that might otherwise seem plausible or at least worth investigating. Citing the Second Law, for example, one can quickly reject any inventor's claim to have discovered a perpetual motion machine.

One finds similar scope and drama in Darwin's formulations of the laws of natural selection. Darwin's great achievement included not just a set of new ideas, but the demonstration that his principle of natural selection could account for the "mystery of mysteries," the diversity of species. Again, the scope of these claims is immense, for Darwin speaks of *all* species, in *all* continents, and for *all* ages. Darwin's image of the endless process of natural selection and its perpetual workings is a secular variation on a theme earlier attributed to an all-loving deity, who neither slumbered nor slept:

> It may metaphorically be said that natural selection is daily and hourly scrutinising, throughout the world, the slightest variations; rejecting those that are bad, preserving and adding up all that are good; silently and insensibly working, *whenever and wherever opportunity offers,* at the improvement of each organic being in relation to its organic and inorganic conditions of life.[3]

The great physiologist Emil Du Bois-Reymond had zealous hopes to place biology on a strictly scientific basis. Du Bois-Reymond was fighting against the Vitalists, a scientific school that held that biological organisms were essentially distinct from physical-chemical interactions. Du Bois-Reymond and his Viennese colleague, Ernst Brücke, fought against vitalism and carried their crusade for a rigorous scientific biology and physiology throughout Germany and Austria. Freud studied under Brücke for six years in the latter's Physiological Institute at the University of Vienna.

In his earliest essays Freud makes his allegiance to Brücke's research program clear and unmistakable: The only processes that occur within the brain (or mind) are physical-chemical. A scientific psychology requires one to discover what energic forces underlay psychological processes.

We should distinguish this ideal from Freud's sense of his capacity to meet it. Freud had no illusions that he had accomplished the final reduction of psychological events to physiological processes. But he did not forsake that ideal. Freud stated in an unpublished essay, written under the influence of Brücke, that he wished to develop a psychology representing "psychical processes as quantitatively determinate states of specifiable material particles."[4]

Freud never abandoned Brücke's physiological ideal. It appears throughout his work. Even in his final papers, written in the late 1930s, Freud speaks about the flow and containment of psychic energies. Yet Freud never claimed that he had accomplished the task of reducing all of psychology to its physiological underpinnings. In all his writings Freud developed concepts that reflected the tension that existed between his physiological ideals and his psychological practice, so most of Freud's basic ideas are two-sided. On the one side they have a physiological reference, on the other a psychological meaning. For example, when he speaks about the "dream work" in *The Interpretation of Dreams,*[5] he refers to both the physical work accomplished by the expenditure of energy and the creative effort expended by the dreamer's unconscious mind.

In a similar way, when Freud talks about the work of culture, he refers to both the actual expenditure of energy by millions of people and the intellectual achievements of the few. Freud *hoped* to found a unified physiological science. He *realized* he had not fulfilled that hope. Rather than forsake that hope, Freud incorporated it into his basic theorems about the human mind. Nowhere is this more specific than in his definition of a fundamental notion, repression.

The concept of repression is so central to Freud's thought and so integrated with other key concepts in his theory that serious scholars have devoted whole books to the task of elucidating its meaning in Freud's clinical theory (how analysis cures) and his developmental theory (how infants grow into children and children grow into adults). Like other core terms in Freud's theory, the concept of repression has no single definition. To explicate some of its meanings, it will help to recall some of Freud's favorite metaphors for repression, metaphors drawn from physics, politics, and journalism. The first metaphor, from physics, is based on a Newtonian model of force and counterforce. Following the principles set down by Brücke, his mentor, Freud asserted that all ideas must have associated with them a certain force, that is, a quantum of psychic energy. If the expression of a certain idea could cause discomfort, the mental mechanism must find some way to prevent its arriving to consciousness. But to do so, the mental mechanism must summon enough psychic energy to counteract the quantum of energy attached to the dangerous idea. One force must be countered by another. If one feels, for example, the sudden impulse to laugh at a colleague's misfortune, one must repress the entire idea if one wishes to avoid being labeled as cruel. But to repress that impulse one must find a force equal to it, for example, the threat of shame, which one can oppose to its expression. To "re-press" an idea is to push it back into a state of nonconsciousness. Repression is the conscious or unconscious effort one makes in order to eject an idea (or feeling) from entering consciousness.[5] The apparatus that accomplishes this ejection (later termed the "ego") must use force against force. Freud calls his theory a "psychodynamic" one because it is a theory of psychic forces. The English word *dynamic* derives from the Greek term *dunamis.* In Greek philosophy, *dunamis* refers to potency or capacity as well as to the underlying physical forces of the universe. In the Greek New

Testament, *dunamis* refers to God's power, represented in Jesus as the Christ. According to the gospel writers, Christ's ability to conquer the power (*dunamis*) of death originates from his being empowered by God.[6]

The second metaphor for repression derives from politics. Politicians must repress opponents who struggle against them, especially if those opponents gain the public's ear and rouse the masses. Freud says something similar can occur within the psychic economy of human beings. By 1920 Freud had developed a tripartite theory of the personality. The first and oldest portion of the personality was the id (*das Es*), the source of instinctual forces. The second was the ego (*das Ich*), and the third the superego (*das Über-Ich*). Ideally, the ego rules. But in moments of chaos or instinctual upsurge, the id might gain control of the reins of self-governance. Or, at other moments, when the ego perceives that it has failed to abide by the superego's demands, the superego might gain control and punish the ego severely, even driving it to death.[7] Like any judicious ruler, then, the ego must organize its defense against the mobs that threaten it with anarchy and against internal threats as well. It does this by repressing ideas that emerge from the id and by repressing condemnations and threats that emanate from the superego.

The third metaphor for repression comes from literature and its suppression. In Freud's time military censors often blacked out large segments of newspapers that gave accounts of maneuvers and battles. In the middle of a large printed page one might find, literally, a large black spot—the product of efficient censorship. When Freud first announced the utility of the concept of repression, he did so in the context of his equally brilliant concept of "the censorship." This term figures prominently in the great theory sections of Freud's masterpiece, *The Interpretation of Dreams*.[8] There, drawing upon yet other metaphors, Freud suggests that a censor operating within the dreamer's mind is responsible for deleting from consciousness ideas that would bring discomfort (psychic pain).

RELIGION AND THE RETURN OF
THE REPRESSED

Throughout this chapter I have wanted to avoid two mistakes in advancing a psychology of occult experience. The first is to confine occult experience entirely to the inner world, to the mental apparatus of the individual who has the occult experience. The second is to confine occult experience entirely to the external world, to agree with the occult actor that the entire event occurred out there, apart from anything that preceded the occult moment. One finds a similar set of approaches to religious experience. One group of psychologists views religious experience as entirely the product of internal experience. A second group views religious experience as entirely the product of external forces (divine forces) impinging upon human beings. Freud belongs to the first group. Many traditional theologians and other religious experts belong to the second group. Our central question has been, Does the concept of repression illuminate occult experience? One way to answer this question is to see if the concept of repression illuminates ordinary religious experience.

Freud used the repression theory to examine all religious experience. I have suggested that the term *repression* has a dual parentage, partly from physiology and partly from psychology. The term is a brilliant solution to technical issues in the psychology of neurotic conflicts because it links together somatic events, like a stomachache, with psychological causes, like one's competitor getting the job instead of oneself. Repression links together, in other words, the two "realms" of experience with which Freud was most concerned: the somatic systems (the body) and the mental mechanism (the mind). With concepts like repression in his conceptual toolbox Freud could construct his revolutionary insights into the hidden meanings of physical symptoms and similar physiological events.

Freud did not stop there. He also sought to explore the meaning and function of cultural artifacts using the same set of conceptual tools. We find Freud writing voluminously not just on neurosis and psychosis, but on art, religion, and history as well. Freud's essays on the art of Leonardo da Vinci, on Moses, and on Feodor Dostoevski are as well known as his essays on dreams and symptoms. When Freud examined religious experience, he employed his chief conceptual tool, the concept of repression.

In Freud's best-known essay on religion, *The Future of an Illusion*,[9] he claims to show that religion is a grand illusion, based on human wish-fulfillment and the universal need to feel loved by divine parental powers that will safeguard us against the dangers of the world, especially death. Freud's lesser-known works on ritual, uncanny experience, and Moses contain far richer psychoanalytic accounts of religion.[10] In these texts one sees that Freud took religious claims seriously. Indeed, as he says in a very late essay, his science, psychoanalysis, has only one great enemy and opponent: religion.[11]

Freud feels that religion is an opponent to psychoanalysis because religion appears to cure the miseries that plague both ordinary folk and neurotics. Miseries such as feelings of depression, worthlessness, bleakness, and similar states of psychic pain afflict the just and the unjust, the neurotic and the normal. These miseries are all based on the frustration of infantile wishes for loving, unceasing protection from divine parents, immortality, preservation from harm, and so on. Religious teachings suggest that one might indirectly fulfill these wishes by carrying out certain actions and affirming certain beliefs. By fulfilling these wishes religion offers a way out of the psychic pain that otherwise seems our common lot. Wishes that a neurotic person has repressed, for example, the wish for immortality, religion seems to grant and declare fulfilled. Religious teachings, according to Freud, are powerful and believable because they reinstate to consciousness wishes and feelings that had been repressed. Religion gains prestige because it sanctions repressed yearnings. Religion seems to contradict the harsh dictates of an unfeeling natural world. Religion, in its Judeo-Christian form, says that the ultimate forces that rule our human world are personal ones, the will of a loving god.

Religious experiences, for example, visions of a deity that appears to be intimately involved with one's life, are often visions of a personal god. Freud explains religious experiences by using his concept of the return of the repressed and a variation, the return of surmounted beliefs. The latter are beliefs one once entertained in childhood but seemed to outgrow. For example, in uncanny experiences like visitations by ghosts, it seems that ideas that one once entertained as a child but later repressed return and are justified by current events. Freud concludes that uncanny moments, and by extension religious experiences, have two sources. Repressed ideas, for example, incestuous wishes, may return to consciousness because they appear to be fulfilled. The heroes of many science-fiction stories, for example, go back in time to encounter their parents, who were then at the hero's present age. Such encounters raise the danger and excitement of an actual incestuous event, for now no age barrier separates child and parent. Other science-fiction stories and ghost stories place their heroes in circumstances in which magic pills, robots, or special fluids grant them powers that were once the stuff of childhood fantasy. The abilities to fly, be invisible, and see through people's clothing are all available in one form of fantasy or another.

These fantasies, long surmounted by adult experience and education, are pleasurable when presented in the proper atmosphere of a movie or novel. In this way surmounted fantasies have little of the danger and thrill linked to repressed fantasies. By definition, such wishes must remain repressed; they cannot be owned directly. Yet the immense quantity of affect associated with them—their "libidinal charge"—remains, therefore, repressed as well. Freud uses his central idea of repression to make a brilliant analysis of the power of religious ideas: They gain their potency through their linkage to ideas long repressed yet to which are attached the most powerful currents of infantile life. As we saw above, a key feature of Freud's theory is the axiom that all ideas have attached to them a quantity of force (or cathexis). When dangerous ideas are repressed, that quantity of force remains attached to them and so unavailable to the ego. When those ideas are liberated, as may occur in primitive cultures that sanction certain forms of sexual license, there are also liberated intense emotional forces.

AN OCCULT EVENT
DURING AN ANALYSIS

I advance a post-Freudian view of occult experience in this book. I do not reject Freud's analysis of religious experience. That is, I think we can find repressed elements in occult experience, and we should examine those repressed ideas as well as the self and selfobject issues that coexist with them. To explain what these two sets of ideas look like in a real story, I discuss a case history published some thirty years ago.

In 1955, Jule Eisenbud, a well-known New York psychoanalyst, published an article, "On the Use of the Psi Hypothesis in Psycho-Analysis." As he had in other writings, Eisenbud wanted to show that psychoanalytic theory could be improved if a new hypothesis about mental functioning were added to it. He called this new hypothesis "psi." Eisenbud advanced his hypothesis as a "construct-fact" like the classic Freudian concepts of the unconscious and repression. He defines psi: "In the absence of any known means of gaining information through normal sensory channels it is nevertheless possible for a person to behave in non-chance correspondence with given events past, present, and future."[12]

Eisenbud claimed that this hypothesis is more scientific than any alternative because it states that there is *some* causal link between a future event and one's ability to predict it, even if we have no way to measure that connection and even if the prediction is made in a way that uses no ordinary channel of communication. Eisenbud uses the psi hypothesis to account for an extraordinary event in the life of one of his patients.

Eisenbud's case history is useful because it actually contains two occult stories, both about birds. In the first story, Eisenbud's patient, a fifty-five-year-old man, imagines that he can predict the appearance of a kingfisher. In the second story, this same patient believes he has predicted the appearance of a much rarer bird, a worm-eating warbler. Eisenbud examines both stories. The first he explains using Freudian concepts of repression; the second he says could not be explained with these concepts. He asserts that the second story can be explained only by using the psi hypothesis. The second story is a genuine occult event, according to Eisenbud. So in this case history we have two birds, two different events, and two different theories used to explain these events.

The first occult event occurred to Eisenbud's patient about a year before he terminated his many-year analysis. He was driving home alone, after a day of birdwatching on Long Island. "Suddenly, while thinking of the fact that he had not seen one Kingfisher during the entire day, the thought came that he was shortly to see one, and this presented itself with a feeling of absolute conviction." Soon a kingfisher flew in front of the patient's car. This sight and the feeling of "fore-knowledge" gave the patient "a wonderful sense of exhilaration as if a miracle had occurred."[13]

Eisenbud does not attack his patient's story. But he does make it clear that the standard repression hypothesis can account for his patient's ability to predict the appearance of the kingfisher. Eisenbud reasons that either his patient had seen the kingfisher out of the corner of his eye or he had heard its distinctive rattle. "In either case he might have *repressed* the perception and then accomplished a 'double-take' precisely in order to give himself the feeling of a premonition coming true."[14]

Eisenbud rejects his patient's claim that he had a premonition because, as Eisenbud says, "the determining psychodynamic forces were clear." In other words, when Eisenbud feels that he can use the standard repression hypothesis to explain his patient's actions, he does not affirm an occult principle. He does not invoke the psi hypothesis.

The psychodynamic forces that brought Eisenbud's patient to create his "slight of mind" are related to selfobject disorders. His patient had struggled for years with severe dependency upon alcohol and drugs and "had finally faced squarely the panic of having to begin to make a living for himself and his family. Just before the [kingfisher] episode he had for the first time permitted himself to experience realistically the impact of a sad state of debt from which he had somehow to extricate himself."[15]

Eisenbud's brief descriptions of his patient's character suggest that the patient suffered intense narcissistic wounds. The man's deep needs for soothing magical substances, like alcohol and other drugs, which he could imbibe whenever he felt close to fragmentation, suggest that one could classify him as a narcissistic character of the "overburdened" type. Ernest Wolf, a psychoanalytic colleague of Kohut's from Chicago, says that such people cannot tolerate any sudden increase in emotional intensity. Such people lack "self-soothing" structures[16] that help them control their emotions. Any upsurge, even of positive emotions, is traumatic. "Even gentle stimuli cause painful excitement, and the world is experienced as hostile and dangerous."[17] Wolf adds that such patients may alternate between making strident demands upon those close to them and total suppression of all demands. I believe that something like this alteration occurred in Eisenbud's patient: His analyst had begun to take away his lifelong solutions to fragmentation anxiety by "analyzing" away the usual rationalizations the patient had about his drinking and drug usage. When Eisenbud says his patient had begun to experience the full "realistic" burden of his debt, it seems reasonable to conjecture that the patient experienced this not only as "his ultimate motherlessness"[18] but also as severely fragmenting. Eisenbud explains his patient's vision of the kingfisher as the expression of a fully regressed ego: The patient hallucinated the bird just as Freud speculated that infants originally hallucinate the appearance of the breast, which they spontaneously call up out of memory.

"The bird . . . represented at once the mother and the breast, and the net result of the patient's manoeuvre . . . was to prove that all was not yet lost when one could think, 'Mother, appear!' and then have the mother actually present herself."[19] It was this deep need for a mothering person, and full-fledged and generous breast, that brought about the patient's "slight of mind."

To use Freud's terms, Eisenbud's patient had only partly repressed his infantile yearning to return to a mothering person who would rescue him from his adult crises. Having given up alcohol and other oral solutions, like drugs, to cure his depression, he was especially vulnerable to the return of the repressed. He regressed to a point that Freud had long before described as infantile autism: He hallucinated the appearance of the very object he desired. Like a wanderer, half-crazed with thirst, alone on a desert island, Eisenbud's patient created out of nothing what he most desired.

Eisenbud describes a second occult instance that initially appears to be identical to the first. His patient, "approaching the termination of his analysis, one day reported an experience of the morning that filled him with awe and gave him a tremendous sense of exhilaration. He had awakened early with a strange feeling of certainty that when he went out to the park he would somehow see a rare bird called the worm-eating warbler."[20]

The story of the second visitation begins with the patient in a twilight state of consciousness. The patient says he dressed, sure that he would see this rare bird. Oddly enough, he does see it three times in Central Park, where other birdwatchers also see it and congratulate him on his good fortune.

Eisenbud claims that this second visitation and premonition illustrate the operation of the extraordinary capacity he labeled psi. Eisenbud offers this theorem only because he cannot otherwise account for his patient's ability to predict accurately that the worm-eating warbler would be in Central Park. He examined his patient's story and found no evidence that his patient used "normal sensory channels" to discover the bird's existence in New York City. Lacking any positive evidence that his patient had used ordinary channels of communication, Eisenbud concludes that he must have used extraordinary channels. These channels must operate in ways contrary to ordinary rules of space and time.

One might dismiss Eisenbud's account out of hand since the psi hypothesis is essentially a negative claim, an ad hoc theorem that if everything else fails, try this. But to his credit, Eisenbud did not suppress additional clinical evidence that his patient's second vision paralleled exactly his first vision. For in the second visitation, by the warbler, Eisenbud records that his patient was once more facing extremely painful losses.

The patient's wife had been out of town for several days, and his part-time maid failed to show up. The patient's female secretary left suddenly to attend to family matters in another city, and it appeared that she would never return to her job. In addition, the patient would soon be losing his analyst: "Small wonder that he had to fall back on the infantile illusion that one could conjure up the mother by sheer force of inner need, the last desperate device of a forlorn child."[21]

Having presented this list of profound losses and the wishes each loss aroused in his patient, Eisenbud says that this was *not* an instance of the return of the repressed. He rejects this Freudian theorem because he finds no easy way to explain how his patient could predict the presence of the warbler. Eisenbud feels that his patient could counter every possible suggestion that he had known, unconsciously, that the warbler was there. One might say, Pure chance! But Eisenbud, like all proponents of occult theorems, rejects that as itself unscientific. To argue for chance is to argue that there is no scientific causal explanation for this remarkable occurrence. Eisenbud presents his psi hypothesis as in fact the most scientific speculation available at the moment.

Eisenbud's solution is to propose that there are powers that operate outside the usual bounds of science as we know it. Is this a good solution to the mystery of occult belief? I think the answer is no. Eisenbud requires us to suppose that there are powers that sometimes operate and that contradict scientific laws discovered over the past two thousand years. A more likely speculation is that Eisenbud's patient deluded himself, just as he forgot his previous experience with the kingfisher. It seems irrational to suppose that he could do anything other than so arrange his memory and experience that he could report, with perfect candor, that a world of grace abounding was revealed to him and that he had direct contact with it.

Eisenbud describes, poignantly, how his patient had lost vital selfobject relationships: the women who took care of him all abandoned him at once. He was also facing the loss of his analyst, who by that time had also become a vital selfobject in the man's life. Facing such immense threats to his self-coherence and needing to overcome fragmentation anxiety, Eisenbud's patient needed to find a replacement object, partly from heaven, partly from earth, that signaled the ever-presence of a transcendent selfobject: the bird. We know that Eisenbud's patient had major weaknesses in his self-structure. These weaknesses, for example, his inability to tolerate long absences, gave rise to immensely painful states in which he felt overwhelming needs. His internal needs were met partly by his drug and alcohol addictions and partly by his extreme dependence upon the women in his life. But the nature of these internal needs was not clear to the patient. Neither was it clear to Eisenbud. For, again to his credit, Eisenbud realizes that he can find no evidence of repression in his patient's account of the second visitation, by the warbler. Eisenbud has no psychoanalytic theorems left to account for the occult moment. Having no psychoanalytic theorems left, he turns to an occult thesis, the psi hypothesis described above.

Is the psi hypothesis an adequate solution to the puzzle presented by Eisenbud's patient? I think it is not. First, the psi hypothesis rejects ordinary reasoning and ordinary modes of validation. If we adhere to the psi hypothesis, we are committed to explaining occult moments using occult hypotheses. Second, the psi hypothesis does not connect Eisenbud's classical (and persuasive) psychoanalytic account of the first visitation with his account of the second. We are suddenly left high and dry. We have no access to Eisenbud's previous clinical insights about the patient's object losses and severe psychic pain. Third, the psi hypothesis does not explain why the patient's visions were about birds, rather than, say, the stock market. Unless we wish to ascribe the patient's fascination with birds purely to chance, it would seem important to explain why he chose to center his occult experience around birds, rather than other objects or things available to him. The psi hypothesis is haphazard. It offers no way to predict what a patient might happen upon. Neither does the psi hypothesis permit us to explain why this object, the warbler, was picked up by the patient's extraordinary sensory channel.

Eisenbud's account of the second visitation is sympathetic to his patient's sense of excitement. Eisenbud does not dismiss his patient's enthusiasm for this great event in his life, which comes at the end of their work together. In this way one imagines that both men enjoyed the story and felt it contributed to the mutual good will with which the analysis ended. The psi hypothesis does not reduce the patient's experience merely to the return of the repressed. But Eisenbud's rendition of the second visitation is not an empathic account of an occult event. Like Jung's similar accounts of similar incidents with his patients, the psi hypothesis merely states that the event remains inexplicable and therefore a legitimate mystery.

Because Eisenbud lacked the concept of selfobject, he could not account for his patient's conviction that he had experienced an occult event. That is, his patient's utter conviction that he had no way to predict the appearance of the warbler gave Eisenbud no hint of repressed motives and wishes. The second story appeared to be faultless. It seemed that the patient could answer every possible explanation for his uncanny ability to predict the warbler's appearance. When Eisenbud applied the repression hypothesis to the second visitation, as he had to the first, he discovered no evidence that his patient had *repressed* knowledge about the warbler. That is, Eisenbud found that there were no intrapsychic events that could account for his patient's experience of the warbler. Because there was no evidence of fully intrapsychic processes, like repression, that could account for his patient's premonition, Eisenbud reasoned that the event must have been a fully extrapsychic one, that is, a matter of the real external world and the operation of an uncanny power which came to operate in his patient's world precisely at a time when his patient required it.

In other words, because the repression hypothesis is tied directly to a point of view that is wholly intrapsychic, it cannot account for events that occur on the boundary line between "inside" and "outside." The repression hypothesis cannot account for events that include the relationships between self and selfobjects.

Kohut's basic theorem of selfobject functioning permits us to explain why occult events are never entirely the products of the return of the repressed. Repression does figure into the production of occult experience, but it is not the sole source of occult experience. Rather, Kohut offers us a way to understand why the profound needs for selfobject functioning are not only *intrapsychic.* The needs for which the occult is the answer cannot be conscious because they are not confined solely to the inner world, the world of a private mind. Therefore, when a person threatened with fragmentation anxiety undergoes an occult event, the source of that event is never felt to be from the inside (the inner world), but always the outside (the external world).

SUMMARY:
THE OCCULT SEQUENCE

I suggest that the following list, using Eisenbud's patient as exemplar, highlights the major events that occur sequentially in any occult event. I present the list first, and discuss each portion of it in more detail in the following chapters.

1. Eisenbud's patient formed an intense relationship to Eisenbud, just as he had to his wife, to his maid, and to his secretary.
2. When the patient feels sure about the security of these relationships he feels secure about his capacity to govern himself.
3. The patient's wife and his female colleagues reflected back to him a positive, sustaining image of his self-worth and a sense of self-cohesion.
4. This complex process of mirroring proceeds unconsciously, that is, it occurs without any party recognizing explicitly that it is taking place.
5. A rupture occurred. The idealized other, whose help and love were so essential and who aroused such intense, unspoken hopes, failed to sustain and mirror these conscious and unconscious needs. The wife, secretary, and maid all failed to be near Eisenbud's patient and sustain him just as he confronted losing his analyst, the man who had also taken away his drugs and alcohol.
6. The rupture is an external event, but its effect is to remove internal supports. The loss of the selfobject induces fragmentation anxiety. The source of the patient's suffering is not evident, that is, there is no apparent upsurge in intrapsychic contents (a so-called id irruption).

    This may seem impossible. Yet we recall that the vital mirroring that occurred between the patient and the women and his analyst was, for the most part, unconscious. Selfobjects function as do internal organs. The selfobject relationship is not evident until a disease process takes place. Most people, for example, cannot locate their kidneys exactly within the abdomen. But a severe kidney infection changes this. Suddenly one can pinpoint the exact location of an organ that otherwise remains merely an abstract name.

7. An internal loss remains unrecognized; instead, the patient seeks to locate the source of his suffering in the external world.

8. That external solution takes the form of an object, person, or personage (like a god) who performs, actively and externally, the same function performed by the now-lost object. Here we may speculate that Eisenbud's patient focused his attention upon birds because they are precisely creatures that connect earth and sky, this world and the heavens. Numerous myths and rituals from both ancient and modern religions describe birds as creatures who carry divine messages. The baptism of Jesus, for example, is marked by a dove sent by God to announce God's pleasure (Luke 3:22).

9. Occult actors understand the occult moments as best they can. For example, Eisenbud's patient attempted to find a scientific-like explanation for his occult moment. Other actors from other cultures will use other forms of discourse, depending upon what myths and other public stories are available. I say *myths* because myths are precisely stories designed to explain what remains inexplicable.

10. Regardless of the mythic system employed to account for the occult moment, occult teachings must attempt to unify the apparent paradoxes of occult experience: an internal event is experienced as if it were external. In cultures like ours, where a radical distinction is made between one mind and another, occult events will tend to evoke powers that transcend the problem of other minds. In the West, occult teachings and beliefs often incorporate references to thought-transference, mind reading, telepathy, and the like. Each of these terms names a power that transcends the usual boundaries that separate one mind from another.

11. Because occult experience occurs as the result of breaches in selfobject relationships, and because these relationships are vital to the sense of self, occult experiences are remembered. To the degree that occult moments actually do help heal the breach in selfobject relationships, they are also treasured.

12. In persons especially vulnerable to fragmentation, occult experiences are treasured and incorporated into larger thought systems or schools. We see this especially in the teachings of Jung.

But we will also see it in the earliest, and some say greatest, spiritual autobiography, *The Confessions* of Saint Augustine.

3

Occult Moments in the Life of Saint Augustine

Augustine's psychological genius has given an account of the trouble
of having a divided self which has never been surpassed.
—William James, *The Varieties of Religious Experience*

William James, America's greatest philosopher-psychologist, made
the above comments about Saint Augustine (354–430) at the turn
of the century. His remarks hold true; today, three-quarters of a
century since James lived, few people would claim that the saint's
descriptions of mental torment have been bettered. But I do claim
that we can offer explanations for the divided self that are better
than those offered by Augustine, and even better than those offered by James himself.

What James calls the divided self, a self in which one part seems
to war against the other, I place within the spectrum of feeling
states we described earlier as the fragmented self. The two terms
are not interchangeable in all instances. James uses his term, the
divided self, to describe experiences that extend from ordinary
moments of indecision to states of severe psychopathology. Kohut's

term, the fragmented self, is more restrictive. It designates not just a moment of conflict or feeling divided in oneself. Rather, to be or feel fragmented is to feel that the central part of one's ordinary self-structure is no longer capable of holding one together. In this sense, the fragmented self suffers more severely a far deeper terror than a self in conflict.

In James's masterpiece of description, *The Varieties of Religious Experience,* he refers to many persons as "divided selves" who we would say suffer severe fragmentation anxiety. I think this is particularly true of Augustine. It is also true of James himself, however. Like other great psychologists of religion, James used his scientific talents to locate and stabilize his own troubled religious spirit. James's difficulties with religion are well known. His father, Henry James, Sr., was a wealthy philosopher-theologian who showered upon his three sons and one daughter an idiosyncratic mysticism. In addition to these familial sources of theological ideas, William lived through the intellectual turmoil of the nineteenth century, in which one form of thought and world view, Christianity, seemed to succumb finally to the onslaughts of science. James experienced firsthand the revolutions inspired by Darwin and Marx. At the end of his life, James met Freud and glimpsed a psychology that was to outlive him.

For personal and cultural reasons, James became a public representative in whom the intellectual conflicts of the nineteenth century found expression. To his credit, James describes in detail one of his own experiences which, using the terms developed above, we can call a fragmentation experience. James gives the account, disguised slightly, in *The Varieties of Religious Experience.* This account was written in 1902; yet it parallels almost exactly some of the feelings that Mr. Z reported to Kohut two generations later. James's account is also very similar, in part, to the account Eisenbud's patient gave of his premonition about the warbler. James and Eisenbud's patient encountered their occult moments in twilight mental states. Eisenbud's patient was just waking up when he had the premonition about the warbler. In the following story, James enters a darkened room at twilight:

> I went one evening into a dressing-room in the twilight to procure some article that was there; when suddenly there fell upon me without any warning, just as if it came out of the darkness, a horrible fear of my own existence. Simultaneously there arose in my mind the image of an epileptic patient whom I had seen in the asylum, a black-haired youth with greenish skin, entirely idiotic, who used to sit all day on one of the benches . . . with his knees drawn up against his chin. . . . He sat there . . . looking absolutely non-human. This image and my fear

entered into a species of combination with each other. *That shape am I,
I felt, potentially.*[1]

James rescued himself from this state by calling upon his knowledge
of biblical texts like "The Eternal God is my refuge" and "Come unto
me, all ye that labor and are heavy-laden." Without these representations of a loving, listening, and compassionate God, James says, "I
think I should have grown really insane."[2] We can reformulate this
proposition using Kohut's terms. To grow really insane means that one's
self has fragmented beyond repair: Humpty Dumpty cannot be put
together again.

Augustine's great text, *The Confessions*, tells a deeply personal story
of his youthful sins and later conversion to Christianity. Alongside his
many well-articulated reasons for writing these detailed confessions,
one also finds a deep need to create an audience who will hear his confession again and again.

In the following sections I discuss Augustine's *Confessions*. I suggest
that we can understand it, in part, as his attempt to consolidate a newly
won sense of unification with his mother's religion and therefore with
her. In the language developed above, *The Confessions* prevented fragmentation anxiety because it provided Augustine with a new selfobject
relationship. Augustine wrote *The Confessions*, I will suggest, in part to
preserve his relationship to his mother, his primary selfobject. He also
wrote *The Confessions* in order to establish a new selfobject relationship
to his readers.

Assuming that this point of view is plausible, we should expect to
find that Augustine will have particularly intense needs to feel united
with his mother, Monica, and that she (or secondary representations of
her) will appear stage center in his struggles. I believe they do.

AUGUSTINE AND THE READER
AS SELFOBJECT

It is difficult to resist books with the title of "confession." Will the author confess to the world those actions and thoughts that shame us most
and so ameliorate our suffering? Following Augustine's great book, similar accounts by Rousseau (1781–88), Goethe (1811–33), Gide (1889–
1949 [1967]), and others have earned a place in literature. The number
of nonconfessional autobiographies is immense: Kaplan lists more than
six thousand titles by Americans alone.[3] Regardless of their literary merits, autobiographies have narcissistic value. Our own need to feel worthwhile and unique is satisfied, in a roundabout way, when we compare
ourselves to these writers.

Confession reduces the distance we feel between ourselves and sublime masters. Yet confession maintains their luster since they have felt
that their inner life was worth reporting to the masses, while few of us
could muster that belief. To this point, Freud's masterpiece, *The Interpretation of Dreams*, achieves authority partly because it contains so
many "confessions." It reveals Freud's jealous, petty, sexualized, and
hostile wishes, his grandiose ambitions, and his severe neuroticisms. In
other words, it reveals a person much like ourselves, the difference
being that Freud and Augustine created intellectual modes that permit
confession but prevent narcissistic abasement.

Henri Ellenberger persuades me that much of Freud's influence stems
from his enormous literary talents.[4] The first dream in Freud's book,
"Irma's Injection," is one of his own. Freud spends seventeen pages of
dense text interpreting its subtleties. It is *his* dream; it deals with *his*
most private feelings, *his* hopes, *his* wishes, and *his* characteristic
defenses, including an ignoble attempt to cover up his friend's medical
errors. Freud's text operates much like Augustine's *Confessions:* an inherently personal story, including dreams or conversion, is made public
and is transformed into authoritative wisdom because of the literary genius of the writer.

Reading *The Confessions*, even some fifteen centuries after its composition and in translation, is like being confronted by an impassioned
speaker who is not above grabbing one by the lapels in order to force
his message home. This is not always a comfortable experience, and it
suggests that Augustine wrote *The Confessions* out of many complex
motives. Some of these he states overtly: to indicate the power of God's
intervention, to demonstrate human folly, and to articulate a coherent
theology that would counteract the pull of Manichaeism. Other motives are less manifest and must be inferred. Eugene TeSelle and other
scholars describe some of the difficulties of assessing clearly all of
Augustine's intentions. TeSelle notes that *The Confessions* argues consistently that God alone provides Augustine with a sense of coherence
for "his life in the past, present, and future."[5]

That makes sense to me, and I believe it accounts for my experience of
being pulled into the text, as a member of Augustine's audience. Augustine's fundamental need to establish a sense of coherence underlies
his use of the reader. I read *The Confessions* as a profound call for us to
join Augustine and affirm his newly achieved sense of self-coherence.
The Confessions is more than an implicit call to Augustine's readers to
help him consolidate his sense of self. But by using the concept of
selfobject we can explain how so ancient a text, one that precedes Kohut
by some fifteen hundred years, reveals narcissistic concerns tied to occult experiences.

To make my claim clear I pay special attention to Kohut's basic concept of selfobject, which we have examined already. My general thesis is that *The Confessions* is written for an audience that Augustine uses as selfobjects. That is, we, his imagined audience, are a crucial, underlying element in his work, and our (imagined) responses help him reconstitute himself and feel coherent in time and space. We can see in the events described in *The Confessions* the earlier stages of occult experiences, which have their denouement in the composition and publication of *The Confessions* itself.

This narcissistic reading of *The Confessions* differs from traditional psychological readings of Augustine's life. These focused on Augustine's thought (his theology) and his object relations, his adult relationships with his mother and other people. Authors of these studies tend to agree with Augustine's self-evaluation that his sexual life conflicted with his spiritual ideals. These studies tend to view sexual conflicts as fundamental. Following Kohut, I suggest that much of Augustine's concern about sexuality is a secondary effort to repair narcissistic wounds.

I do not formulate a diagnosis of Augustine's personality. Since *The Confessions* covers most of Augustine's life, it is difficult to know exactly what represents Augustine's essential character. More important for our concerns is Augustine's denunciation of ordinary narcissistic yearnings. Throughout *The Confessions* Augustine attacks himself for being selfish, vain, self-centered, and in search of glory as a scholar and rhetorician. Augustine's vehement attacks upon his own narcissistic yearnings parallel Freud's denunciation of narcissism fifteen hundred years later. Both men believe that self-love grows at the expense of the love of others. To use Freud's language, in order to reach a stage of "object love," one must forsake narcissism. Augustine's *Confessions* is a text with many audiences and many readers. Yet, in a sense, it amounts to Augustine's treatise upon the evils of narcissism and its eventual demise in favor of a higher love, Christian self-sacrifice. As we have seen above, Freud teaches us that repressed yearnings must reappear, perhaps in a disguised form. Universal needs to feel esteemed and loved by a wholly good object reemerge in Augustine's theology and in his grand, public confessions.

Splendid Self-abasement in
The Confessions

I cared for nothing but to love to be loved. But my love went beyond affection of one mind for another, beyond the arc of the bright beam of friendship. Bodily desire, like a morass, and adolescent sex welling up within me exuded mists which clouded over and obscured my heart. (*Confessions*, p. 43)[6]

The splendor of Augustine's self-denunciations obscures a split self. One part identifies with the Lord, who judges everyone with infinite demands, and the other part is a contrite petitioner. *The Confessions* is written, therefore, for two audiences. The manifest audience is the Lord, God, to whom Augustine addresses his pleas. The other audience is the world of human beings. Augustine's *Confessions* asks distinct favors of these audiences. Of God, Augustine seeks forgiveness, followed by a sign of union with him. Of human beings, Augustine asks, I suggest, that they mirror back to him their esteem for his moral courage in composing *The Confessions*.

To make these claims clear I discuss portions of *The Confessions* that deal with occult experience. In a number of places, for example, Augustine discusses astrology and other occult teachings that assert that one can predict future occurrences. In a famous scene that marks the turning point of the story, Augustine hears an unearthly voice telling him to pick up and read the New Testament. I also compare a Freudian reading of *The Confessions* with a reading that incorporates basic ideas we developed from Kohut's self-psychology.

Two kinds of anxiety are evident in *The Confessions.* Freud terms one "oedipal," the other "pre-oedipal." Oedipal anxieties concern fears about one's fate at the hands of persons more powerful than oneself. Pre-oedipal anxieties refer to fears the very young child has about the stability of parental figures without whose support he or she cannot survive. Pre-oedipal anxieties are variations on the theme of fragmentation: the loss of a strong enough selfobject precipitates not just loneliness, but the dread of internal collapse.

Augustine's *Confessions* is a text that addresses both kinds of anxiety. I focus my attention on those portions of *The Confessions* that contain Augustine's covert plea for selfobject relationships with both God and his readers. Finally, I suggest that the extreme fascination with sexuality that Augustine says marked his adolescence may be understood not only as the product of "libidinal" drives, but also as unconscious attempts to undo fragmentation experiences. Like Mr. Z, the young Augustine used sexualized forms of experience to consolidate a self prone to despair and fragmentation. I believe that Augustine becomes engrossed in sexual matters when he needs to repair rents in his self-esteem. Even as a man and as the great author of *The Confessions*, Augustine concentrates upon sexual experiences and sexual thoughts whose magnitude seems unworthy of the brilliant polemics Augustine raises against them.

Both Augustine and Freud view such eruptions of sexuality as breakthroughs of repressed, primal instincts. Augustine calls them inherently sinful. Freud avoids such moralism, but retains the metaphysical assumption that extremely sexualized behavior represents the outbreak of something immensely powerful and beyond the ego's control. Kohut's reevaluation of narcissistic needs and their fulfillment in selfobject relationships offers an account of such sexualization that is less moralistic than Augustine's own.

OEDIPAL ANXIETIES AND
SELF ANXIETIES

Freud chose to name the central conflict of late childhood after King Oedipus because that Greek story is about relationships between "whole objects," that is, mother, father, and child. In its psychoanalytic usage, oedipal problems center around the child's impulses to compete with its parents, to replace one of them and to gain exclusive dominance over the other. Freud's use of the oedipal legend illuminates the child's struggles to feel manly or womanly compared to others, like one's parents, who *are* more powerful, more "manly" or "womanly" than the child. The great unconscious symbols of such struggles therefore revolve around genitals, for genitals are what distinguish men from women and adults from children. Therefore, classical psychoanalytic theory uses terms that underscore the central importance of the genitals, that is, penis envy, castration anxiety, and so on. For the very young child, genitals are the dominant signs of difference and power. Who is big and who is little? Who has authority over whom? Oedipal conflicts occur between whole persons who feel vulnerable to damage (to being wounded, hurt, or diminished) by other whole persons who will respond to one's demands for authority with vengeance (or seduction). Most psychological commentators on Augustine use terms taken from oedipal theory when they analyze *The Confessions* as dealing with Augustine's conflicts over sexuality and aggression. These commentators ask, How did Augustine's idealized and absolutist mother affect his sexual life? How should we understand the disdain Augustine shows for his biological father? How should we compare this disdain for an earthly father with Augustine's adoration of the divine Father?

To these oedipal-level readings we can add a pre-oedipal analysis. Toward the end of his life, Freud realized that the next great task of his science was to investigate pre-oedipal history, that is, the child's experiences and traumas prior to the formation of a whole and complete self, before the age of three or fours years. With the scope of analysis broadening beyond neurotic patients to the treatment of children, psychotic persons, and other patient populations, analytic theory has expanded to encompass these dynamics as well. At that level of work, one finds that the fundamental anxieties are *not* castration (or its many variants). Rather, they center around the infant's needs to receive mothering from a person whose ministrations and empathy resonate with the infant.

Among those primary needs is the infant's requirement to be held internally and externally. Using adult metaphors, we may say that the empathic parent contains the infant's experience of self. The empathic parent does those things, like regulate self-esteem, which will come gradually under the control of the child's internal world, his or her ego. The famous "gleam in the mother's eye" is a nice, if homely, example of precisely such holding. The gleam in the mother's eye mirrors back to her child the child's own need to feel special. Children whose parents realize that this is the best baby in the world receive such holding and are better for it. Those who do not, whose parents have a "realistic" assessment of their child, cannot reflect back and so validate the child's fundamental need to feel worthy of existence. Such children live in a constant state of narcissistic tension.

Fragmentation Anxiety as Pre-oedipal Anxiety

Oedipal anxieties are experienced as external attacks upon bodily integrity. Oedipal anxieties utilize metaphors of external harm to a treasured body part, like the eyes or the genitals. The dominant imagery of oedipal conflicts, for example, in fairy tales and dreams, centers around the fate of a highly cathected aspect of the body: losing or gaining a penis. Freud elucidated basic theorems of castration anxiety and penis envy in his neurotic patients whose conflicts he analyzed at this level of development.

Pre-oedipal anxieties emerge as internal attacks upon the self, either from a persecutor, like the Wicked Witch, or through unbearable feelings of worthlessness. Fantasies that one's mind is dissolving, that one's body is made of soap or some other substance that might disappear, or that one is turning into a machine dominate pre-oedipal pathology.[7] As we saw in our discussion of Kohut's case, "The Two Analyses of Mr. Z," pre-oedipal anxieties are often symbolized by the attack upon a human face, that of the patient or another person. A colleague described a middle-aged patient who felt that his feet, legs, and torso were changing sequentially from flesh into metal. When this transformation reached the patient's head, the psychosis was complete.

Pre-oedipal anxieties are often variations of "Humpty Dumpty." As we know, Humpty took a great fall and no one could put him together again. These fears of fragmenting into pieces appear directly in the psychotic's fear of going to pieces, and the same fears appear in severely traumatized children. Since everyone was first an infant, then a child, and so on, everyone will have faced and mastered to some degree these fundamental anxieties. Like castration anxiety, fragmentation anxiety defines one dimension of the human condition.

Western religious teachings have struggled to alleviate fragmentation anxiety by articulating a portrait of a deity in whose image we are made, who knows our deepest thoughts, and will not permit us to fall out of the world into nothingness. Unlike the poor astronaut in the film *2001: A Space Odyssey,* whom the evil computer sends off, alone, into empty space, we cannot be separated from God's love.

Because fragmentation anxiety is ubiquitous and intolerable, humans try to avoid it at all costs. The first line of defense against fragmentation is the presence of a good-enough mother (parent) who can perform selfobject functions. Slowly, over time, the infant becomes a child who can sustain the child's self for longer and longer periods of time. To use a phrase from D. W. Winnicott, a great child psychiatrist, with good-enough mothering the child slowly acquires the capacity to be alone without feeling lonely. At those moments when the child can no longer sustain an internal sense of coherence, the child turns toward loving adults who will provide those ego functions of synthesis and coherence that are not yet within the child's purview. In theological terms, good-enough parents instill hope. In psychoanalytic terms, good parents act as selfobjects, as persons who perform internal functions for an ego still forming.

Do Adults Need Selfobject Relationships?

But what about adults? Should we not outgrow such needs and such relationships? Is not adulthood precisely what Freud said it was—the forsaking of neurotic fantasy solutions for actual, inexact, and imperfect real solutions? Again, in contrast to Freud's basic stance, Kohut argues that no person is immune to the need for others to fulfill these selfobject functions throughout the lifespan. Happy adults will be neither as needy nor as vulnerable as infants, but they will require selfobjects just as they require food and water.

Kohut and Freud do not share a common valuation of such needs. This illustrates a profound difference in scientific outlook. Freud views castration anxiety as the ego's weak response to powerful drives, the intensity of which threatens the ego. With ego development comes an increased capacity to battle against those drives and their associated wishes. In a real sense, neurotics of all ages misperceive their actual situation: they are childish and afraid of childish forces that now cannot overwhelm them as they once did.

In contrast, Kohut asserts that persons always need selfobjects. Fragmentation anxiety in very sick patients is not a misperception or a carry-over from an infantile past that will dissolve upon analysis. On the contrary, healthy adults will recognize that they too need others, both as whole objects and as selfobjects, that is, as persons who can help "hold" the self together. In drive-theory terms, selfobjects are persons who act on the side of the "ego instincts" that aim at survival. In more phenomenological terms, they share, momentarily, our deepest narcissistic feelings that our unique self is worthy of living, of being whole and powerful. From the outside such needs may appear grandiose and irrational. From the inside they feel equivalent to our need to breathe.[8] In a telling metaphor, Kohut refers to the "psychological oxygen" that selfobjects give us.[9] To deny the validity of such needs, on the grounds of "objectivity," for example, is equivalent to demanding that a person drowning in high seas calm down and learn to breathe water.

Failure to respond to such needs in others elicits in them a great deal of rage. Failure to salute colleagues, or cite their work, can gain one lifelong enemies. Kohut elaborates the varieties of narcissistic rage along a continuum that extends from momentary anger at being snubbed, to the extended and deep anger that dominates many borderline patients who feel misheard and misperceived.[10] (A typical history of such patients shows a depressed mother whom the child struggled to revive in order that she might then reflect back to the child the child's sense of worth.)

Problems with Applied Psychoanalysis

Like Freud's, Kohut's discoveries were in the field of analytic treatment of psychic suffering (so-called mental illness). Like Freud, Kohut realized quickly that his narrow discoveries were relevant to larger, nonpathological realms, including religion. Unlike Freud, however, Kohut does not view his discoveries as metaphysical competitors with traditional beliefs. Freud knew there was no God, and he drafted his clinical theories into philosophic refutations of all those who believed otherwise. Kohut does not leap from clinical theory to metaphysics this way.

This has an important consequence for humanists familiar with reductive readings of great books done under the guise of "applied analysis." While there are brilliant examples of such applications, beginning with Freud's comments on Oedipus Tyrannus, more are disappointing. Why would it be otherwise? Since the genius of psychoanalysis is an observational, empathic science of actual behavior, utilizing its terms abstracted from clinical practice forfeits that genius. More important, applications of the classical theory tend to be written from on high, without interacting with the text. Basic clinical values, such as neutrality and abstinence, seem to support this stance.

Kohut's theory and his innovations in technique counterbalance these classical points of view. First, by grounding analytic work upon empathic immersion in the other's world, he places the center of gravity *not* in the analyst's perception of reality but in the interactional field that exists between patient and analyst. Second, Kohut's core concept of selfobject requires the analyst to comprehend the patient through the patient's effect on the *analyst's* interior life. By definition, the analyst cannot assume a stance outside of, and certainly not superior to, the patient.

No analyst would dare interpret a dream without the patient's continuous cooperation, ideally with as little defense as possible. Yet applied analyses of static works of art are never dialogical. The novel, the painting, and Augustine's *Confessions* cannot respond, cannot correct, and cannot deepen the initial interpretation.[11]

At a more profound level, to the degree that one is removed by time, culture, and language from one's subject, one has fewer and fewer resources with which to generate an empathic response. For Kohut this is the *first* order of business. Should the analyst fail to establish a semblance of empathic understanding, all subsequent formulations will be extraneous to the deep need of the other to be understood. "Concretely speaking, whenever a patient reacts with rage to the analyst's interpretations, he has experienced him from the point of view of the archaic self that has been activated in analysis, as a nonempathic attacker of the integrity of his self."[12] Many people experience traditional analytic readings of a text like *Hamlet* as nonempathic attacks on themselves, for they see a favorite piece of literature or autobiography treated as if it were a pathography, short and simple.

Having protested that, I plunge ahead and describe *The Confessions* as a selfobject generated by Augustine to consolidate a newly won sense of coherence. Since everyone needs selfobjects throughout their lives, this is not pathologizing the text. On the contrary, it may help us understand Augustine's immense status in Western thought.[13]

OCCULT EVENTS IN AUGUSTINE'S *CONFESSIONS*

Augustine describes a number of occult instances in *The Confessions.* The first occult instance occurs in Book III, when Augustine describes his mother's dream. We learn that this dream foretold Augustine's conversion to the Christian faith some nine years later. Although he knew that his mother was adamant about her faith, Augustine avoided Christianity and explored instead the numerous philosophies and mystery religions that were its competitors. In response to her prayers to bring her son into Christianity, Monica was sent a dream:

> She dreamed that she was standing on a wooden rule, and coming towards her in a halo of splendour she saw a young man who smiled at her in joy, although she herself was sad and quite consumed with grief. He asked her the reason for her sorrow and her daily tears, not because he did not know, but because he had something to tell her, for this is what happens in visions. When she replied that her tears were for the soul I had lost, he told her to take heart for, if she looked carefully, she would see that where she was, there also was I. And when she looked, she saw me standing beside her on the same rule. (*Confessions*, p. 68)

The dream foretells a future in which Monica's beloved and idealized son will be reunited with her on the same singular, narrow "rule." At that moment their spiritual separation will be undone.

In Book IV Augustine describes his intellectual development and his flirtations with astrology, a universal mode of occult experiencing. In a passage that presages the famous conversion scene in Book VIII, Augustine describes his fascination with astrology. He then compares his initial enthusiasm with the wisdom of an older friend: "He said that people sometimes opened a book of poetry at random, and although the poet had been thinking, as he wrote, of some quite different matter, it often happened that the reader placed his finger on a verse which had a remarkable bearing on his problems" (*Confessions*, p. 74).

This "kind and fatherly" advice (*Confessions*, p. 73) had no effect, and Augustine continued to accept astrological claims up to the period of his conversion. That the famous scene in the garden begins with his looking into the New Testament in a random way only highlights the centrality of occult issues in *The Confessions*. Of course, for Augustine the difference between the two is absolute: astrology is both illogical and anti-Christian. He reports in detail how he reasoned out the absurdity of astrological claims in Book VII. Augustine noted, for example, that twin children born at exactly the same time, under identical astrological conditions, have lives determined primarily by their individual characters, their upbringing, education, and environment, not by the stars (*Confessions*, pp. 141–43). If astrology were a science it should predict identical lives for persons born under identical signs. But that is irrational. Augustine concludes that astrological predictions are merely matters of luck, not proof of wisdom.

Augustine's Conversion: Signs from Above

The drama of Augustine's conversion is undeniable. Augustine insists that it occurred only at the end of a long and bitter internal struggle with himself against himself.

> When I was trying to reach a decision about serving the Lord my God, as I had long intended to do, it was I who willed to take this course and again it was I who willed not to take it. It was I and I alone. But I neither willed to do it nor refused to do it with my full will. So I was at odds with myself. I was throwing myself into confusion. (*Confessions*, p. 173)

Augustine denies the Manichaean belief that such confusion illustrates the existence of two opposed souls. Rather, such confusion illustrates a single soul that has two conflicting wills (*Confessions*, p. 174). Augustine draws upon Aristotle and other ancient authorities who elaborated the nature of habitual actions so powerful that they can counteract even the truth of Scripture. But more important, in his habitual pride Augustine wished to conquer his bad habits himself rather than rely upon God, who had loaned his strength to others who recognized their own weakness.

These other people's solutions, therefore, came from on high. These solutions were given freely, bestowed by an infinitely greater yet personal power, which requires only obedience. Just before receiving God's sign, Augustine abases himself, raging against his weakness: "Why not now? Why not make an end of my ugly sins at this moment?" (*Confessions*, p. 177).

The Scene in the Garden

The stage prepared, Augustine hears a child singing, "Take it and read, take it and read" (*Confessions*, p. 177). To indicate that he has not lost his reason and that his story is true, Augustine says that he first asks himself if this is a common children's song. Obviously, if it were it would not count as a divine command. But, "since I could not remember ever hearing them [these words] before," Augustine reasoned the song could only be "a divine command to open my book of Scripture and read the first passage on which my eyes should fall" (*Confessions*, p. 177). He reads a passage, "Not in revelling and drunkenness, not in lust and wantonness, not in quarrels and rivalries. Rather, arm yourself with Lord Jesus Christ; spend no more thought on nature and nature's appetites" (Romans 13:13–14). Augustine applies this immediately to himself (although he seems to have given up wantonness already) and rushes to tell his mother that he and his friend Alypius have both received divine summons to the faith. His mother's dream was ful-filled, and Augustine himself "no longer desired a wife or placed any hope in this world but stood firmly upon the rule of faith" (*Confessions*, p. 178) by his mother's side.

In other words, Augustine returns to his mother's side, but this time standing upon a narrow ledge of righteousness. His mother's dream is fulfilled, and his struggles against adopting her faith are over. One might question the validity of this solution since Augustine felt it nec-essary to compose *The Confessions*. That is, taking a view that is cer-tainly one-sided, one might challenge the adequacy of Augustine's solution because it seems to depend upon the veracity of an occult message.

Contrary to his previous denunciations of occult reasoning, Au-gustine here seems compelled to create an argument that requires him to justify occult occurrences. In an earlier passage, quoted above, Au-gustine said that he could not support people who claimed that ran-dom passages from a text could be of any value. Yet in the garden scene Augustine seems to do exactly what he criticized in others: he seeks an occult solution.

Augustine's Unempathic Attitude
Toward Himself

Kohut, again, permits us to ask questions about such religious reason-ing that we could not otherwise even consider. Are occult solutions to basic narcissistic needs ever fully empathic to the believer's needs? That is, if occult solutions are always "transcendent," sent from an-other realm to us, it seems that they cannot be discovered either through one's own introspection or through vicarious introspection, that is, empathy. Transcendental answers to fragmentation anxiety, like the answers Augustine develops in *The Confessions*, place the center of gravity outside the self, and in the hands of a Wholly Other. But this Wholly Other is not an ordinary person. His or her presence must be inferred, just as Augustine had to infer the meaning of the child's song. Can such an Other respond to one's intense needs for selfobject relationship directly and empathically? To answer this question we consider, again, Kohut's fundamental concept of selfob-ject. In a sense, Augustine's great achievement in the composition of *The Confessions* contrasts sharply with his unempathic attitudes to-ward himself and others. That we can even question the adequacy of Augustine's attitude toward himself is a measure of Kohut's achieve-ment in advancing beyond Augustine, and beyond Freud.

THE CONFESSIONS AS PLEA FOR
SELFOBJECT RELATIONSHIP

The Confessions illuminates a great mind interrogating itself and demanding a response from both God and humans. Augustine touched on this theme, his profound need to find an audience, but rejected it in Book X: "Why, then, does it matter to me whether men should hear what I have to confess, as though it were they who were to cure all the evil that is in me?" (*Confessions*, p. 208). His theological answer is that if his readers share his own striving after charity, they will discern the truth of his account: "But charity believes all things—all things, that is, which are spoken by those who are joined as one in charity—and for this reason I, too, O Lord, make my confession aloud in the hearing of men" (*Confessions*, p. 208).

This capacity for charity would seem to derive from the noblest portion of human being, the soul, which is the "better part of me because it animates the whole of my body. It gives it life, and this is something that no body can give to another body. But God is even more. He is the Life of my soul." How can we know God? Only through the soul and its unique capacity to interrogate its memories and its "vast cloisters." It is the "great force of life in living man, mortal though he is" (*Confessions*, pp. 213, 215, 224).

The Confessions rings with Augustine's great pleasure in recalling his past, even the errors of his youth. One cannot doubt Augustine's sincerity. But neither can one doubt the tremendous intellectual pleasure he gained in composing the account. Augustine's denunciations of ordinary boyish pranks, for example, are far grander and more eloquent than the deeds warrant. Of course, Augustine could not say so, since that would amount to another sin, intellectual pride, which, in turn, would have to be punished. This obsessional quality runs throughout *The Confessions*, as it does throughout any account dominated by a superego as severe as Augustine's. (One thinks of the obsessive moralist who, having performed a good deed, takes pleasure in that fact, and in turn recognizes that pleasure as a sin that must be punished, and then takes pleasure in that new bit of godliness.)

The Pleasures of Self-examination

In Kohut's terms, Augustine's unending self-analysis and his unending complaints about his moral failings derive from his repression of self-object needs, especially his need to contain his genius. Contrary to

Augustine's manifest rejection of the pleasures of being read by mere mortals, *The Confessions* represents a covert plea for selfobject relationships with an audience whose responses Augustine treasures deeply. Given his immense talents and a culture that seems to have offered every opportunity for self-debasement, Augustine's struggles and solutions are remarkable. From Kohut's point of view, the young man's efforts to come to terms with his talents revolved around precisely narcissistic issues: How could he control himself and channel his skills in ways that would restrain him and keep his feet on the ground?

The Confessions tells us that Augustine's natural father was not equal to the task. Consequently, an extraordinarily talented boy searched for other persons whom he could idealize and then trust with that task. In Kohut's terms, Augustine needed to find suitable selfobjects. He looked to a great non-Christian, Faustus, then to a great Christian, Ambrose, and finally to God, the most ideal of fathers. Augustine says, in effect, if it is God, not I, who commands such powers, then surely God will tolerate Augustine's genius and hear his confession. "Because you first willed that I should confess to you, O Lord my God. For you are gracious, your mercy endures forever" (*Confessions*, p. 253).

SELFOBJECT RELATIONSHIPS IN
THE CONFESSIONS

Kohut's conception of the development of infants into children and children into adults is like other psychoanalytic theories of pre-oedipal development. These theories, especially those that deal with the earliest events in the development of the self, assume something that most nonpsychoanalysts do not believe. For Kohut and theoreticians like him believe that human beings must construct slowly their understanding of themselves as whole complete beings.

Augustine does not agree with this contemporary view. Throughout *The Confessions* he describes himself at every age as if he were a fully adult human being. The most famous example of this kind of "adultomorphism," that is, ascribing adult characteristics to infants, occurs in chapter 1 when Augustine recounts how he learned to speak: "I taught myself by using the intelligence which you, my God, gave to me" (*Confessions*, p. 29). This is an odd view of language since it presupposes that a very young child, as young as eighteen months, learns to speak language by comparing what it wants to say against what it hears. Ludwig Wittgenstein, the great Austrian-American philosopher, pointed out that this could occur only if Augustine knew a kind of inherent language to which he could then compare his parents' language.[14]

Both common sense and traditional metaphysics assume that individuals are independent and coherent singularities. William James had described "subliminal selves" as early as 1900, as we have seen.[15] But it was child psychoanalysts who investigated the pathways that lead from relatively diffused, partial selves to an adult sense of continuity and coherence. Erik Erikson said that ego identity, the capacity to be and feel like a coherent self, grows slowly.

There are numerous difficulties each person must face before his or her sense of identity is complete and consolidated.[16] Before this level of maturation is reached, infants, children, and even adults must pass through developmental stages, which Kohut terms selfobject forms of relationship. From an adult's perspective, selfobject relationships appear either psychopathological or sinful. Contrary to common sense, "Selfobjects are objects which we experience as part of our self; the expected control over them is, therefore, closer to the concept of control which a grown-up expects to have over his own body and mind than to the concept of the control which he expects to have over others."[17] Augustine wrote *The Confessions* as an adult looking toward his childhood. Lacking the concept of selfobject, he naturally interpreted infantile behavior toward others as identical to adult behavior. From that perspective, with its stringent superego, infantile needs for selfobject relationships will appear pathological (or sinful).

Yet just as repressed sexual needs return in the form of symptoms, repressed narcissistic needs for selfobject merger return in adult life. These great needs, to feel worthy in oneself (an aspect of the "grandiose self") and to feel bonded to an idealized other ("idealized parental imago"), cannot be ignored since they constitute the basic drive to attain and retain a sense of coherence. However, unlike sexual impulses, which may take circuitous routes, including abstinence, Kohut argues that narcissistic yearnings are vital and require an actual, external other for their fulfillment.

This has led some of his critics to charge Kohut with environmentalism. They charge that he ignores the traditional psychoanalytic emphasis upon vicissitudes of unconscious fantasies and instead explains psychopathology by blaming bad parents or a bad environment. An extreme critic might contend that Kohut ignores the patient's responsibility for his or her neurotic condition. This misses Kohut's point. Narcissistic wishes may be neuroticized and therefore distorted. But since they represent fundamental needs, one cannot and should not hope to analyze them away. In other words, narcissistic needs are not symptoms that will disappear upon correct interpretation. In one of his major papers, Kohut speaks about the transformation of narcissistic hopes, not their dissolution.[18] Needs to feel worthy, creative, and linked to a shared center of infinite value will not disappear.[19] Psychoanalytic therapy is a situation in which "the damaged self begins to strive to achieve or to re-establish a state of cohesion, vigour and inner harmony."[20]

Erikson says of Martin Luther that if one has no psychology of the unconscious, one must have a theology of heaven and hell.[21] We may say the same about selfobject needs. If one's developmental psychology is like Augustine's, assuming that infants and children are wholly formed selves from the beginning, then the child's needs to find and use selfobjects will emerge as the work of a dark power. From an adult's perspective, a mature, morally developed person does not use other people as if they were parts of the self. When, contrary to these moralistic demands, persons exhibit needs for selfobject relationship, these narcissistic wishes will seem extraordinary to themselves and to other people. In order to control these dark and unnamed forces, which seem to arise out of the depths of the psyche, the conscious self must call upon an equally uncanny and extraordinary power of light.

Augustine's Developmental Psychology

Augustine shares this moralizing attitude toward wishes for selfobject relationship. We see this directly in Augustine's speculations about human development in the first chapters of *The Confessions*. The harshness of his views suggests a strong reaction to the needs for bonding, merger, and selfobject relationships Kohut describes. Augustine's initial hymn to God might equally well describe the infant's experience of the good-enough mother merged with her adoring child:

> [S]ince nothing that exists could exist without you, does this mean that whatever exists does, in this sense contain you? If this is so, since I too exist, why do I ask you to come into me? . . . I should be null and void and could not exist at all, if you, my God, were not in me. Or is it rather that I should not exist, unless I existed in you? But if I exist in you, how can I call upon you to come to me? (*Confessions*, p. 22)

Augustine solves this problem by envisioning God in ways that are strikingly female (even though he uses masculine names):

> And when you pour yourself out over us, you are not drawn down to us but draw us up to yourself: you are not scattered away, but you gather us up. You fill all things, but do you fill them with your whole self? . . . You support, you fill, and you protect all things. You create them, nourish them, and bring them to perfection. (*Confessions*, pp. 22–23)

Augustine deepens this metaphor and at the same time shifts from a hymn to autobiography by linking God's infinite desire to love creation with his mother's breasts:

But neither my mother nor my nurses filled their breasts of their own accord, for it was you who used them, as your law prescribes, to give me infant's food. . . . All this I have learned since then, because all gifts you have given to me, both spiritual and material, proclaim the truth of it. But in those days all I knew was how to suck, and how to lie still when my body sensed comfort or cry when it felt pain. (*Confessions*, p. 25)

From our contemporary vantage point it is easy to see how Augustine misconstrues the infant's experience. He constantly views infants and children as if their psychological organization were identical to that of adults. Infants, according to Augustine, are basically adults who are very small, inarticulate, and consequently helpless. They are like foreigners in Gargantua: captives of superior gigantic figures whose language they must comprehend slowly. Wittgenstein took Augustine to task for this notion of language.[22] But these passages of *The Confessions* show equally well Augustine's unempathic view of infant psychology and the baby's inner world, where the wishes are inside and no faculty can penetrate its mind. Since babies are miniature adults, according to this belief, they too sin and have faults which must be "rooted out" (*Confessions*, p. 27). Just as the capacity for signification is present from the beginning, infants are capable of gluttony and other sins.

At a manifest level Augustine recognizes that these ideas about children are speculations, based on his observations of infants, and not part of his conscious memory. At the same time he wants to inculcate the truth of the doctrine of original sin (*Confessions*, p. 28). To do that, Augustine attacks precisely those pre-oedipal yearnings that Kohut (and others) has designated as the crucial needs that must be satisfied before the infant and child can develop into full-fledged mature adults.

Augustine is not a patient, and his account is not a case report. *The Confessions* is a complex polemic, apology, and theological treatise. Yet it articulates an understanding of human development so contrary to Kohut's understanding that it will be valuable to us to contrast Augustine's consistent condemnation of narcissistic wishes with Kohut's clinical approach to such wishes.

Sources of Augustine's Disdain for Infantile Needs

How did Augustine come to feel so strongly the moral failings of infants? Augustine's story of his boyhood sickness suggests a mother who shared the absolutist superego of her son, and perhaps of the entire epoch. Young Augustine is very sick. His mother, Monica, fears for his life. She makes plans to have him baptized. But the boy recovers and "So my washing in the waters of baptism was postponed, in the surmise that, if I continued to live, I should defile myself again with sin, and, after baptism, the guilt of pollution would be greater and more dangerous" (*Confessions*, p. 32).

The world view Augustine espouses here is directly opposed to the empathic point of view we have formulated above. In psychiatric parlance Augustine's theology is similar to a radically paranoid world view: forces of evil inhabit everyone, including infants, and these must be met by forces of good. The ego is a weak, lonely hero struggling to align itself with good against evil. Augustine uses a beautiful metaphor that describes well this metapsychology: Tides of temptation beat upon him who is yet "unmolded clay rather than upon the finished image which has yet received the stamp of baptism" (*Confessions*, p. 33).

This passage recalls the Genesis account of Yahweh, the potter who molded human beings into Yahweh's image (or *eikon* as the Septuagint expressed it). Yet it rejects that relative security by evoking also the evil effect floods of temptation may have upon weak and unformed characters.

Liquid metaphors appear throughout Augustine's account, as they do in Freud's general account of the drives. Although separated by language and world view, both men believed that a constant battle rages between upsurging eros and the rational self. Augustine described his sexual impulses as filthy lust, brewed in a cauldron of passion (*Confessions*, pp. 52–53). Less poetically, Freud described the channels in the mind through which the libido flows, carving out an ever deepening bed of habit.[23]

Freud does not moralize about these currents of libido. He does not say, directly, how one should direct them. But his basic stance toward sexuality is identical to that of Augustine: One must acquire the strength necessary to overcome and subdue currents of libido. Toward this task Augustine invoked God's power. Freud invoked the power of reason and the forces for change liberated by positive transference. Freud and Augustine both view human life as constituted by profound conflict. Freud differs from Augustine only in that he reduced the ontological status of the combatants from divine forces contending for the human soul, to powers within the soul contending between themselves. Kohut's contribution has been to advance this chain of moral reasoning (in the sense of moral philosophy).[24]

Given Augustine's epoch, then, *The Confessions* is an immense achievement. It advanced a new intellectual model of the Socratic ideal of self-knowledge and self-control.

The Confessions *and Augustine's Need to be Constrained*

Many commentators have remarked upon Augustine's lack of empathy for his opponents and for his concubine. These are striking features of Augustine's personality, yet seem typical of his time and culture. A culture that turns to transcendental solutions for selfobject needs will remain unempathic to the inner life of an individual. That is, transcendental solutions necessarily leap outside the individual's actual interior experience and invoke the authority of an idealized Wholly Other whose face is always obscure and whose intentions are mysterious. According to this reading, therefore, Augustine's implacable self-accusations are reasonable attempts to make God mirror him, even if to condemn him. The incessant, compulsive quality of *The Confessions* derives, perhaps, from this profound need.

One might see the law of the return of the repressed operating with remorseless logic in the latter part of *The Confessions,* where we read that Augustine continued to invoke a transcendental solution to his sexual conflicts. In his and Freud's psychologies these struggles are eternal. The drives themselves are immortal powers that strive always to overthrow the ego's better judgment. The battle between drives and ego, between eros and reason, will never cease. Freud usually avoided transcendental language. But he uses it when he describes the sexual and aggressive instincts against which the ego must grapple in an unending struggle against these immortal substances.[25]

Freud's basic theorems about the two great instincts (or drives), eros and destructiveness, parallel Augustine's fascination with Manichaeism. This religious philosophy swept through the ancient world and by the fourth century claimed numerous influential persons among its adherents. Manichaeism appealed to Augustine and others who shared his training in rhetoric, for it seemed to show that the human world is one of inherent conflict. According to Mani, the founder of the religion, human beings are two-souled because the divine world is twofold. At the beginning of human history forces of darkness challenged forces of light. Now all human beings are the battleground over which these ancient divine powers wage constant war. Only at the end of time, after the last great battle, will human beings achieve unity. For then absolute goodness and the light will conquer darkness. Augustine was fascinated by Mani's teaching. As a young man, Augustine burned to associate himself with the great leaders in the intellectual circles that espoused Manichaeism. Freud had a similar fascination for dualistic metaphysics. Freud's essay on the metaphysical foundation of the personality, *Beyond the Pleasure Principle,*[26] is compatible with the dualisms that permeate Manichaeism.

Kohut counters both men's implicit metaphysics by tracing sexualization not to some fundamental drive that requires transcendental solution, but to deficits in a self-selfobject relationship:

> Instead of the further development of a firmly cohesive self able to feel the glow of healthy pleasure in its affectionate and phase-appropriate sexual functioning and able to employ self-confident assertiveness in the pursuit of goals, we find throughout life a continuing propensity to experience the *fragments* of love (sexual phantasies) rather than love and the *fragments* of assertiveness (hostile fantasies) rather than assertiveness and to respond to these experiences . . . with anxiety.[27]

Parents like Monica, who attend primarily to the control of these fragmentation products, systematically deny that the child has a coherent and cohesive self. Kohut does not claim that human beings are not sexual. He does not deny that human beings are aggressive. He does deny that sexual and aggressive fantasies express the ultimate constituents of human nature, the bedrock of our animal natures, which all honest persons must recognize. Augustine, like Freud and most Western moralists up to our times, increased this sense of fragmentation by taking for granted that sexual impulses, that "hissing cauldron of lust" (*Confessions,* p. 55), are irreducible forces that civilization must constrain, just as the Olympians jailed the Titans. Augustine describes how a close friend, Alypius, who had given up his fascination for gladiatorial combat, fell back into that fascination. In his description Augustine relies upon the metaphor of upwelling drives: "When [Alypius] saw the blood, it was as though he had drunk a deep draught of savage passion. Instead of turning away, he fixed his eyes upon the scene and drank in all its frenzy, unaware of what he was doing" (*Confessions,* p. 122).

In contrast, Kohut views sexualization as a product of prior narcissistic injury. Sexualized and aggressivized images, as well as perverse actions, are attempts to repair a wounded self.

Selfobject "Transferences"

A selfobject transference is a relationship in which the patient treats a contemporary as if that person were the long-lost parent who failed to provide "selfobject" support. Once a selfobject transference is established, the patient (or child) responds to alterations in it with fragmentation anxiety. As we know, because fragmentation anxiety is so painful it elicits frantic, sexualized efforts to repair the breach in self caused by that empathic failure. Given the subtleties and variety of selfobject transferences, empathic failures occur frequently. Some patients, like some children, may experience a two- or three-minute delay as sure signs of the analyst's disinterest. In response to that perception, they withdraw their deep wishes for merger with the analyst. Since that wish formed part of the armature, as it were, around which they wound their psychic structure, withdrawing it causes a deep feeling of incoherence. Kohut calls such moments "mini-fragmentations." Because fragmentation is so painful, patients seek relief from it immediately in characteristic ways.

The broadest and most obvious route to effect such repair is through frantic sexual activity, hypersexualization. In phenomenological terms hypersexualization seems especially attractive because it permits one to establish an intense feeling of body integrity and wholeness, even if it is temporary. To speculate further, it seems likely that increased sexual excitation, especially orgasm, serves to concretize and validate the underlying unconscious fantasy. Kohut permits us to account for the perverse action as an attempt to use physical experience (orgasm) to temporarily replace psychological structure.

These are not radical psychoanalytic conclusions. Numerous ego psychologists have made similar comments about the fantasy structures underlying perverse (and normal) sexuality. Kohut's contribution has included the clinical insight that perversions, especially in narcissistically vulnerable patients, occur as the consequence of empathic failures. I think that this is an extremely helpful point of view.

Kohut describes many such sequences in his texts. I suggest that we see an intergenerational sequence in *The Confessions.*

TWO GENERATIONS OF
EMPATHIC FAILURE

Augustine describes the upbringing of his mother, Monica, as well as his own. In Book IX of *The Confessions* he gives us an intimate portrait of his mother's early life under the care of a very severe nurse, and her death at age fifty-six. Monica was brought up in "modesty and temperance" (*Confessions*, p. 194). At least, this is what Augustine says. A more complete description should include the remarkable fact that Monica's nurse raised her in an extremely unempathic way. In fact, Monica was raised to become immodest and intemperate in her drinking. Most of the caretaking fell to an older woman servant who was "conscientious in attending to her duties, correcting the children when necessary with strictness, for the love of God, and teaching them to lead wise and sober lives" (*Confessions*, p. 193). Yet, as part of her teaching, Monica's nurse inculcated into her charges extraordinary yearnings for drink. The nurse did this by enforcing the bizarre rule that children should not drink water, no matter how thirsty, except at meals: "She used to give them this very good advice: 'Now you drink water because you are not allowed to have wine. But when you are married and have charge of your own larders and cellars, you will not be satisfied with water, but the habit of drinking will be too strong for you'" (*Confessions*, p. 193).

Augustine fails to see the irony in his celebration of this nurse. For, looking back, we can see that the nurse actually induced in the children under her care an immense urge to drink all forms of liquid. When Augustine says that his mother developed a secret liking for wine in spite of her excellent nurse we must pause. First, we must challenge his assessment of Monica's nurse. Second, we must underscore how unempathic Monica's entire childhood was. For, on the one side, she was confronted with a nurse who delighted in rationing out water (in a very warm climate) and, on the other, Monica's parents sent her to "draw wine from the cask" (*Confessions*, p. 193). So we must imagine the interior experience of a child who is thirsty, as thirsty as one can be in the middle of an Italian summer day, sent to draw liquid refreshment for her parents and not for herself. What will she do?

"She used to dip the cup through the opening at the top of the barrel, and before pouring the wine into the flagon she would sip a few drops" (*Confessions*, p. 193). She did this, we suppose, not because an interior evil spirit prompted her to, but because she was thirsty. Indeed, it was not the alcohol that lured her, "because she found the taste disagreeable" (*Confessions*, p. 193), as do all children. Monica became a secret drinker, stealing drops and then cups of wine from her parents' stores. Like his mother's nurse, Augustine explains his mother's alcoholism as a fated illness, a "secret disease" that only an infinite parental power could cure. God accomplished this cure by providing Monica a young servant girl who, in a moment of rage, called Monica a drunkard.

From a contemporary psychoanalytic point of view, Monica's addiction was probably created by her nurse's extremely unempathic care. The nurse's terror of the young girl's appetites, symbolized by thirst, is similar to the terror with which unempathic parents greet manifestations of narcissistic needs in their children. Such needs and their expression are to be stomped out, pulled out by the roots, and destroyed on an altar of selflessness. When they return in one form or another in adult life they are always greeted, as Augustine says, as the work of dark spiritual forces which can be conquered only by more powerful spirits, as God did by using Monica's maid to shame her into abstinence. The nurse's premonition of Monica's addiction, manifested in the nurse's obsessive efforts to train her ward to ignore normal thirst, guarantees precisely such dependency.

Like the nurse, Monica and her son disdain those feelings and needs for an internalized "good object" (a selfobject) that would sustain her internally. These needs for ongoing maternal reflection of her narcissistic wishes become symbolized by the beverage, wine, which gives Monica a temporary sense of elation, power, and internal warmth. In this sense, Monica's addiction to wine and her son's addiction to hypersexual actions represent their responses to intergenerational failures. Nurse, mother, and son disdain these internal needs and seek to alienate themselves from that part of themselves. Augustine calls such needs the product of a "despicable fault" (*Confessions*, p. 194).

This issue reappears in the dramatic conversation between mother and son, which Augustine reports immediately following this account: "No bodily pleasure, however great it might be and whatever earthly light might shed lustre upon it, was worthy of comparison, or even mention, beside the happiness of the life of the saints" (*Confessions*, p. 197).

Their conversation mounts in spiritual fervor: "At length we came to our own souls and passed beyond them to that place of everlasting plenty, where you feed Israel forever with the food of truth" (*Confessions*, p. 197). Finally, "for one fleeting instant we reached out and touched it. Then with a sigh, leaving our spiritual harvest bound to it, we returned to the sound of our own speech, in which each word has a beginning and an ending" (*Confessions*, pp. 197–98). When a fleshly, human mother cannot provide a sense of inherent worthiness and narcissistic wholeness, God, the great mother who feeds Israel, will.

This passage precedes Augustine's account of his mother's death. It looks forward to that immense loss and serves to prepare author and reader for it. Its overt message is that of a better life beyond this one, where words would not have a beginning and an ending, but the fleeting moment would last forever. Mother and son engage in a kind of spiritual ecstasy that unifies them in a common bond of selfobject merger with God. "For all these things have the same message to tell, if only we can hear it, and their message is this: We did not make ourselves, but he who abides forever made us" (*Confessions*, p. 198).

SUMMARY:
THE SEARCH FOR GOD

From an analytic point of view Augustine's notion of God's presence corresponds directly to the universal human need to find, somewhere, another who knows us to our depths, recognizes our faults, yet loves us completely. Using Kohut's terms, we can say that the debate between Augustine and Freud centers on the question of to what degree God is a selfobject or a Wholly Other who has instilled in God's creatures an ineradicable longing to see their creator face to face.

Freud, as opposed to Kohut, was sure that religious beliefs were essentially false. Augustine erred, from Kohut's point of view, because he demanded too much of abstract representations of relationship. Freud erred because he repressed selfobject needs. Consequently, Freud himself, the great opponent of irrationalism, often took up its cause in a variety of interests in the occult. This horrified many of his colleagues, especially his English biographer, Ernest Jones. As we shall see, Freud was not alone in maintaining a lifelong fascination with the occult. His great colleague, and later, great opponent, Carl Jung, made the occult a central part of his grand philosophical psychology.

4
Freud, Jung, and the Return of the Occult

When Augustine heard himself addressed by a voice from on high, he looked back to Paul's similar experience on the road to Damascus. Paul, in turn, looked back to numerous Jewish authors who had described similar events. Looking even further back, we find that Adam and Eve were also addressed, first by God, later by the serpent, in the same way. Similar visitations appear throughout the history of religion. Some visitations or visions appear to great saints and scholars; others appear to ordinary religious people. Less well-known is the fact that religious persons are not the only ones to whom such visitations or revelations are made. Artists and even scientists also report occult events in which they felt themselves addressed by transcendent beings and granted transcendent powers like telepathy.

Within religious traditions can be found detailed techniques used to distinguish the source of a vision, for example, and to establish if it comes from benign or evil forces.[1] However, I do not propose to distinguish between the sources of transcendental messages. This is not to deny that one might accomplish that task.

Certainly, religionists have never avoided it. Even psychologists, most notably William James and his students, have tried to find ways to assess the spiritual worth of a particular vision. James proposed to do so by elaborating a pragmatic test: Does the vision enhance one's life? Does it create a new sense of harmony, balance, and openness?[2]

Yet not all occult events are religious, nor are all religious experiences occult. In this chapter I discuss occult experiences that are not religious, at least not in any obvious way. Yet they were powerful moments in the lives of those who experienced them. More important, they occurred in the lives of brilliant psychologists, Sigmund Freud and Carl Jung. Each, in turn, attempted to explain these occult events. To advance my Kohutian explanation of occult experience it will pay us to consider carefully how Freud, Jung, and other psychologists explain it, too.

NONRELIGIOUS OCCULT EXPERIENCE: HENRY MILLER AND GIUSEPPE VERDI

One can find dramatic accounts of occult events in numerous nonreligious sources. Indeed, the autobiography or biography with no reference to any occult events in the hero's life would seem rare. This is true of great artists, too. Before discussing Freud and Jung it will be helpful to consider some briefer examples from Henry Miller (1891–1980) and Giuseppe Verdi (1813–1901). Chronologically, Henry Miller comes after Verdi, but I begin with Henry Miller because his simple anecdote about an astrological event links him to Augustine, whose opinions on astrology we know.

In many biographies occult and ordinary events occur side by side. Such a sequence appears in Henry Miller's *Reflections*. Miller describes seeing Jupiter in the night sky above Paris. His friend Moricand had identified the planet and told him to observe it. After going home, Miller mounts a ladder to the roof of his apartment:

> [I] stood gazing at the heavens for a long time. I think I even wept a little as I communed with my lucky star, beautiful jewel of a planet. I was so happy, ecstatic, exalted, almost in a kind of trance.
>   On my way back down the ladder, I slipped and crashed through a glass door which happened to be standing ajar. There was glass everywhere. I took off my clothes, got into the shower, and as I looked down into the drain, the water was full of blood. And I didn't stop bleeding.

Miller tries to sleep, cannot, and has a friend take him to the hospital. After he is bandaged and fed he goes home to sleep for forty-eight hours: "Then Moricand came over with his astrological charts to show me how close I'd come to killing myself. Every single planet in my chart had been badly aspected except for Jupiter. Jupiter, my lucky star, had saved my life!"[3]

To this vivid anecdote Miller brings his storytelling skills, but, unfortunately, no previous history. We cannot show a causal sequence of separation issues followed by despair and occult repair. But we may speculate about Miller's reasoning. In an obvious sense Miller describes a massive parapraxis, that is, an error committed with unconscious intent. It was he who climbed the ladder, he who left the glass door ajar, and he who happened to slip, then crash through the door. Even supposing that Miller was profoundly inebriated (which he does not indicate), the errors leading up to the disaster are all products of his judgment. In addition, contrary to the astrologer's interpretation, it would seem that Miller's intention to gaze longingly at his lucky star, Jupiter, was the source of his accident. Rather than save his life, in this sense, Jupiter was responsible for his near death.

Miller wishes to assign to Jupiter an occult power that is without question maternal. His lucky star, his jeweled planet, somehow watches down on him, like a mother gazing at her child. Like the child who scans the mother's face, Miller gazes longingly at Jupiter. This distant inhuman object, seen rarely in Paris, has a special, loving interest in Henry Miller and, like any devoted parent, intuits his need for special protection. It gazes back at him. Unfortunately, we do not know the events that preceded Miller's accident and cannot show, directly, that it was a profound longing for a maternal presence that led up to the parapraxes, a challenge to fate and an appeal to Lady Luck.

A different example permits us to be more explicit. Giuseppe Verdi reported how he came to agree to compose the music to his first great opera, *Nabucco*, in the early part of 1841. Following a series of tragic deaths, two children in the previous two years, and his wife in June 1840, Verdi's comic opera, *Un Giorno di Regno*, failed miserably in September 1840. His friend and director of La Scala, Merelli, persuaded him to read the libretto for an opera that dealt with the fate of the Hebrews under the dominion of Nebuchadnezzar.

According to Verdi's own account, his eyes fell first on the chorus of the Hebrew exiles, "Va, pensiero, sull'ali dorate" (Arise, sad thoughts, on golden wings), which left an indelible impression: "I was much moved, because the verses were almost a paraphrase from the Bible, the reading of which had always delighted me." He spent a sleepless night reading and rereading the whole libretto.[4]

Like Augustine and like those whom Augustine emulated, Verdi invokes the theme of divine intervention. In the midst of his suffering he understands that the first passage to present itself to him will be significant because it will have been sent for that purpose. It will be a sign, just as the children's voices were signs for Augustine, that his tribulations are done. As we have seen, such signs convey tremendous authority because they seem to match perfectly emotional needs that, as Wordsworth says, lie too deep for tears. A portion of the ecstatic feelings such events arouse seems to derive from the uncanny way in which the signs sent match these inner, unspoken needs. Verdi tells us that this particular verse reminded him directly of the Old Testament book Lamentations, a profound and beautiful evocation of mourning and loss. Reading it even in the best of circumstances is not easy. For Verdi the text evoked not only his own severe losses, but also memories of a time long past when he had read Lamentations in the midst of loving friends.

Lamentations is a Hebrew text that describes the Babylonian captivity of the Jews, which followed the destruction of Jerusalem by the Babylonians in 587 B.C.E. Written in five brief chapters, Lamentations describes the utter devastation wrought by the Babylonians upon the Jewish homeland and its most sacred institutions. The text is replete with terrible scenes of bloodshed. But these descriptions are also masterful accounts of the destruction. This literary mastery, it seems, gives to the Hebrews as a people a degree of control over their story, and their past, that would otherwise not be available. Lamentations was composed for public recitation on those special days set aside to commemorate the disaster. The terrible indictment of Jewish failures is also a supreme example of Jewish achievement, namely, the spiritual integrity of the text itself. Verdi did not write the libretto to his opera. Yet his special feeling for Lamentations, especially during his period of recovery, suggests that Verdi attended to its theme of profound loss contained and made tolerable by artistic transformation.

When Verdi's eyes fell upon the chorus of the Hebrew exiles, he felt that this chance encounter was actually a direct intervention in his life by God. God had seen his suffering, so similar to that of the Hebrews, and after hearing Verdi's lamentations gave him a way to resolve his grief: the composition of a great opera.

Although we have minimal information about Verdi's thoughts at the time he began the composition of *Nabucco*, we can see in this short episode the sequence of loss and repair evident in other occult experiences. First appears the loss of a person who provides one with the loving, caring, and holding we can call mothering. Verdi suffered this and, in sequence, manifested the mourning and search for solace evident when he scanned the libretto waiting for the proper text to reveal itself to him. Having discovered that sign, he responded to it with renewed creative effort. Verdi composed his first operatic triumph "one day one line, another day another. . . . "[5]

Finally, Verdi felt compelled to display the opera even though his producer, Merelli, had no place for it in his program, having already established the season's repertoire. Unlike previous instances of rejection when he had acquiesced, Verdi showed an "angry insistence to bring *Nabucco* to performance. Self-doubt had been replaced by self-confidence."[6] The sources of Verdi's new-found strength no doubt are many. Yet we may suggest that he insisted on the opera's immediate performance because it satisfied his need to consolidate the sense of place and mission revealed to him when a benign force brought the lines from Lamentations to his attention.

Objectively speaking, we should not expect to find that the opera matches perfectly Verdi's internal state. Neither Lamentations nor the story of Nebuchadnezzar (Nabucco) was created by Verdi. However, from an empathic point of view, the opposite should be true. That is, as argued above, the occult event is shaped exactly and directly by the subject's profound internal needs. From his or her point of view, the text or the sign should fit perfectly. Part of the work involved in the scanning involves assessing, perhaps unconsciously, the degree to which the external signs match internal needs.

In a clinical setting one can reconstruct with the patient precisely how this matching occurs. Since that match is often accomplished on idiosyncratic lines, it is difficult to predict how an individual will interpret his or her experience. In other words, it is hard enough to comprehend a patient whom one may see for six or seven or eight hundred hours. To attempt to comprehend the interior states of persons known only through their writings may seem foolhardy. But having attempted this for Augustine, I plunge ahead and consider occult moments in the lives of two great psychologists, Sigmund Freud and Carl Jung.

FREUD AND THE OCCULT:
THE RETURN OF THE REPRESSED

Freud's antipathy toward religion is well-known. Beginning with his earliest comments on religious rituals and their similarities to obsessive actions, and through his last book, he attacked religion consistently. The fascination that religion held for him seems incongruous with his absolute claim that such beliefs and actions were obviously infantilisms that the human race was destined to overcome. If that were so, one wonders why Freud found it necessary to write so much about religion. A partial answer to this question may be found in his less well known essay on religion, "The Question of a *Weltanschauung.*"[7] There Freud says that rather than propose a grand world view, a *Weltanschauung,* psychoanalysts should remain faithful to the aims of science, which are always pointed toward a program, "the fulfillment of which is relegated to the future."[8]

A *Weltanschauung* gives emotional security because it seems to answer every possible question and leaves us, therefore, satisfied that there is nothing beyond our understanding. A mature, scientifically grounded person will tolerate the unknown and sustain a hope for eventual understanding, won after years, or perhaps generations, of struggle to comprehend the laws of nature. However, Freud says, mature persons ought not to feign a liberal generosity toward the religiously devout. To tolerate religious claims is to give them a dignity and weight that will prove dangerous.

Freud attacks religion, therefore, under the banner of zealous regard for the truth. For of all the opponents that scientific persons will encounter in their struggles toward understanding, "religion alone is to be taken seriously as an enemy."[9] These are not accidental remarks made by a bitter old man. On the contrary, I believe that they undergird all Freud's better-known treatises on religion, for example, *The Future of an Illusion* and *Moses and Monotheism.*[10]

Freud's Attacks on Religion: Manifest and Latent Reasoning

In addition to the manifest reasons Freud advances against religion, I believe that we can find additional latent issues as well. Within his short essay on *Weltanschauung* there is one hint. He describes an error that religion and philosophy share. Each group clings to "the illusion of being able to present a picture of the universe which is without gaps and is coherent."[11] In order to feel that the outside world is coherent and without gaps, one must feel that one's inner world, one's self, is also coherent and whole. Freud's discoveries about projective mechanisms validate the folk truism that people see in others what they cannot bear to see in themselves.

Freud attacks religious beliefs primarily because they contradict, at a manifest level, scientific discoveries. Yet he also attacks them because they appear to afford the devout a "crooked cure" for their neuroses. That is, religious beliefs permit people to feel "coherent and without gaps" because they assert the existence of a benign, loving deity who gazes down upon them and responds to their deepest needs.

Of course, religious authorities say that God often seems not to hear our prayers. But in the end we will see that there is meaning even in our worst suffering and loss.

There are, no doubt, idiosyncratic reasons for Freud's animosity toward religion. His biographers and later commentators have often pointed out that he suffered acutely upon hearing that his father had once tolerated being humiliated by a Gentile. Some argue that Freud's Catholic nanny and her curious role in his early religious education played a part in his later criticisms of Roman Catholicism, for example, in *Group Psychology.*[12]

In contrast to these biographical explanations for Freud's hatred of religion, his reasoning about religion is consistent with his fundamental belief that religious solutions are public instances of a private neurosis.[13] Religion preserves a semblance of healthy ego functioning, but at the cost of sacrificing a large portion of ego autonomy in favor of belief. Religiously devout persons may be safeguarded against certain obsessional neuroses, precisely because they already manifest a cultural obsession: religious beliefs and practices.

Psychoanalytic authors who came after Freud, like Kohut and, especially, David Winnicott (1896–1971), permit us to reexamine Freud's attack on religion. These authors also permit us to distinguish occult beliefs from other claims about transcendental events, that is, religious beliefs. This distinction, advanced in the Introduction, states that occult beliefs are held to be valid accounts of a realm that is essentially unknowable by ordinary means. Occultists typically align their beliefs with some form of scientific argument. This contrasts with religious beliefs, which are advanced as matters of faith, not knowledge.

Kohut and Winnicott permit us to account for occult beliefs with theorems that are clinical, not philosophic. One such theorem, advanced above, is that occult beliefs occur as consequences of failures in self and selfobject relationships. They emerge, therefore, as the products of a long, complex chain of events, personal losses, emotional responses, and creative solutions to those perceived losses.

FREUD'S OCCULT EXPERIENCES

It will prove instructive to examine Freud's own life to see if we can discover there evidence to confirm or disprove this theorem. We find that Freud himself always maintained some degree of interest in the occult throughout his life, even during his later years when he rejected entirely all religious beliefs.

Freud's fascination with the occult has always embarrassed his strait-laced followers. Ernest Jones, author of the semiofficial three-volume biography, *The Life and Work of Sigmund Freud*,[14] summarizes these interests in an entire chapter devoted to the topic.[15] In those instances where we have some knowledge of the events that preceded an occult event, we see the sequence of loss of the selfobject followed by occult reparation.

Freud's involvement with occult matters may be gauged by the frequency with which he reported occult events in his life and practice,[16] and by the shame he suffered when his wishes for validation of occult reasoning were not fulfilled. He saw for himself how hopeless were his scientific explanations, which fall into a category of speculation about the possibility of thought transference. Assuming that many traditional occult claims about clairvoyance or telepathy might be true, Freud reasoned that documented psychoanalytic evidence of thought transference between patient and analyst might give additional weight to the argument. That is, the naive reception of telepathic communication, and similar perceptions in the trained analyst, might be products of an as yet undescribed mental process by which brain waves are transmitted from one person to another. This would not be, Freud says, "a psychical phenomenon, but purely a somatic one—one, it is true, of the first rank in importance."[17] It is curious that Freud's reasoning here and elsewhere about occult matters is so nonanalytic. Freud imparts little information about a patient's previous thoughts, emotional state, or wishes, all of which must be connected to the occult event.

Freud did advance more analytic theorems about a small class of reported occult events, those associated with death wishes toward close relatives and friends. These premonitions of another's death or misfortune commonly hide aggressive feelings toward the victim, which are then masked under a veneer of concern.[18]

Jones reports that Freud's most significant occult experiences, and the first reported by him, were associated with his fiancée, Martha. As a boy Freud had chosen, in a lottery that predicted one's character, the number seventeen, which he associated with the term "constancy." As Jones puts it, "Now, lo and behold, that was the very number of the day of the month when he got engaged."[19] This would seem to be an instance of numerology, a belief that held Freud in thrall all his life. Freud's many well-known interchanges with his friend, mentor, and alter ego, Wilhelm Fliess, are filled with Freud's calculations of the numerological significance of certain events, especially those associated with Fliess's special numbers, twenty-eight and thirty-two.

A more direct example of occult reasoning is Freud's experience of telepathic communication with Martha. Jones's account cannot be made more succinct:

A month after being engaged [Freud] accidently broke the engagement ring [Martha] had given him. At the moment he thought nothing of it, but soon mysterious doubts assailed him and he wrote to ask her on her honor whether she had been less fond of him "at eleven o'clock last Thursday." He said it was a good opportunity to put an end to a superstition.[20]

The longer story behind this short account suggests that Freud's mysterious doubts link him far more closely to Augustine (and later to Jung) than Jones might appreciate. Again, Jones provides sufficient evidence in the first volume of Freud's biography to reconstruct a likely sequence of events culminating in Freud's occult experience.

To set the stage, even briefly, requires contemplation of Freud's intense character, well-delineated in 1882 when, at age twenty-six, he became engaged to Martha Bernays, five years his junior. Jones reports that Freud wrote more than nine hundred love letters to Martha during their four-and-a-quarter-year engagement.[21] Recalling Freud's literary skills, which are comparable to those of Augustine, we are not surprised that many of these letters are longer than ten or twelve pages. Some run to more than twenty. We are a little more surprised when we read them and see how completely Freud invested in them his scientific and intellectual thoughts. Freud's devotion to Martha is undeniable, but he is not blind to her ordinary features and skills. That is, the letters are not filled, Jones tells us, with exuberant romanticisms colored by grandiose claims about Martha's beauty. Freud addressed Martha rather as Augustine addressed his mother, as a fellow novitiate on a long road to eventual self-fulfillment.

To call these narcissistic goals is not to disparage them. It should be clear now that I use this term in Kohut's sense as pertaining to one's overall feeling about the worthiness, coherence, and continuity of one's self. Such goals emerged in the conversation that Augustine reported between himself and his mother when they contemplated their ideal relationship:

At length we came to our own souls and passed beyond them to that place of everlasting plenty, where you feed Israel forever with the food of truth. . . . For one fleeting instant we reached out and touched it. Then with a sigh, leaving our spiritual harvest bound to it, we returned to the sound of our own speech, in which each word has a beginning and an ending.[22]

Object Love and Selfobject Love

Side by side with Freud's adamant "object love" for Martha is an intense expression of her value to him as a selfobject, a person with whom he can feel in special communion and whose presence, either in the flesh or in some visible sign, helps him feel fully constituted, real, and optimistic. Among many possible examples, the following illustrates one aspect of Freud's self-selfobject relationship to Martha. He wrote, "And when you are my dear wife before all the world and bear my name we will pass our life in calm happiness for ourselves and earnest work for mankind until we have to close our eyes in eternal sleep and leave those near us a memory every one will be glad of."[23]

Aside from the superior mind and literary style, one finds that Freud's feelings toward Martha are normal and expectable. That is, they manifest intense object love and intense selfobject demands. These sometimes alternated in a furious manner. Jones says of their early relationship that Freud felt "their relationship must be quite perfect; the slightest blur was not to be tolerated. At times it seemed as if his goal was fusion rather that union."[24] Fusion occurs between self and selfobject. The latter must submit itself to the demands of the former. Freud rebuked himself numerous times for making such demands upon Martha; then he would make similar demands of her again. In the midst of a jealous torment Freud tells her, as Jones translates Freud's German letter, "She is no longer the eldest daughter, the superior sister: she has become quite young, a sweetheart only a week old, who will quickly lose every trace of tartness." Following this episode, Freud apologized and said that the "loved one is not to become a toy doll, but a good comrade who still has a sensible word left when the strict master has come to the end of his wisdom."[25] When the selfobject refuses to obey the demands placed upon it by a person in this state of narcissistic vulnerability, its disobedience enrages the other, who now feels deprived of what he or she needs most. As we have seen, Kohut sometimes calls positive relationships between self and selfobjects "psychological oxygen" without which one suffocates and dies.

With these thoughts in mind we return to Freud's occult experience. In response to Freud's proposal of marriage, Martha had given him a ring that her father had apparently given her mother under similar circumstances in their courtship. A month later, Jones tells us, Freud happened to break the ring under a peculiar circumstance. In order to relieve anginal swelling, a surgeon had pierced Freud's throat and "in his pain he had banged his hand on the table" and so broke the ring.[26] One might speculate that Freud did not enjoy the experience of feeling himself stuck in the throat, fully conscious, in an effort to reduce an intense pain, all the while removed from his devoted Martha. Thoughts of death and impalement could not have been far away.

Banging his hand down upon the table may also have been a superstitious act designed to placate evil forces. Freud described other such acts in letters to friends.[27] Also, one might speculate about obvious castration themes associated with having his body pierced and bled in order to reduce a painful swelling, all the while thinking about his fiancée and her supposed falseness.

Freud's associations seem to lead to occult beliefs, which he states but then denies by overstating the case and disowning his superstitious thoughts: "Now I have a tragically serious question"—when the ring broke, was Martha, at that very time, less fond of him? Freud hastens to add, "I was *not* seized by forebodings that our engagement would come to no good end, no dark suspicion that you were just at the moment occupied in tearing my image from your heart."[28]

The urgency of Freud's request for reassurance and soothing is not diminished by these intellectual defenses. Needs for selfobject relationships, even in a person as robust and insightful as Freud, can be as frightening and disorganizing to one as sexual needs. In both cases, if needs seem too strong, that is, not controllable, the person erects defenses against them as against any other repressed set of wishes. When needs for selfobject relationships emerge, as they do in instances when Freud felt threatened, they elicit embarrassment. To defend himself against this embarrassment he uses humor or intellectual formulas. These efforts, like all defenses, can only be partly successful. Freud tried but failed to discipline himself and deny these needs.

Freud's Fascination with the Occult

Freud's fascination with the occult did not diminish over time. It persisted long after his self-analysis (begun in the last years of the last century) had ended. In fact, it persisted throughout his life. Freud did waver as to what degree he ought to permit occult research conducted by Sandor Ferenczi to be linked directly with psychoanalysis. Yet he remained sympathetic to Ferenczi's fascination with thought transference and telepathy. Jones reports that Freud often felt he had received special telepathic communications from his eldest son, who was away during the war. Of special importance to us in these instances is that such communications occurred when the loved one was at some distance, his exact status unknown, and in some danger. At a manifest level that danger would seem to be an objective one of being harmed in battle. Yet, turning back to Martha, Freud's occult experiences with her revolved around the issue of her availability to him as a selfobject. Her supposed disinterest in him might, he feared, have caused the sacred ring to break—as happens in fairy tales.

A striking occult moment occurred to Freud during his stay in Paris, away from Martha. He often hallucinated her voice, and reported to her that he often heard her calling his name. He wrote her, "I then noted down the exact moment of the hallucination and made anxious inquiries of those at home about what had happened at that time. Nothing had happened."[29] To indicate how irrational these beliefs are, Freud notes also that he received no messages and suffered no presentiments when one of his children actually was in danger of bleeding to death. Freud does offer an explanation for the appearance of such superstitions: They represent the return of disguised wishes for harm to the beloved. "A person who has harboured frequent evil wishes against others, but has been brought up to be good and has therefore repressed such wishes into the unconscious, will be especially ready to expect punishment for his unconscious wickedness."[30]

This might well be true of some instances of superstitious actions. Yet, in his own experiences, it seems farfetched to suppose that he heard Martha's voice precisely at a time when he wished her ill. It seems more reasonable to suppose that these hallucinations manifested his direct wish to have Martha with him in Paris, a city famous for its sexual temptations. A young obsessive Austrian scientist had much to face while living in the midst of French eroticism. Did the fact of their separation, coupled with his severe intellectual demands upon himself and the loneliness of his stay in a foreign country, induce in Freud moments of fragmentation? If so, we can better explain his hallucinations as responses to narcissistic deficits in which he felt intensely the lack of a soothing, holding selfobject.

In support of this explanation, we note that even following these momentary lapses, Freud felt compelled to write Martha and inquire as to exactly what she had been doing at the precise moment he heard her voice. Freud suggests that these inquiries were in the nature of scientific tests of the occult hypotheses. Yet his letters suggest that they were much more in the nature of anxious expressions of narcissistic vulnerability: Did she still love him? Was he in her mind and heart? Was their "fusion," to use Jones's term, still strong and unbroken by mere time and distance?

Occult Beliefs as Embarrassment to Freud

The embarrassment Freud evinced about his lifelong fascination with the occult, and the shame over his hero's concerns with these matters obvious in Jones's account, appear throughout traditional psychoanalytic works on the occult. I believe that one source of Freud's and Jones's embarrassment is that traditional analysts have found themselves in a dilemma. They can affirm occultist claims to have special knowledge about extraordinary powers, rather as Eisenbud did in suggesting the concept of psi. But these claims contradict common sense and the discoveries of modern science. To affirm occult beliefs is to side with the mystics and others who argue against the dominance of reason, at least reason as it is known by the majority of scientists of our time. But most psychoanalysts, and certainly Freud himself, wanted to dissociate themselves from mystical teachings. This leaves the second alternative: to reject mystical claims. But this then seems to marry psychoanalysis with a crude materialism that holds that mind is fully reducible to brain. This form of materialist psychology offended Arthur Conan Doyle. Freud abandoned it when he wrote his first truly psychoanalytic works in the last years of the nineteenth century. In addition, if psychoanalysts align themselves completely with physicalist theories of mind, they become colleagues of people who find psychoanalytic claims to be as untestable as those of mystics. Freud was acutely aware of this issue, and he warned Ferenczi about it when Ferenczi became more and more vocal about his occult experiments and beliefs.

Kohut permits us another explanation of Freud's embarrassment. Given the argument advanced in this book, occult claims draw upon self and selfobject needs that are linked to narcissistic issues. Freud and his followers saw no way to advance a strict psychoanalytic explanation of such issues. In the absence of a valid, clinically based theory of selfobject needs, Freud and many other psychoanalysts denounced "narcissism" with a fervor that matched anything Augustine wrote.

Kohut offers us a way to advance a truly psychoanalytic perspective on occult experiencing without falling into either side of this dilemma. Some of Freud's followers did accept occult claims and set about to unite them with the discoveries attributed to psychoanalytic research. Ferenczi made numerous attempts to link the two disciplines. So great was Ferenczi's fervor that he sometimes exhorted his patients to recognize exactly how his private thoughts matched their unconscious communications. Ernest Jones describes how Ferenczi "used his powers of suggestion to the full and almost tearfully begged me to perceive the significance of the resemblance between my associations and his unspoken thoughts, however remote the connection might be."[31] Jones, who knew Ferenczi both as a patient and later as a member of the circle around Freud (to each of whom Freud gave a ring), alludes to many of Ferenczi's passionate concerns with occult matters, from fortunetelling to telepathy to astrology. Jones only touches upon a far more compelling example, that of Carl Jung.

CARL JUNG AND THE
OCCULT REBORN

From the beginning of Jung's relationship with Freud and his followers, the two invested each other with tremendous importance. For Freud, the younger Swiss psychiatrist was the heir apparent to his position as leader of the psychoanalytic movement. For Jung, Freud was the ideal hero, like Wagner's Siegfried. Jung hoped that Freud's revolutionary discoveries would give rise to a radical doctrine that would reinvigorate Western spirituality.

Looking backward at their union and their stormy intellectual divorce, we can see more easily than they how it could not last. Many excellent accounts of their relationship are now available and I will not repeat the story here.

Of more direct relevance is the nature of Jung's never-abandoned fascination with the occult in all its forms. That fascination is evident in Jung's scientific works, which begin with his medical dissertation on a young female medium who was distantly related to him. This devotion to occult issues persists throughout his later works, when Jung wrote extensively on spiritualism, religious experience, astrology, Eastern mysticism, alchemy, and UFOs, to name but a few.[32]

Jung's view of occult issues is directly contrary to that of Freud. Freud asserts that as he matured he had fewer "uncanny" experiences.[33] According to Freud, overcoming infantilisms meant overcoming the propensity to see the world in one's own image. According to Jung, the capacity to see deep meaningful connections between our inner world and the outer, between our wishes and the fall of a sparrow, marked spiritual achievement.

In his many volumes on religious psychology Jung advances a sophisticated set of explanations, not a mere apologetic, for traditional occult claims. It would be unfair and dismissive to treat Jung's work as if it were nothing more than intellectualized versions of ancient heresies. Jung should be judged in himself and according to his own goals: to elaborate a scientific account of myth that respected its ability to give human life depth and joy.[34] However, our goals are to understand Jung's own experiences and to see how a contemporary psychoanalytic theory can help us explain them. To accomplish this, we consider passages from his autobiography, *Memories, Dreams, Reflections.*[35]

In his autobiography Jung recounts many occult events, one of which, involving Freud and some mysterious sounds in the kitchen, has become widely known. We consider these reports below. From my point of view, the first chapters of *Memories, Dreams, Reflections*, in which Jung describes his earliest memories and his boyhood fantasies, are more important. There we see laid the groundwork of his later fascination with what Freud once termed "the black mud of occultism."

Separation and Mother
in Memories, Dreams, Reflections

Jung never wished his autobiography to be included among his scientific works. Reading it, one can see why. Jung rambles along, speaking directly to the reader, with none of the Latin and Greek quotations with which he laces his scholarly pieces. However, his rambling is vivid and evocative of the man, and the story he tells is, I think, touching.

Speaking in the first person Jung describes "perhaps the earliest [memory] of my life":

> I am lying in a pram, in the shadow of a tree. It is a fine, warm summer day, the sky blue, and golden sunlight darting through green leaves. The hood of the pram has been left up. I have just awakened to the glorious beauty of the day, and have a sense of indescribable well-being. I see the sun glittering through the leaves and blossoms of the bushes. Everything is wholly wonderful, colorful, and splendid. (*MDR*, p. 6)[35]

This would appear to be a memory that presages a wonderful account of boyhood. At a manifest level we do not doubt that Jung meant this, nor that he recalled such an event. At a latent level, which he himself always assumed in his own work, a patient's claim about earliest memory takes on significance. It amounts to a statement of the original time, the genesis of all later self-experiences. Like a nation's beginning or the birth of a child, the first recollected experience is always important. For this reason an analyst might ask a patient to describe the patient's earliest memory in addition to describing the patient's family.

An obvious feature of Jung's memory is the intense feeling manifested toward nature, especially the warm brilliant sun that peeks through the leaves. An equally obvious feature is the complete lack of other people, especially his mother. We can see the young boy, perhaps still an infant, in his pram, yet there is no hint of another person near him, taking care of him.

A second memory is of himself, sitting in his family's dining room, spooning up milk: "This was the first time I became aware of the smell of milk. It was the moment when, so to speak, I became conscious of smelling" (*MDR*, p. 7). In another memory, an aunt points out the Alps, glowing in the sunset: "I can hear her saying to me in Swiss dialect, 'The mountains are all red.' For the first time I consciously saw the Alps" (*MDR*, p. 7).

Where is his mother in all these moments? Each memory centers upon a part of himself, his vision, taste, or skin, upon which he places tremendous importance. These things, particularly the skin, are normally associated with the infant's bond to its mother. Most studies of mother-infant interaction describe the infant's intense gaze upon the mother's face.

We might question whether Jung's retrospection back some seventy years is a valid history. Yet the fit between Jung's earliest memories, the boyhood neurosis, and Jung's later devotion to occult experiencing is exactly as we would predict. In the face of his mother's inability to care for him and sustain him during moments of anxiety, the young boy reconstitutes himself, in part, by focusing his attention upon his body and its sensations. To feel the sharp color of the trees, or the strong smell of milk, is to feel the boundary separating himself from the world. That is, sensations establish a boundary and so help establish a sense of inner coherence and stability. People pinch themselves when they feel overwhelmed by disturbing news, such as the death of a loved one or sudden good fortune. As Keats said, the issue in these cases is: Do I wake or do I sleep? We find a psychopathological instance in certain types of perversions in which one must submit to masochistic suffering, often inflicted by a woman who masquerades as a sadistic mother.

Each of these perversions, even the painful humiliations of sexual masochism, prevents worse suffering: fragmentation of the self into bits and pieces. As suggested above, this deep sense of fragmentation is allayed only by the continuous presence of a good-enough mother who loans to her child a sense of coherence in time and space. In Kohut's terms, the good-enough mother makes herself available as a selfobject. She permits her child to establish a self-selfobject relationship and so prevents the catastrophe of fragmentation.

Fragmentation and Defenses
against Fragmentation

We may distinguish the experience of fragmentation from defenses against it. Fragmentation occurs along a continuum ranging from minor disturbances that one overcomes quickly to major lifelong patterns of such severe disturbance that the person requires prolonged psychoanalytic therapy in order to feel relatively secure and complete.

Prolonged exposure to vivid pornographic films, which focus upon body parts, the genitals, also may engender an uneasy sensation of unreality and displeasure. In these films the actors hypersexualize all modes of relationship. Part of the dreariness of such films is their absolute inability to portray whole, complete persons engaged in significant relationships with other full-fledged persons. The relentless pull toward fragmenting sexual experience makes pornographic films unsatisfying.

Another example of ordinary fragmentation is the twinge of anxiety and confusion that comes over a speaker when the audience seems uninterested and unappreciative. To remain faithful to one's text and refrain from bitter, rageful response takes a special effort.[36]

More debilitating examples of fragmentation experiences may be found in numerous case histories of persons diagnosed as manifesting narcissistic personality disturbance. Following Kohut, I have argued that there is a continuum between ordinary fragmentation experience and the suffering of persons with these particular difficulties. Yet one should not underestimate the sometimes unbearable pain the latter suffer. Any clinician might point to patients who would choose suicide rather than suffer again the intense loneliness and despair that follow a severe fragmentation occurrence. Ritual suicides occur following massive narcissistic losses in which to recover one's "face" one must take one's life. Ritual suicide is often directed against others as well and so entails motives that are object directed.

Assuming with Kohut that narcissistic needs are universal and that fragmentation anxiety is as well, we can delineate a range of defenses against it. So-called normal healthy adults invest their work, family, neighborhood, child's baseball team, favorite actors and politicians, and particular religion with a large amount of "idealizing affect." All these things, people, and ideas are the "best." By associating themselves with them, these people have demonstrated their inherent worthiness—and probably superiority, if modesty did not forbid even thinking such things. The variety of such narcissistic yearnings is a major topic in its own right, and numerous people, including Freud, have addressed it. In narcissistically vulnerable persons, a large portion of their energy is spent defending themselves against fragmentation. One middle-aged woman, for example, was addicted to supplying her friends with hard-to-find household items. She prided herself on this capacity to give her friends these special items: "The importance of this to her and her dependence upon it had a desperate quality which she later began to recognize for what it was—a vehicle for maintaining an experience of uniqueness of her self."[37]

Not surprisingly, many of this woman's bitterest feelings toward her mother and her mother's lack of investment in her centered around food, that is, the kitchen. Her mother was dedicated to altering her daughter's figure: "The mother relied on the reassuring solidity of her own physique to give her a sense of solidity she lacked and for which the fullness of body had become the reliable representative. The patient's slenderness seemed to the patient's mother a symbol of her own inner insufficiency and inability—qualities she could not abide in her child."[38] This woman's nightmares centered around the kitchen and food, especially blueberries. As with any good case history, the subtle connections between the patient's history and the patient's relationship to the analyst, and the complex events constituting the patient's past, cannot be summarized easily.

Jung and His Mother: Splits in the Self

To return to Jung, our general claim about occult experience lets us predict that the idyllic mood of his initial memory will not persist and that we should discover major separations between child and mother. This is precisely what Jung describes. When he was about three, his parents separated, and his mother spent several months in a hospital while the boy suffered a general eczema, a painful condition of the skin which makes it especially sensitive to touch. Jung reports: "I was deeply troubled by my mother's being away. From then on, I always felt mistrustful when the word 'love' was spoken" (*MDR*, p. 8).

Immediately following the memories of natural beauty and his mother's criminal actions (she abandoned him for some months), Jung informs us that he had many painful accidents: a fall downstairs, a burned leg, a scarred head. More ominous is his memory of nearly falling into the river: "I already had one leg under the railing and was about to slip through" (*MDR*, p. 9).

Jung describes these "overwhelming images" (*MDR*, p. 9) and identifies these serious accidents as suicidal or "a fatal resistance to life in this world" (*MDR*, p. 9). One must doubt that the latter "resistance" pertains to the experience of a four-year-old child. It is more likely that Jung reacted to his mother's depression. His suicidal gestures were dramatic actions that both punished the boy for his aggressive thoughts and brought his mother, or her substitute, his nurse, to his aid. Deepening this portrait of the nurse as his savior is another early memory: "She [his nursemaid] had black hair and an olive complexion, and was quite different from my mother. I can see, even now, her hairline, her throat, with its darkly pigmented skin, and her ear" (*MDR*, p. 8). In retrospect Jung connects this woman with his anima, that is, with that contrasexual component which is a portion of the archetypes.

Like his other early memories, this memory also focuses on part of a person's body, not on the whole person. In fact, Jung does not focus upon the nurse's entire face, but only on the parts of the face that a very young child would see, either nursing or being held closely against breast and face. Unfortunately, most people do not have Jung's capacity for recalling such events, nor his literary skills. Yet there is something poignant about the intensity of these memories of the maid's ear. It suggests how much the young boy attended to these parts of the woman who held him, cared for him, and pulled him away from certain death.

We finally meet Jung's mother, but only through a prayer that she taught him and that contributed to Jung's "first conscious trauma" (*MDR*, p. 10). That prayer and the boy's interpretation of it pertain directly to Jung's later fascination with the occult:

> Spread out thy wings, Lord Jesus mild, And take to thee thy chick, thy child. "If Satan would devour it, No harm shall overpower it," So let the angels sing! (*MDR*, p. 10)

At a manifest level, this prayer, like its English equivalent "Now I lay me down to sleep," assigns an evil intention to Satan and a heroic, salvific role to Jesus, whose wide wings will protect the child against Satan. Perhaps, as do most children, the young Carl interprets Satan's devouring along a line of "oral aggression": "Satan . . . had to be prevented from eating them" (*MDR*, p. 10). Yet I would suggest that unlike most readers of this prayer, Jung implicates Jesus in the eating as well. Lord Jesus "took" children to himself, "like bitter medicine" (*MDR*, p. 10). Even more solemnly, the boy concludes, "So, although Lord Jesus did not like the taste, he ate them anyway, so that Satan would not get them" (*MDR*, p. 10). Compounding this horrible vision of Jesus was the boy's association of "taking" to the "taking" Jesus was said to do when a devout member of the local church died, and the boy heard his father, who was a pastor, or another preacher explain that the lost person had been taken back to Jesus.

Jung's First Conscious Trauma: The Jesuit

These scary, nightmarish elements entered into Jung's first trauma. When he was very young, he spied a strange figure, a man, dressed all in black, with robes like a woman's, walking toward his house. His fear grew into terror as he recognized that this was a Jesuit, about whom his father had complained, and whose title obviously linked him to the horrible actions of Jesus. Jung's father and a good many of Jung's uncles were Lutheran pastors. This abundance of religiosity might explain, in part, the boy's precocious concerns with theological distinctions (he was between three and four at the time). Yet the boy's response to this walking nightmare, again, seems idiosyncratic: Jung rushed to the darkest part of the attic and hid there under a beam. "For days afterwards the hellish fright clung to my limbs and kept me in the house" (*MDR*, p. 11).

One might assume that a terrified three-year-old boy would rush to his mother's arms, or to his father or nursemaid. Obviously, from this single report we cannot interpret the boy's feelings. Yet this piece of the story fits closely with the others we have already considered: the boy feels overwhelming anxiety about a figure that is neither clearly female (maternal) nor male (paternal). Rather than turn to either of his parents, or another adult, Jung retreats into a solitary state in which he effects self-repair. The attic and its darkness (normally not a place where a three-year-old would play) represented an environment of rigid security. Hiding there, no one could see him, no one could attack him, but neither could anyone help him. He was safe but alone, secure but convinced he was under the attack of evil forces.

JUNG'S UNDERGROUND GOD
AND FRAGMENTATION

The importance of this attic and Jung's retreat to it whenever he felt vulnerable to fragmentation reappears in his story when he feels himself challenged by other children. Before discussing that, however, we should keep in mind his mother's role in these earliest accounts. Jung's mother was associated with the monstrous bird, Jesus, who eats little children before Satan does. She does not appear as a warm available object to whom the boy can retreat when faced with overwhelming anxieties. Both aspects of her role in these memories appear in a famous dream Jung says he had between ages three and four.

In his dream, Jung walks down into an underground crypt made of stones, where he sees a huge chamber across a meadow; then its ceiling arches, and a platform or throne appears. On it is a huge treelike thing some twelve feet high:

> But it was of a curious composition: it was made of skin and naked flesh, and on top there was something like a rounded head with no face and no hair. On the very top of the head was a single eye, gazing motionlessly upward. The thing did not move, yet I had the feeling that it might at any moment crawl off the throne like a worm and creep toward me. I was paralyzed with terror. At that moment I heard from outside and above me my mother's voice. She called out, "Yes, just look at him. That is the

man-eater!" That intensified my terror still more, and I awoke sweating
and scared to death. (*MDR*, pp. 11–12)

A dream as condensed, overdetermined, and dramatic as this yields
a surplus of possible interpretations. Since Jung reports it as an old
man looking back through some fifty years of theoretical development,
he himself feels that its meaning is clear: The dream represents an
upsurge of archetypal images. The ritual phallus links it to Greek and
Egyptian mystery religions; the vault is a grave (or tomb or catacomb);
the carpet is blood-red; the meadow symbolizes "the mystery of Earth
with her covering of green vegetation" (*MDR*, p. 13). Other commentators have advanced other interpretations.[39]

Jung calls this dream a "frightful revelation" (*MDR*, p. 13) into the
true nature of spirituality. Contrasted to his father's dry, rationalized
religiosity this dream seemed to demonstrate the existence of an underground deity. The gigantic phallus belonged to a deity who lived below
the earth, where he ruled and opposed himself to the Lord Jesus who
reigned in heaven, on the right hand of God. One might offer a more
extensive Jungian reading of this dream. However, for our purposes, I
would note that Jung does not look for a causal sequence of the sort
Kohut has taught us to expect. Jung's excursions into metaphysics and
other intellectual realms are valuable in their own right. His scientific
works on the history of religious symbols demonstrate remarkable parallels between archaic religious thought and the ideas that torment psychotic persons.

However, in his own story he does not focus upon the boy's relationship to his mother.

> I could never make out whether my mother meant, "*That* is the man-
> eater," or, "That is the *man-eater*." In the first case she would have meant
> that not Lord Jesus or the Jesuit was the devourer of little children, but
> the phallus; in the second case that the "man-eater" in general was sym-
> bolized by the phallus, so that the dark Lord Jesus, the Jesuit, and the
> phallus were identical (*MDR*, p. 12, emphasis in original).

On this reading Jung's confusion mirrors exactly his emotional
dilemma: he felt estranged from his father, as symbolized by the anti-
Christian elements in the dream and by the gigantic phallus, yet could
not rely upon his mother to save him. Her voice alone seems available
but its message is also confusing, rather like the Delphic oracle. This
confusion was already manifest in Jung's terror at seeing a man dressed
like a woman, that is, an ambisexual being, and it is compounded by his
mother's ambivalent response to him. Jung's mother partly perceived
his need to give the gigantic penis a name, that is, to control it and make

its powers his own. But the dream mother fails to respond to him fully and directly. Not accidentally, Jung's dream is about a sexual part-object, which defines what a boy is (it proves he is not a girl), yet which is grotesque. The boy is faced with fragmentation anxiety that his mother seemed unable to prevent. The boy reverted back to an archaic image of masculine power and strength. As master of the secret underground penis he would find himself whole and complete.

The gigantic penis is hidden just as Jung hid himself when he perceived the real possibility of an evil Jesus-figure who manifested an ambisexual attitude in his clothing. Although he does not say so directly, we may suppose that associated with this vision of the gigantic penis was another fantasy of incorporating it into himself, through some body orifice. The opposite idea is stated directly: If that is the man-eater and he is a man (male), then it will incorporate him.

This fantasy of incorporation into or by a gigantic penis is not rare. It appears frequently in boys and men whose sexual orientation is significantly homosexual and who have suffered a major narcissistic loss. Some narcissistically disturbed patients, for example, find themselves compelled to seek out homosexual liaisons when they feel on the verge of fragmentation. And, as we would expect, such moments of fragmentation anxiety are precipitated by the threat of separation from their analysts, with whom they now have an intense self-selfobject relationship.

In descriptive psychiatric nomenclature, each of these episodes is distinct, and as a class homosexual yearnings are distinct from heterosexual ones. However, from the point of view advanced in this book, they all represent a reflexive effort to prevent fragmentation experience. The clinical literature on severe narcissistic disturbances has many examples.

TWO SECRET SELVES:
JUNG AND MR. I

Jung's account of his internal world reveals a number of split-off portions of himself. He felt that these portions of himself were secret and must remain secret. Otherwise, their power to keep him sane would disappear and he would, once more, face immense anxieties. It will be helpful to compare Jung's account of his secret self with a contemporary case history of a patient who also has a secret self. This case history, about a patient called Mr. I, appeared in a collection of case histories published by some of Kohut's colleagues.[40] Mr. I's case history reveals two striking parallels to events Jung narrates in his autobiography. The first parallel is the tremendous emphasis each man places upon the penis as a sign not only of masculinity, but of a coherent and consolidated self. The second and more important similarity is Mr. I's need to affix someone inside himself and thereby feel safe and coherent. This remarkable need and its corresponding fantasies find a striking parallel in Jung's autobiographical account.

In the middle phase of his analysis, the patient, Mr. I, begins to contemplate the upcoming summer vacation in which his analyst will be unavailable to him (just as Jung's mother was unavailable to him in his boyhood and later during her depressive spells). From thoughts of homosexual coupling (which would be direct physical union with a man representing his analyst), Mr. I shifts to memories of summer camp. He was sent away when he was six and recalled hating his mother for pushing him away. Separations were especially difficult: "He recalled that in college, after a lecture was over in the large auditorium and the student body began to leave, he would feel very much alone and have an erection. Only if he masturbated right then and there could he leave."[41]

Masturbating meant handling his penis, feeling its "aliveness" and, perhaps of equal importance, validating the rich set of fantasies that underlay the compulsion. We also sense a part of the needs fulfilled by this kind of action if we note how such sexual actions might easily be discovered and become a source of intense shame.

On another occasion, as his parents pulled away after visiting him at college, Mr. I felt an intense need within his abdomen: to masturbate, vomit, or get some kind of release.[42] Alongside these numerous instances of painful disorganized response to traumatic separations, Mr. I elucidated a series of childhood fantasies and current wishes, all precipitated by the real fact that his analyst was soon to be absent. One set of fantasies dealt with two girls whom Mr. I kept hidden and locked up where he alone could be near them. One would be like Superwoman and he would be like Superman; flying together but not engaged in any kind of sexual relationship. During the early phases of his treatment, he felt compelled to maintain a number of liaisons with different women. In a wonderful expression of true selfobject relatedness, Mr. I refers to them as "comfort stations" that helped him get through the day.[43] However, an additional fantasy is directly relevant to Jung's own story:

At camp, when he was alone at night, awake and frightened, he fantasized about S.L., a boy who lived next door and was three years older—tough, intellectual, and a leader—whom he hero-worshipped. He felt that S.L. was in his chest, in a secret compartment that he carved out. He was smaller and would fit in there; and whenever he ate, he would feed S.L. too. "S.L. was someone who could not leave me, Superman. When I was picked on in camp, I would call upon him in fantasy for help. In our family, leaving was a tragic thing."[44]

In this powerful image, Mr. I, as a desperate boy shunned by his mother, recreated a symbol of inner strength. He would *have* his idealized boy's strengths and security because he would have the boy himself inside his chest. We note again how this was a secret fantasy, and the miniature ideal object was placed in a secret interior compartment. This image also makes vivid many of Kohut's more abstract terms. Concepts like selfobject, internal structure, idealization, and narcissistic regression are illustrated by this single elaborate fantasy.

Mr. I, as a boy, needed to idealize the older boy, to have him become an internal part of himself, and to do so as a selfobject, that is, to make up for a family environment that had deprived him of precisely such relationships. Lacking that age-appropriate set of experiences, the boy regressed to infantile fantasies whenever he felt jeopardized by fragmentation. In other words, when Mr. I's tenuous relationship to his mother was broken by her actual absence, he had nothing "inside" himself that would preserve an image of himself as loved and coherent (as idealized and esteemed). Lacking a constant external source of such validation, Mr. I could not fall back upon an internal, fully integrated sense of his own worthiness and coherence. The tiny secret other person sitting in his chest would serve to repair that internal deficit because that secret other *was* complete, whole, and secured.

Jung's Secret Self: The Manikin

Roughly a century before Mr. I created the secret S.L., the little person inside his chest, Jung had created a similar figure and used him in a similar way. By the age of six or seven (which was Mr. I's age during his summer camp experience) Jung felt threatened and endangered from the world outside his family circle. He turned to nature and the "golden sunlight" filtering through the trees, but this route was inadequate (even though he took it again in repeating his earliest memories) for "at the same time I had a premonition of an inescapable world of shadows filled with frightening, unanswerable questions which had me at their mercy" (*MDR*, p. 19).

Jung's difficulties increased as he entered school, and he felt threatened by the demands of his age-mates. He went through a series of depersonalized experiences which, when retold by the distinguished psychiatrist, sound more philosophical and less frightening than I think they really were. Jung describes sitting on a large stone, for example, wondering whether it was correct to say that he was sitting on a stone thinking about it, or, from the stone's point of view, that it was lying on the ground and this boy was sitting on it: "The question then arose:

'Am I the one who is sitting on the stone, or am I the stone on which *he* is sitting?'" (*MDR*, p. 20, emphasis in original).

One cannot doubt that Jung was a man of extraordinary mental and emotional energy. Yet one does doubt that the boy sitting on the stone could have been quite so full of equanimity. That he was not is suggested by the little man that he found necessary to invent. Unlike Mr. I, who only imagined such a figure, Jung actually created one. Jung tells us that when he was about ten, he carved a little manikin out of a ruler and dressed it in frock coat, top hat, and black boots (the garments he associated with funerals conducted by his father or other clergy). Jung made the little man a bed and gave him a long black stone that he had found near the Rhine and had painted so as to create two halves. "This was *his* stone. All this was a great secret. Secretly I took the case to the forbidden attic . . . and hid it with great satisfaction on one of the beams under the roof" (*MDR*, p. 21, emphasis in original).

In this beautiful gesture lies much of Jung's later creativity: he responds to internal suffering by creating an artifact, from bits and pieces, from found objects as well as synthetic ones, which when complete and whole makes him feel better: "No one could discover my secret and destroy it. I felt safe, and the tormenting sense of being at odds with myself was gone" (*MDR*, p. 21). We also see aspects of his paranoid response to others in his adult life whom he felt were bent on destroying his discoveries of ancient occult secrets.

There is also a kind of double identification in the act: Jung creates a secret representation of the very figure, the man in black, who frightens him and so contains him. Yet he clearly loves this figure because he gives him a special stone. This special stone, itself divided into two parts, as the boy so often felt himself to be, represents something solid, imperishable, and coherent which the manikin will treasure. The ten-year-old Jung can treasure the manikin, protect it from harm, and, in turn, be soothed by its constancy and perfection: it cannot be destroyed by the fickleness of others (for example, a depressed mother).

Indeed, Jung so loved the little man that he gave him his own stone, which would preserve the manikin as it preserved Jung. The manikin mothers Jung, and Jung in turn mothers it. The importance Jung attached to the manikin and its stone is evident in his use of it: "In all difficult situations, whenever I had done something wrong or my feelings had been hurt, or when my father's irritability or my mother's invalidism oppressed me, I thought of my carefully bedded-down and wrapped up manikin and his smooth, prettily colored stone" (*MDR*, p. 21).

Using Kohut's terms, we can reformulate this to read: Whenever Jung felt threatened by fragmentation anxiety induced by an unempathic parent, he called up the memory of an object, the manikin that was indestructible, unharmed, and secret. He alone knew it existed and he alone controlled its fate. The boy's love for the manikin (his narcissistic investment in it) was therefore preserved, and he felt himself needed by it in return. This second feature, which occurs fleetingly in many children, became part of the solemn rituals Jung performed for his manikin. He wrote to it little scrolls, using a secret language of his own invention. These secret letters became part of the manikin's secret library. In other words, Jung felt that the manikin, like himself, needed intellectual stimulation and would need, therefore, to acquire a library of the various sayings and quotations that enchanted the manikin's creator.

The Prevention of Fragmentation

This artistic-religious achievement marked the end of his boyhood, according to Jung, and effected a substantial consolidation of his character. As Kohut would help us predict, Jung did not abandon his creature, his imaginary selfobject. He often felt narcissistically wounded, especially by his mother when she failed to see his wishes to present "as irreproachable an appearance as possible" (*MDR*, p. 26) in a public gathering. Gyrating between feelings of grandeur and impoverishment, Jung acted to discredit his mother's demands: "If things became too bad I would think of my secret treasure in the attic, and that helped me regain my poise" (*MDR*, p. 26).

One could spend much more time on *MDR* and show, again and again, how Jung was able to transform these early severe traumata into the basic themes of all his later works.[45] Jung reports, for example, that the "annoying" rumor of his being a direct descendant of Goethe may be related to his boyhood fantasy of living in his grandfather's time, the end of the eighteenth century. He often wrote, he tells us, the date 1786 instead of the correct date, 1886, when he felt himself living in that former time.

However, I restrict this account to a discussion of Jung's relationship to his mother and her peculiar treatment of him. His relationship to his father seems clearer: the older man was severely depressed over his own lack of faith in the doctrines he preached. In Carl's eyes, the elder Jung was without hope because he perceived only the superficial aspects of religion and knew nothing of the underground gods whom the boy had met firsthand in his dreams. In Kohut's terms, Carl dismissed his father as unworthy of bearing up under his son's idealizing demands. His father could not give him a sense of living Christianity: "He would shrug and turn resignedly away" (*MDR*, p. 43). In Jung's account his father had abandoned all hope of ever achieving valid insights into Christianity; he was a poor man, suffocating under a religious repression. He did not dare think, "I was seized with the most vehement pity for my father" (*MDR*, p. 55). This, of course, contrasts with the boy's special revelations beginning with his discovery of the underground god.

Jung's Mother: Separation and Loss

Jung's portrait of his mother is much more complex. In retrospect he attempts to explain her idiosyncrasies and sudden mood changes upon her own special access to the "underground world." As a boy, Jung felt that he was divided into two personalities, a number one and a number two. Throughout the first three chapters of *Memories, Dreams, Reflections*, Jung assigns to his mother a number one and a number two personality, precisely as he did to himself. This division of the personality into distinct parts accords with his adult theories about the psyche. But here one suspects it also covers up the anxiety he must have suffered when he realized that she and her husband were not happy in their married life. One might suggest that in this circumstance the boy would be pleased since it would afford him a kind of oedipal victory: the old man is put out of the couple's bedroom, leaving the mother available. However, this did not occur. His parents' separation from one another, and his mother's consequent depression, damaged the boy far more than a simplified oedipal theorem would predict.

A hint of the boy's deep wish for his parents' reunion is found in an early memory from the crucial age of six. His parents had taken him on a holiday. His mother wore a dress that "I have never forgotten, and it is the only dress of hers that I can recall" (*MDR*, p. 16). This earliest memory is not of an oedipal conquest, but of an attractive woman, happily linked to her husband and son.

Later memories of his parents' obvious sexual difficulties have no sense of triumph. On the contrary, they revolve around the anxiety he felt and his occult attempts to soothe himself. Around the time that Jung first manifested pubertal changes, he had a series of nightmarish visions. His parents slept apart and he hallucinated his mother "coming from her door a faintly luminous, indefinite figure whose head detached itself from the neck and floated along in front of it, in the air, like a little moon" (*MDR*, p. 18). Many of these visions suggest a sexual anxiety (things suddenly grow larger, his mother's decapitation). Others suggest infantile fears of suffocation at the mother's breast: "I saw a tiny ball at a great distance; gradually it approached, growing steadily into a monstrous and suffocating object" (*MDR*, p. 18).[46] However, we need not depend upon these speculations about the dreams' meanings. Jung says directly that the hallucinations of fairies, for example, or his mother as the moon "allayed my fear of suffocation. But the suffocation returned in the anxiety dreams" (*MDR*, p. 19).

Having discovered that he consisted of two persons, the one a schoolboy easily humiliated and deeply anxious, and the other a grand Goethe-like figure, Jung attributed the same split to his mother. "I was sure she consisted of two personalities, the one innocuous and human, the other uncanny" (*MDR*, p. 48). When Jung felt humiliated and forlorn, for example, when his mother compared him unfavorably to better dressed children, his mother's second self emerged to comfort him. In a most roundabout way Jung first blames his mother for shaming him, and then, following his attack on the superior child, believes she shares his grandiose needs: "To my relief I realized that she too regarded those odious children as inferior whelps, and that the scolding need not be taken at face value" (*MDR*, pp. 49–50). To rescue himself and prevent severe fragmentation, Jung projects onto his mother a split that duplicates his own. He discovers what he had to find: that her secret self parallels exactly his secret self. Using this logic, Jung binds up his own psychic wounds and links himself to the single person whose presence he requires: his mother.

Just as he preserved the secret manikin and the manikin's stone, and the secret dream of the underground god, so too Jung preserves this secret belief. When his mother seems to speak about religious or occult topics associated with these other secrets, the boy feels a special joy: "I pretended that I had not heard and was careful not to cry out in glee, in spite of my feelings of triumph" (*MDR*, p. 50).

That triumph is partly a victory over his father, whom Jung felt never saw into the depths as he and his mother had. Yet the intensity with which the boy keeps these secrets and the anxiety against which they preserve him are not oedipal. Again and again, we see Jung describe fragmentation anxiety: bodies falling apart, his mother growing six heads, himself suffocating, himself and his mother cut into two parts. And, again and again, we see him leap to occult solutions and attribute occult powers to his mother as well as to himself.

I think that Jung's autobiography describes severe narcissistic impairment. Jung's later works and intellectual achievements are significant efforts to repair these deficits. In so doing he illuminates a realm of narcissistic issues in religious thought that Freud, for example, could not have understood. One could pursue that line and document the thread of occult reasoning that runs throughout *MDR* and all Jung's writings. From his earliest memories to his last reflections on life after death Jung dedicated himself to understanding his occult experiences. We consider his core theorem about such events in the next chapter. Before turning to that it may help to summarize my presentation up to this point.

Occult events occur as a consequence of perceived threats to self-selfobject relationships. When the other person seems unable to perform the selfobject functions without which one suffocates (to use Jung's term), their threatened separation elicits a massive effort to reinstate those functions. We have now read a number of occult stories and seen their relationship to perceived loss. With these in mind we can summarize my argument and prepare a way to analyze Freud's encounter with Jung's number two personality.

From within the experiencing subject, the selfobject performs functions that eventually come under the rule of the ego. That is, the good-enough mother soothes the child when something seems to scare it, just as later she will reflect to the child the child's basic needs to feel unique, loved, and invincible, that is, not subject to sudden fragmentation. As Jung says, this experience of making contact with the selfobject is one of sudden coming together: "At such times I *knew* I was worthy of myself, that I was my true self" (*MDR*, p. 45, emphasis in original).

In this gradual, many-year process, infants slowly acquire the conviction that the world of others will not crush and humiliate them and that they rightfully feel at the "center" of their experiencing self.

Selfobjects reflect back to the person this crucial message and so help reconstitute the self again and again. Kohut does not tire of pointing out that, to an outsider, it seems the child (or adult) utilizes the selfobject as if it were an extension of the child's own body. This occurs because, from the inside point of view, the selfobject does perform functions, such as regulating self-esteem, that eventually come under the dominion of the self. When a selfobject fails to perform these vital functions the person searches desperately for a suitable substitute. As suggested above, this sequence of first losing and then searching for a suitable selfobject constitutes the first and second stages of occult experience.

SUMMARY:
SHARED OCCULT MOMENTS

Occult experiences are not rare. It is difficult to imagine a person who has not felt bereft of selfobject sustenance at some point and, consequently, wanted to receive some sign that the world and the person's self would not come to an end. Even though they were great psychologists and clinicians, both Sigmund Freud and Carl Jung suffered fragmentation anxiety at different points in their lives. Consequently, each also experienced occult moments in which their anxieties about the integrity of their selves was overcome.

In the following chapter we see both men confront their needs for the other and we compare how each responded to the loss of that selfobject relationship. Our previous discussion would lead us to predict that the collapse of their relationship yielded an occult event. First, we examine that event; then we compare each man's response to it.

5
Jung's Occult Psychology: A Synchronistic Moment

Freud and Jung needed each other with an intensity that far exceeded ordinary scientific collegiality. From the beginning of their relationship in 1907, through their careers and into our time, their meaning for each other has been subjected to detailed analysis. Freud and Jung began this process by submitting to one another's interpretive efforts, including a stint of mutual dream interpretation, and then by writing about their relationship after its demise.[1]

Many authors, some explicitly Jungian, others explicitly Freudian, have since continued this tradition of using the theories of one to interpret the actions of the other. I find many of these persuasive.

Each man fulfilled profound selfobject needs of the other, and each responded to the collapse of their relationship in characteristic style. Jung retreated into himself and explored, with much pain, his inner world of psychotic-like images. From that period of intense self-scrutiny he created one of his most representative works, *Symbols of Transformation*.[2] Freud expanded his own scientific works to include his first major essay on narcissism and narcissistic development.[3] In a sensitive essay on the correspondence between the two men, Hans Loewald remarked that it takes no special acumen to see that the relationship foundered on the "father complex."[4] This seems true only of the aspect of their relationship that emerges directly in their letters and later in their separate accounts. Freud felt that Jung had courted him and that Jung was to carry out Freud's great scientific projects, but that Jung betrayed that trust. Jung reacted vehemently to Freud's accusations of betrayal. Freud said directly that the younger man had failed to become the heir and single claimant to the leadership of the analytic movement.

Thanks to Kohut's elucidation of selfobject relationships and their repetition in selfobject transferences, we can amplify Loewald's analysis. Both Freud and Jung needed the other to complete a part of themselves that they felt was bereft, that is, subject to fragmentation. Of course, knowing what we do now of Jung's early history, we can see that he was far more threatened by severe fragmentation than was Freud. We also know, however, that Loewald's assessment of Freud's indifference to occult reasoning, that he abhorred occultist beliefs, is overstated.[5] In fact, if we add Kohut's point of view to this interpretation of both men, we can explain their extreme importance to one another and their fascination with the occult.

THE FREUD/JUNG LETTERS

It is not possible to summarize accurately the complete range of feelings and thought that characterizes the letters between Freud and Jung.[6] Both men perceived that they shared a rare moment in the development of a radically new way of thought, and both wrote with a verve and command of language that render any summary inadequate. Jung and Freud also exhibit feelings toward one another ranging from formal scientific comparisons to bitter remonstrations of each other's hurtful attitudes.

However, a consistent theme runs throughout the letters, beginning with letter 11 (from Freud to Jung). In that letter Freud soothes Jung, "You are quite mistaken in supposing that I was not enthusiastic about your book on dementia praecox" (*Letters*, p. 17). Following a visit, Freud confides that Jung has inspired him as a successor now that he realizes that "I am as replaceable as everyone else" (*Letters*, p. 27). Responding to Freud's gift of his book on Jensen's *Gradiva*[7] and to Freud's complaint that Jung had not sent him his opinions on it, Jung says, "I gulped it at one go. The clear exposition is beguiling, and I think one would have to be struck by the gods with sevenfold blindness not to see things now as they really are" (*Letters*, p. 49). In another letter, "I rejoice every day in *your* riches and live from the crumbs that fall from the rich man's table" (*Letters*, p. 56, emphasis in original). Freud immediately objects to this portrait: "I am very much surprised to hear that I am the rich man from whose table you glean a few crumbs" (*Letters*, p. 58).

Jung's boundless admiration for Freud and the importance he placed on their relationship appear in the letters that follow this exchange. Thanks to the publication of Jung's autobiography[8] we can look back to these letters and see in them the seeds of Jung's affection for the older man and a hint of his later dissatisfaction. In a letter written on 28 October 1907, Jung confesses that his veneration for Freud is a "religious crush. Though it does not really bother me, I still feel it is disgusting and ridiculous because of its undeniable erotic undertone" (*Letters*, p. 95). Jung then describes how, years earlier, a man had made a sexual assault upon him. This thought is obviously linked to his concern about his own erotic feelings toward Freud and his anxiety that Freud might be seduced by the force and power of Jung's sexual feelings toward him. Jung tells Freud quite honestly, "I therefore fear your confidence" (p. 95).

To this heartfelt letter Freud gave no immediate reply, and Jung wrote again, four days later: "I am suffering all the agonies of a patient in analysis, riddling myself with every conceivable fear about the possible consequences of my confession" (*Letters*, p. 95). A hint of the uncanny power Jung attributed to Freud occurs in the way he describes Freud's "*dangerousness*" (p. 96, emphasis in original). He prefaces this word with three crosses, a symbol Freud had used earlier in their correspondence to refer to superstitious signs peasants drew on doors to ward off supernatural dangers. Jung continues, "I hope to goodness the subterranean gods will now desist from their chicaneries and leave me in peace" (p. 96).

Although this is written in a jocular vein, an attitude Freud assumed in his own occult moments, it seems quite real to Jung. We cannot forget what Freud did not know: As a boy Jung had confronted the "underground gods" face to face, and his occult practices with the manikin, the manikin's stone, and other rituals had protected him from severe fragmentation.

Our discussions of such needs and their relationship to occult practices prepare us to understand the last paragraph in Jung's letter. He describes his election to the American Society of Psychical Research (ASPR) and adds, "I have been dabbling in spookery again. Here too your discoveries are brilliantly confirmed. What do you think of this whole field of research?" (*Letters*, p. 96). It took a great deal of courage for Jung to write this letter, for it evokes Freud's uncanny ability, his godlike powers, to bring Jung's different selves together into a complete whole. Jung has put himself, his potentially fragmented self, into Freud's hands and asked him to meld the pieces together. Given this profound hope, Freud's silence appears to Jung to prove that Freud disdains him. This further traumatizes Jung, who turns immediately to occult issues: first in their scientific form, the ASPR, and then to his direct "dabbling in spookery," that is, the direct experience of selfobjects— ghosts—who verify the existence of spirits who cannot abandon him.

Freud's delay in answering Jung amounted to a threat to the latter's stability. It threatened to impose a new burden on him and become a new source of fragmentation for Jung. In response to this severe anxiety, Jung invoked, naturally and automatically, his lifelong resource: occult experience.

Unfortunately, Freud's reply to this dramatic letter is missing. Jung's reply to Freud's letter, however, permits us to conclude that Freud's advice was to "extol humour as the only decent reaction to the inevitable" (*Letters*, pp. 96–97). As we have seen, this was Freud's characteristic defense of his own occult leanings, but it did not serve Jung as well.

Jung's Service to Freud

The two shared a furious attachment to the psychoanalytic movement. Of course, this is equivalent to championing Freud, who was identified completely with psychoanalysis. What Freud said became psychoanalysis, and what he said was not was banished from the realm. It does not denigrate the scope of Freud's achievement to recognize, at the same time, his narcissistic investment in his science. Everything in Freud's life was subordinated to its advancement. Jung represented a tireless, brilliant, Swiss "Aryan" (to use Freud's terms) who could help Freud with that great crusade. Again and again, the two men employ military metaphors to describe their political conflicts. Together they planned strategies, established outposts, made conquests, and defeated their enemies: the outmoded professors, obstinate publishers, competing psychiatric organizations, and all others who seemed to oppose their efforts to reveal the power of psychoanalytic thought. By the time he knew Jung, Freud had, for his part, assumed an understanding of his science that permitted him to feel optimistic about its future. In contrast to his usual serenity, Freud was not above making severe and sometimes abusive attacks upon his opponents. When he did so, that is, when he felt narcissistically vulnerable to criticisms of *his* science, as opposed to himself, Freud looked to Jung for selfobject responses. In other words, when Freud felt that his great task, the advance of

psychoanalysis, was jeopardized by attack, he utilized Jung as a selfobject who would employ his talents to defend Freud.

A sequence of letters regarding such an attack on psychoanalysis appears in November 1908. Commenting on "the recent wave of abuse"
(*Letters*, p. 175), Freud notes that some of these attacks are directed
toward Jung, probably out of ignorance. Jung's immediate response is a
vehement letter of shared outrage and shared grandiose belief, beginning with the words, taken from the Apocryphal text 1 Esdras: *Magna
est vis veritatis tuae et praevalebit!* ("Great is the power of your truth
and it shall prevail").

One doubts that Freud would have known this verse as well as Jung.
It probably would not have been available to Jewish readers. Jung
would have come across it in his studies of noncanonical traditions,
especially the repressed traditions with which he later so completely
identified. This verse is manifestly one of grand salutation, almost a
"hallelujah." Why would Freud's letter precipitate this kind of outburst? As Jung notes, one might think that Freud's report of continued
attacks would be bad news, but Jung adds, "Your last letter . . . has
bucked me up no end" (*Letters*, p. 176). I suggest that Jung was
deeply taken by Freud's willingness to share the burden of the attacks
with him, that is, to identify Jung with himself as the object of the
outsiders' unbelief and outrage. Jung is bucked up because he feels
empowered by Freud's gesture of merging himself (a great man with
great truths) with the younger man. Jung invokes this passage from an
Apochryphal text (1 Esdras 4:41) and so seeks to associate himself
with that royal, though noncanonical, tradition. This Latin phrase concludes a well-known hymn to truth, which was written to compete
with similar hymns to wine, women, and the king himself. The entire
hymn became well-known; even Christian authors quoted it. We learn
that St. Augustine interpreted it as a prophecy of the coming of
Christ, who would personify Truth and make its rule supreme.[9]

It seems appropriate that Jung would invoke a text associated with
Jewish Wisdom literature, but not Jewish traditional beliefs, just as
Freud's discoveries are those made by a Jew but contrary to Jewish
orthodoxy. Following his break with Freud, Jung came to identify himself directly with both heretical doctrines and underground traditions
like alchemy and astrology.

A Mysterious Knocking:
Occult Moments between Jung and Freud

The most dramatic exchange of letters between the two men describes
their meeting at Freud's house in late March 1909. In this meeting,

toward which Jung was looking with joy (*Letters*, p. 214), he raised again his deep concerns about occult matters. At the meeting's conclusion, according to both men's accounts, Jung believed that he had a premonition of an uncanny event that in fact occurred. Some people are persuaded that Jung had direct access to spiritual powers not normally under the control of human beings.

A careful retelling of the sequence of events that led up to the occult event suggests that it occurred in response to Jung's crushing realization that Freud failed to respond to his deepest needs for merger and sympathetic resonance; that is, it occurred as a consequence of a perceived failure in Jung's selfobject transference to Freud. (We learn that Freud had a very similar occurrence in his relationship to Wilhelm Fliess, the man who preceded Jung as Freud's closest spiritual and scientific companion.)

By combining the various sources available we can construct the following sequence on the night of 30 March 1909: Jung told Freud of his recent experiments in parapsychological matters, especially precognition, which he had always found fascinating and verified in his own life. At the same time it fit perfectly the major concepts of psychic integration, psychosynthesis, and the synthetic function that Jung was developing and toward which he naturally felt a tremendous sense of ownership. In addition, as we know from Jung's *Memories, Dreams, Reflections,* these concepts were intellectual formulas that touched upon Jung's deepest concerns from childhood. What for Freud were passing issues, relevant to himself only in extreme circumstances, toward which he later responded with characteristic humor, were for Jung the core of his life. At the same time, Freud represented an ideal father to Jung, especially when Jung compared Freud to his perception of his own miserable preacher-father. Compared to Freud, Jung's father seemed to possess none of the heroic qualities Jung needed to find in an idealized other.

When Jung presented the results of *his* discoveries into matters that he alone recognized for their true value, he expected from Freud some measure of admiration. Like all people who expose such deep aspects of themselves, Jung wanted a nurturing, holding environment first, and "reality testing" second. As Kohut notes in another context, to challenge the right of a patient to use a therapist as a selfobject is equivalent to challenging the patient's right to breathe. Such a challenge becomes an affront and can yield only one response: narcissistic rage. In people like Jung, who have struggled to preserve a sense of coherence through occult methods, that rage will follow a riverbed already laid down in traditional occult teachings. The "inner explosion" of narcissistic rage is externalized and perceived as if it occurred outside, and now at the behest of angry spirits whose feelings and wishes happen to parallel exactly those of the offended party.

But Freud did not reflect back to Jung the wonderment and admiration for Jung's achievements that Jung hoped to find. Jung reports that Freud "rejected the entire complex of questions as nonsensical, and did so in terms of so shallow a positivism that I had difficulty in checking the sharp retort on the tip of my tongue" (*MDR*, p. 155). Freud's failure to take pleasure in his brightest follower evokes a rage that Jung chokes back.

Jung's rage finds another route, namely, an occult one. Jung's urge to give a sharp retort turns into a sharp report: "While Freud was going on this way, I had a curious sensation. It was as if my diaphragm were made of iron and becoming red-hot—a glowing vault. At that moment there was such a loud report in the bookcase, which stood right next to us, that we both started up in alarm, fearing the thing was going to topple over on us" (*MDR*, p. 155).

In Jung's account, he then predicts that another "catalytic exteriorization phenomenon" (*MDR*, p. 155) will occur, and it does. Freud looks aghast. Jung attributes this occurrence to their eventual division some four years later: "I had the feeling that I had done something against him" (*MDR*, p. 156). And Jung had, although it was not his exteriorization experiment. He had rejected, earlier in the evening, Freud's most fervent wish. Freud made that wish clear in his own long account of the evening in his letter of 16 April, two weeks following the late-night meeting.

"It is strange that on the very same evening when I formally adopted you as eldest son and anointed you—in *partibus infidelium* [in the land of the unbelievers]—as my successor and crown prince, you should have divested me of my paternal dignity" (*Letters*, p. 218). These metaphors are all grandiose expressions of supreme power: the Pope who grants a bishopric to a man who confronts the pagans; the king who announces the next divine personage who shall wear his immortal crown. These images represent one aspect of Freud's intense narcissistic use of Jung against which Jung felt he had to rebel. Jung, the esteemed eldest son, was to carry on the immortal work of analysis and, by extension, preserve Freud's most important portion of himself, his creation.

In the same letter in which he announces his unbelief in the exteriorization hypothesis, Freud comments upon his own occult experiences. As if in anticipation of our concerns he notes that his own fascination with numerology occurred directly upon his loss of the intense selfobject relationship he had with Wilhelm Fliess (*Letters*, p. 219).

Freud's Previous Selfobject Relationship: Fliess

It may seem unfair to say that Freud had intense selfobject relationships with Jung and, earlier, with another colleague, Wilhelm Fliess. Yet if one examines Freud's earlier relationship with Fliess, between his thirty-first and around his forty-sixth year, one finds in it all the markings of intense narcissistic needs in Freud during a phase of creativity, which Fliess fulfilled to his utmost. The large amount of literature now available on this period of Freud's life documents with remarkable consistency the listening, consoling, soothing, reflecting role that Fliess carried out for Freud. In turn, Fliess inculcated into Freud his own idiosyncratic theory that neuroses were caused by certain nasal impairments, and that one could document twenty-eight-day cycles in males and females to which numerous diseases were attached.

In Max Schur's detailed report of Freud's relationship to Fliess it becomes clear that Freud needed Fliess as an idealized other.[10] Freud attributes to him an "extraordinary optimism" (in contrast to his own pessimism). Fliess is a "healer," a "magician," and when he fails to respond to Freud's letters, a "demon" who fails to see how much his every word and gesture mean to Freud.[11] Schur and other biographers are puzzled by the degree to which Freud invested Fliess with powers and skills that the latter did not possess. These authors tend to see the relationship between the two men as an object-level transference. In other words, these authors interpret Freud's feelings toward Fliess as if Freud had no selfobject needs and therefore treated Fliess wholly as an independent object.

Kohut's brief comments on Freud, and our use of his basic theorem of selfobject transferences, let us add to these biographical insights the additional insight that Fliess served selfobject functions as well. This becomes abundantly clear in the letters Freud wrote to Fliess and in his need to see him as an ideal correspondent whose mind was equal to his own and who would sanction Freud's genius. We can make these claims with confidence by noting two distinct aspects of Freud's response to his own creativity (a paramount narcissistic issue) and any change in his relationship to Fliess. Schur documents continuously how Freud struggled through his great discoveries of dream interpretation, in the last years of the nineteenth century, and his own analysis by relying on Fliess's constant intellectual companionship.

One vivid instance of Freud's narcissistic reliance upon Fliess occured when Freud drafted his famous "Project for a Scientific Psychology"[12] upon leaving Fliess after one of their intimate congresses. It is no exaggeration to say that the "Project" predicts many of Freud's later refined theoretical achievements. A contrasting, yet equally important, example of the selfobject dimension of their relationship occured when Freud discovered that he could not attend one of their private congresses. Freud's father took ill, and it appeared that Freud would have to call off his planned meeting: "Certain things should not even be mentioned in jest, otherwise they come true."[13] Schur says that this is a rare instance of Freud's recording a superstition. Yet it fits exactly the pattern we have come to expect. Following a major break in a self-selfobject relationship, one responds to the consequent suffering with an appeal to occult powers: fate, the gods, or some other transcendent, maternal force that will make good the internal deficit.

Given this line of inquiry, we should find that Freud suffers a recurrence of occult events when he makes an ultimate break with Fliess. Freud himself hinted at this when he informed Jung that he, Freud, had abandoned occult beliefs, including numerology, when he broke off with Fliess. Schur offers a surplus of corroborating evidence. In letters and family postcards which were not published during Freud's lifetime, for example, it is clear that Freud's famous "Disturbance on the Acropolis"[14] occurred in response to an exchange of letters between Fliess and Freud regarding Fliess's bitter feelings that Freud had betrayed him.[15]

It is not possible to summarize the relationship between Freud and Fliess in a few words. What they meant to each other, especially the way in which Freud needed Fliess to reflect back to him his creative genius, is a subtle issue. Kohut and other psychoanalysts have noted, for example, the intensity with which Freud pursued Fliess, making him read his drafts, share his speculations about psychology, and become his champion when, to Freud's mind, everyone else seemed to be against him. But we can note that there is a direct link between Freud's disturbance of memory and his loss of Fliess's friendship, that is, his loss of Fliess as a selfobject. Following the exchange of letters with Fliess, Freud traveled to the Mediterranean. By happenstance, he visited the Acropolis, literally the high point of Greek civilization. Alongside Freud's tremendous pleasure at visiting this great monument was a feeling of "unreality." It was "too good to be true."[16] Schur notes that this moment was so overwhelming that Freud found it necessary to ask his traveling companion, his brother, to verify that he was indeed on the Acropolis.[17] Freud links the "too good to be true" feeling immediately to his guilt at having surpassed his father: "For, as has long been known, the Fate which we expect to treat us so badly is a materialization of our conscience, of the severe super-ego within us, itself a residue of the punitive agency of our childhood."[18] Certainly, Freud's own associations support his interpretation that a portion of his

and his brother's disturbance was due to these repressed oedipal striv-
ings and the consequent guilt. Yet, in invoking the dealings of Fate and
our relationship to its supreme power, Freud seems to have forgotten
his own insight that Fate is a female, a mother, to whom we look for
guidance and love. Fate, Ladyluck, and Fortuna are all female god-
desses whose good graces we hope to receive. Freud made this association directly in his essay "The Theme of the Three Caskets" and his
pessimistic essays on civilization.[19]

The sequence of events linking the loss of Fliess's good will to
Freud's "uncanny" experience strongly suggests a typical occult moment. Yet the episode remains murky and open to debate. Far less
murky and far less debatable is the sequence of events experienced by
Freud and Jung that culminated in a famous occult moment between
the two. Schur links that episode to Freud's moment of unreality on
the Acropolis and so do I.

EMOTIONAL AND
INTELLECTUAL DIVORCE

To the credit of both Freud and Jung, their falling-out over the occult
moment in the bookcase did not mark the end of their relationship.
They maintained their correspondence and completed an enormous
amount of work up to and through their final personal break in the fall
of 1913, some four years later.

The bookcase affair did mark the end of a period in which each man
hoped the other would fulfill his deepest wishes. Jung wished to find
in Freud an idealized father who would bless his scientific ventures
into areas that, we now know, were at one time terrifying to him as a
child. Freud wished to find in Jung his intellectual heir who would
protect his great creation from the infidels. Jung intuited Freud's
hopes and describes the embarrassment it cost him to recognize that
Freud's wishes for him could never be fulfilled. This was so primarily
because Jung's whole program had been set before his meeting with
Freud. Jung's lifelong work, the elaboration of his religious psychology,
lay ahead.

Even after the disastrous bookcase affair, both men remained important to one another. Jung sent Freud a draft of his most original work,
Symbols of Transformation.[20] To this gift Freud responded with technical asides and minor stylistic criticisms saying, as from on high, "I
don't know whether this will make me popular with you. But I'm sure
you didn't send it just for applause" (*Letters*, p. 334).

Jung responded to this cool reception with cool, scholarly concern to effect any reasonable change he thought pertinent. A wide swing in feelings occurs throughout the remaining letters until the final drama in October 1912, through the winter, and into the new year, when Freud wrote, in response to Jung's vigorous protests of his unfairness, "I propose that we abandon our personal relations entirely. I shall lose nothing by it, for my only emotional tie with you has long been a thin thread—the lingering effect of past disappointments—and you have everything to gain . . ." (*Letters*, p. 538). These short excerpts cannot convey adequately the depth of feeling in both men's letters, and I urge the serious reader to examine the entire set, certainly those covering this last period. For our purposes, it is vital to point out the direct consequences of Freud's abandonment upon Jung.

In his autobiography, Jung writes as if the concluding chapter of *Symbols of Transformation*, "The Sacrifice," was the source of his break with Freud. In that chapter Jung minimizes the universality and psychopathological aspects of incest and instead argues that the incest theme has a religious character: "I knew he [Freud] would never be able to accept any of my ideas on this subject" (*MDR*, p. 167). Jung completed the book and "it did indeed cost me Freud's friendship" (*MDR*, p. 167).

Yet the letters between the two men around this period do not support Jung's prediction. Jung is enraged by Freud's attitude toward his intellectual struggles. Yet he hopes to maintain a two-part correspondence. In one part, he will write as he feels directly—which is often angry and critical of Freud's neuroticisms. In the second part, he will be formal and correct, as one scientist writing to another. Jung calls the first kind of correspondence "secret letters." Clearly, they amount to a direct expression of his hopes for a continued relationship with Freud.

A touching event unfolds on 3 January 1913, when Freud composes the letter quoted above, disowning the friendship. On the same day Jung writes to Freud, saying anxiously: "Don't hesitate to tell me if you want no more of my secret letters" (*Letters*, p. 539). Upon receipt of Freud's letter, Jung writes back on 6 January, "I accede to your wish that we abandon our personal relations . . ." (*Letters*, p. 540). Jung then quotes Hamlet's famous line at his death, met at the hands of a cruel man who replaced an ideal father, "The rest is silence."[21]

This final break with Freud did not precipitate all at once Jung's fascination with the occult and with primitive religion. Nor did it directly cause the severe psychological trials Jung underwent beginning in the fall of 1912 and lasting, he tells us, through 1918. During this six-year period Jung severed his last remaining ties with formal psychoanalytic organizations, many of which he had developed. Instead, he pursued an ever-deepening set of fantasies that, in a lesser person, might have led to psychiatric hospitalization.

However, this final break with Freud did contribute to Jung's disorganization. As he says directly: "It would be no exaggeration to call it a state of disorientation" (*MDR*, p. 170). His "great dreams" of archetypal images, like those found in medieval religious paintings, began in December 1912, not afterwards. That is, the importance Jung placed on Freud, sometimes attributing to him a demigod status, and his disappointment with Freud, contributed to his occult experiences. Jung dreamt of himself "sitting on a gold Renaissance chair; in front of me was a table of rare beauty. . . . Suddenly a white bird descended, a small gull or dove" (*MDR*, p. 171). This dream has undeniable associations to a grandiose vision of himself receiving an annunciation (like Mary) sent from above for his special understanding. It is a personal telling of an ancient myth and from the side of ordinary life contains an element of deep narcissistic repair.

Jung's subsequent achievements in psychiatry, the history of religion, and the occult branches of thought are well-known. His resolution of his "creative illness" has been analyzed in detail by many thoughtful people.[22]

Jung's central concepts were also born in this period. If one has worked through his basic theory, presented in later books, one can read *Memories, Dreams, Reflections* as an illustrative case history of all the major Jungian principles. The fact that Jung's visions and his wrestling with the underground gods occurred in his middle life illustrates his notion of individuation, that is, the process of becoming an individual, as opposed to an obedient member of society. This process usually begins in the middle of life's journey. Thus Dante opens his account of a similar descent, and continues on toward death—and the hope for resurrection.

Jung's explanation of occult events, like the exteriorization phenomenon and his prophetic dreams, relies on his notion of synchronicity. In brief, synchronicity refers to the meaningful linkage that one can observe between events that have no causal relationship to one another. For example, Jung describes a series of nightmares he had in the fall of 1913 in which the Alps are flooded with a tide of bodies, rubble, and blood, all products of a great catastrophe. Initially, he wonders if this presages a psychotic collapse. As political events unfolded in the summer of 1914, he construed his nightmarish visions as occult previews of the coming war, which began in August 1914. Using Jung's terms, one would say that his acute sensitivity to great psychological currents operating at that time, that is, collective psychological events, made his dreams operate like an antenna that perceived and broadcast them prior to their actual occurrence. Jung believes that his dreams were connected to the Great War synchronistically: they resonated with the same psychic energy. Note that they were not *synchronic*: his dreams did not occur at the same time as the war broke out. His dreams prefigured the war's outbreak. Obviously, one could use Jung's notion of synchronicity to describe prophecies and other occult knowledge that seem to permit some people to predict the future. It will be instructive to consider what this term denotes and compare it, as theorem, to alternative accounts of empathic understanding.

JUNG AND SYNCHRONICITY

I have suggested that occult events occur as the consequence of a chain of events culminating in a person's feeling threatened by fragmentation anxiety. I have tried to show how this sequence explains many features of Augustine's calling, Verdi's discovery of the passage from Lamentations, and other events in the lives of the great and the ordinary. In all these cases, I feel that we can find a clear pattern of cause and effect that replicates the same pattern Kohut found in his patients who had severe narcissistic impairments. A mistake on the therapist's part, a failure in empathic immersion, yielded in succession a threat to the self-selfobject transference; this elicited fragmentation anxiety; and fragmentation anxiety in turn elicited a set of characteristic defenses. For some patients, those defenses include bizarre sexual habits; for others, they include icy aloofness and grandiose images of themselves. In response to a perceived slight, the latter feel it necessary to assume immediately a posture of wounded royalty or, in more extreme cases, that of a messiah upon whose message the infidels have trampled.

Clearly, each patient responds to perceived harms according to individual history and style. Not all narcissistically vulnerable people have occult experiences (just as not all find themselves caught up in perverse sexual exploits). Some people respond to narcissistic wounds by arranging a week-long drunk. The interesting question in each case is, Why does one person choose one solution to narcissistic suffering and another person choose another solution? That is, what distinguishes one person from another such that the first finds the occult irresistible but alcohol intolerable, while the second finds the occult laughable but a drunken binge exactly what is needed?

While this is a central question, I have no single answer. The issue of character, in all its complexity, pertains to narcissistic issues as well. The particular family, physical endowment, and culture that make up a person's character all constrain and shape that person's response to narcissistic wounds. With regard to the occult, it seems fair to say that intellectual fashions come and go. In some groups at some times fortunetelling, mediumship, and ghost hunting may become *de rigueur*.

An excellent way to answer the question of character would be to convey the complete psychoanalytic treatment of an occult devotee. Jung's vivid and courageous autobiography is an excellent alternative to such a case history, and we have examined it at some length.

Another way to address the question of who chooses the occult, compared to those who do not, is to examine traditional occult teachings and argue backward to reconstruct the needs they seem to have met. I have begun this in part in our discussions of Augustine, Freud, and Jung. I propose to continue in this way below, when we consider Jung's central concept of synchronicity. If we treat this theorem as a rational, well-rounded statement of occult faith, we may examine it as itself an occult event.

In treating the concept of synchronicity as itself a statement of occult faith, it may appear that I have prejudged its adequacy as a scientific claim without having shown it to be invalid. Jung and many others who profess this principle might protest my use of it as unfair. However, I do not pretend to judge the scientific credibility of the concept. Rather, I treat it as an analyst would treat the fact of a patient's vocation or lifework: we assume that the choice of profession (however noble or ignoble) demonstrates a person's resolution of the major conflicts that surround everyone who grows up, leaves home, and struggles to fulfill his or her inmost needs.

Synchronicity and Mirroring

The general theorem of synchronicity parallels with uncanny accuracy Kohut's basic account of the mirror stage of development. To clarify this point, I first discuss synchronicity and then Kohut's account, which I link to other psychoanalytic theorems about child development.

Jung's first formal pronouncements on synchronicity appear very late in his writings. "On Synchronicity" derives from a lecture series he gave in 1951. However, as we know from *Memories, Dreams, Reflections*, he had experienced "meaningful connections" between otherwise disconnected events while he was a young boy in the Swiss Alps in the 1880s. In his formal paper Jung defines the concept: "a *meaningful coincidence* of two or more events, where something other than the probability of chance is involved."[23]

If two items seem to be related, for example, one's phone number and one's license plate number, but one can show that it is a highly probable accident, then one sees no synchronistic event. As mentioned above, Jung employs the term to cover all those occult moments when two events that cannot be causally connected are, nevertheless, meaningfully connected. Synchronicity is an "acausal" principle of interaction between persons or events with no possible physical connection, nor one dictated by chance.

Given this principle, Jung can arrange many typical occult terms, like precognition, telepathy, prophetic dreams, ESP, mind reading, and the like under the rule of synchronicity.[24] In each case, the occult moment seems to convey the existence of meaningful connections that one knows cannot be explained by any causal theorem. When friends and family call on one's birthday, it is not synchronistic. Nor is it synchronistic if they happen to call when it is not a special day. It only becomes uncanny and memorable if they should call when we are thinking intently about them and they respond to this needful state. In all the examples given above, from Eisenbud's patient to Verdi to Jung, an event, like chancing upon a passage from Lamentations, is occult only if the event fulfills a wish that preceded it.

From the point of view advanced in this book, this state of neediness, particularly when a self-selfobject relationship has been disturbed, makes us demand of our environment some sign that we are loved, esteemed, and worthwhile. As noted above, this point of view parallels that which Kohut advanced in his clinical theory about narcissistic impairments. That is, Kohut believes that he advances *causal* principles, as any other scientist would, in explaining why a patient with keen narcissistic vulnerability reacts with intense rage to even a brief delay on the part of the analyst.[25]

This is precisely the point of view I have advanced. A perceived failure in the selfobject dimension of a relationship causes one to scan one's emotional environment searching for a clue or sign from a transcendent power. That transcendent power is given the task of reorganizing the self and repairing the breach in it caused by the failure of the selfobject. Is this transcendent power identical to that set of forces Kohut identifies with a positive self-selfobject relationship?

Synchronicity and Narcissistic Control

If we return to the principle of synchronicity, again we see that it describes a situation in which one feels suddenly linked to another person (or Person) in a way that merges ordinary boundaries between us and them. They become part of us and we become part of them. Each depends upon the other, not just as friends or colleagues or team members, to use a few obvious metaphors, but as essential parts of one another.

In one sense, this is an aspect of what Freud termed, following a hint from an educated patient, the "omnipotence of thought." Yet it is more than that. Occult powers, like mind reading, demonstrate that one has crossed the ordinary boundaries that separate one person from another, or oneself from another. Kohut's discussion of the control that one expects to wield over another, treated as selfobject, is especially pertinent to this topic. That control is identical to that which we expect over a part of our body, for example, a hand, which we expect to obey our demands.

Looking at Kohut's analogy from the outside, it may appear ethically suspect to treat another person as an extension of oneself. In philosophic terms, it seems to violate Kant's great dictum that human beings ought to be treated as whole and complete selves—not as means to an end, but as ends in themselves. Kant concludes that a rational and just society would be a kingdom of ends, where no person or class of persons would be used as if they were means toward certain aims. This profound principle rules out slavery, which is among the most glaring of ethical faults.

Yet from an empathic point of view, that is, from within the point of view of the needy individual, the selfobject performs functions closer to that of a vital internal organ than that of a slave who serves the whims of a master. One may well find examples of narcissistic disturbance, especially in narcissistic rage, in which other persons are treated unethically or, in extreme pathological instances, monstrously. But more typically, and certainly in the occult instances described in this book, selfobject relationships are experienced not as master to slave, but as self to internal organ.

We need only recall the examples of fragmentation anxiety that we have considered in which the selfobject has the distinctive role of preserving the self. The selfobject that loves the self guards it against a fatal split that would otherwise yield a fully developed psychosis.[26] In these cases the person used as selfobject may well feel enslaved, but the aim of that enslavement is not to inflict suffering upon an object perceived to be negligible. On the contrary, the selfobject has no peer in its importance as a life-preserver to a self threatened with fragmentation.

Synchronistic events are strikingly parallel to selfobject transferences in that both exemplify a merger of oneself with another such that ordinary boundaries are dissolved: in union there is strength. This strength increases almost geometrically, it appears, as the number of participants increases. Two people engaged in an occult event, for example, a séance, may serve one another as selfobjects.

A Synchronistic Event in Psychotherapy

Jung's favorite example of synchronistic events in a therapeutic context concerns a highly rational young woman who, he says, avoided letting herself become involved with the irrational parts of herself. She dreams that someone has given her a piece of costume jewelry, a scarab beetle. She and Jung then consider the dream. While trying to find a way to free her of her "Cartesian rationalism,"[27] Jung hears a knocking on his window by an insect "in the obvious effort to get into the dark room." It is a scarab-like beetle. Taking his cue from the beetle that seemed to importune Jung to catch him, Jung does so and hands the beetle to his patient: "Here is your scarab." This dramatic enactment "punctured the desired hole in her rationalism and broke the ice of her intellectual resistance."[28]

There are many ways to evaluate this episode. Jung feels that it illustrates a typical synchronistic moment, like those that appeared throughout his own life, and like those more commonly placed under occult rubrics, especially telepathy, telekinesis, and premonition. Using these terms, one might say that his patient's dream about the scarab (not accidently an ancient symbol of Life from Death) shows a kind of precognition since it seems to predict the subsequent episode. The beetle's insistence upon entering the room suggests that it was influenced by the patient's state of psychic need, that is, a kind of telekinesis. That Jung heard it and gave it to the woman suggests his extreme sensitivity to all these currents.

While Jung alludes to these standard parapsychological claims, and to J. B. Rhine's claims about ESP, he cannot do so and at the same time affirm the acausal principle of synchronicity. That is, if one argues that the beetle episode illustrates the particular sensitivity of a dreamer to predict the future, it would seem that this is a causal event or, if not causal, at least rational. Similarly, one might explain Jung's visions of blood and destruction in the fall of 1913 as the products of his special sensitivity to the currents of the collective mind. Like a sensitive political weather vane, he responded automatically to the otherwise unnoticed forces that were shaping European history.

This is a conceptual dilemma of the first order. On the one side, Jung and his followers wish to claim that their psychology is scientific (they refer often to portions of contemporary speculations in physics that seem to support an acausal principle). On the other side, they must affirm that the relationship between occult events, like the beetle's knocking on the window and the young woman's dreams, is not causally related. Jung discusses, for example, possible physical causes that may explain astrological predictions about a person's personality. If these are correct, then "it is probably a question here of a causal relationship, i.e., of a natural law that excludes synchronicity or restricts it."[29]

In other words, synchronicity refers only to those events that another age might call miracles. They must be events that one knows could not have any reasonable, causal connection. Jung states his principle as clearly as possible: "[Synchronicity] explains nothing, it simply formulates the occurrence of meaningful coincidences which, in themselves, are chance happenings, but are so improbable that we must assume them to be based on some kind of principle, or on some property of the empirical world."[30]

Jung does not rule out the possibility that empirical explanations for synchronistic (occult) events may be discovered. But he does rule out causal explanations, that is, explanations that claim that the occult event was caused by a previous event. Many of Jung's students and colleagues have offered explanations that they feel are scientific: "During or because of emotion, the threshold of consciousness is lowered, and the unconscious and its content—the archetypes—gain the upper hand."[31] Freud predicted that healthy people would have fewer and fewer occult experiences; Jung predicts the opposite. As a person individuates, that is, matures and has increasing access to the collective drama of human history, more and more meaningful connections will make themselves evident.

INTERPRETATION OF
SYNCHRONICITY

Jung's ability to link events that appear chaotic and unrelated to one another under the single rubric of synchronicity has helped consolidate occult thought. Jung felt that the concept permitted him and others to search for corresponding discoveries in the natural sciences that would corroborate his psychological discoveries. He was particularly interested in the more abstract portions of Einstein's theory that seemed to alter the ordinary conceptions that causal relationships are bound by a linear time flow. In other words, Jungian theory takes the principle of synchronicity as a given and seeks to find explanations for it. I do not.

For our purposes I propose to treat the concept itself as a highly condensed psychological event. I suggest that we interpret the concept as a rational theorem that denotes a state of need: it names a class of experiences in which one needs to discover the existence of a new selfobject relationship. Lacking the theoretical tools Kohut has offered us, as well as basic formulations in child psychiatry developed by David Winnicott, Jung sought to locate his concept in the outer world, the world of natural phenomena. I believe that we should locate it in the inner world of the child's relationship to the child's mother.

To make this claim understandable, we have to consider a few more technical terms. By now, the reader will have become familiar with Kohut's basic theorem about self and selfobject relationships. My discussion does not exhaust the meaning of this theorem, nor does it do full justice to the rich clinical issues it addresses, many of which remain obscure to even the most enlightened clinicians. We will also consider the following terms: the mirror stage of development (Lacan and Winnicott), mirror transference (Kohut), and transitional object and transitional phenomena (Winnicott).

Looking at Synchronicity: The Mirror Stage

As do all psychoanalytic theorists, Kohut bases his claims upon a genetic point of view. To explain why a certain patient treats him as if he were a machine, rather than a human being, Kohut looks to that patient's past and attempts to discern there what traumas occurred such that this patient needed to experience people around him as if they were machines, that is, predictable, uninvolved, unlovable, and unloving. And while Kohut did no direct observation of children, he, like Freud, argues consistently that his clinical discoveries with adult patients permit us to explain how early failures in the child-parent relationships give rise to defects in the child's self-structure. These, in turn, give rise to extreme narcissistic vulnerability.

I have employed this point of view consistently throughout this book, and the reader will not find it alien. However, it is worth stressing again because to explicate Kohut's and Winnicott's central concepts of the mirror stage we must permit them to speak about very early mental states, access to which is severely limited.

This would seem to be a request, on my part, for a leap of faith or at least the suspension of critical reasoning. Nothing would be more disastrous or contrary to the spirit of analytic science. Unless one has seen at first hand behavior that Kohut terms selfobject transference, these terms become just another set of ideas. And this is a subtle disease in which psychoanalytic discoveries, transported out of their clinical matrix, enter the intellectual milieu where they are treated as things in themselves and become "ideas." Granted that ideas are the stuff of academic discourse, they are not identical with the events and processes they name. Yet since most people have had some kind of occult experience, and have been raised by human beings, most people can examine their own experience and see if this discussion proves helpful.

We may now address a question raised in the Introduction but not answered: If everyone needs selfobject relationships, and everyone experiences failures in those relationships, ought not everyone to have major occult experiences? In other words, how do we explain the interesting fact that some people, like Jung, live a life full of fantastic occurrences, while others do not?

We have hinted at the answer a number of times. That answer, or partial answer, relies upon the genetic point of view described in the Introduction. Following Kohut, who follows traditional analytic practice, we assume that in the history of someone whose life is consumed by occult experience we will find major difficulties in their relationship to their parents and other important people along the lines of narcissistic maturation. We expect the opposite to hold true as well—that in a life where the occult is unimportant, and where no other narcissistic repairs seem to create severe suffering, the person was able to find in his or her parents sufficient narcissistic validation. In making these two generalizations I have not pretended to blame parents, nor praise them, for raising children who grow up to become adults with especially vulnerable narcissistic constitutions or with especially firm and cohesive senses of themselves.

THE MIRROR PHASE IN
CHILD DEVELOPMENT

I have suggested that persons who have not navigated the mirror phase of psychological development will be prone to occult experiences. Since I have made this claim, arguing backward, as it were, from documents of adult behavior (e.g., Augustine's *Confessions* and Jung's *Memories, Dreams, Reflections*), it remains a speculation and not a demonstrated truth.

However, given our analysis of these many instances of occult experience, and of synchronicity that summarizes occult belief, I believe that we can show a striking resemblance between them and early childhood issues. These issues all revolve around what different psychoanalytic authors call the "mirror phase." We consider three views of this phase: those of Jacques Lacan, David Winnicott, and Heinz Kohut.

Jacques Lacan

Jacques Lacan used the term *mirror phase* as early as 1931.[32] We focus on Lacan's efforts to formulate a way of understanding how human beings first come to understand themselves as an "I." Using current work in animal studies as well as his own clinical experience with severely disturbed psychiatric patients, Lacan suggests that at around the age of six months, or later, the human infant perceives that it is a subject by seeing itself reflected in a mirror. Some of the higher apes also notice themselves in mirrors, but they cease to find that interesting after a short time.

Only human beings latch onto this experience. One source of their fierce attachment is the discovery that the mirror validates the appearance of the self as whole and complete, that is, not fragmented. Following Freud, who felt that an entity as complex and as sophisticated as the ego could not exist at birth,[33] Lacan argues that there must be, therefore, a period of time in which the infant acquires the profound capacity to comprehend itself as a unity, even if for a short time. He calls this period the mirror stage. By seeing itself in a mirror, complete and integrated as an external object, the infant experiences a total unity. In Muller and Richardson's words, "This totality becomes idealized into a model for all eventual integration and, as such, is the infant's primary identification—the basis for all subsequent 'secondary' identifications."[34]

Yet precisely because the experience of unification is so powerful and so desirable, the infant assumes that this is the only way to retain its newly won state of coherence. To do this, the infant assumes a character armor that is now shaped around the external image of self. Yet this very image subtly alienates the infant from itself because the image with which it identifies itself is an inversion of reality. The mirror image inverts "reality," for left hand becomes right hand, and it presents a two-dimensional image of our three-dimensional world.

In a brilliant move, Lacan then generalizes a psychological principle out of this bit of natural law, that ordinary mirrors invert the image. Because persons first discover themselves in an external image (the mirror image), the ego's experience of all other realities is based on this alienated (because distant from self and inverted) image: "This confusion leads to a misidentification of himself with the other and has far-reaching effects."[35]

Lacan's argument is far more involved than this summary. In particular, he wishes to marry elements of Hegel's metaphysics with Freud's epistemology: Hegel spoke of the human subject as an element of world history, coming to know itself through philosophy; Freud seems to have described the same process in individual history. Again, for our purposes, Lacan's essay helps us understand why severe narcissistic conditions so often seem to occur when another fails to mirror our internal needs. If we think of the actual experience of peering at ourselves in a mirror, whether as an infant, adolescent, or adult, we realize that the entire relationship between self and mirror image is one of self and selfobject.

Ordinary experience and language tell us that people who spend a great deal of time peering at themselves in mirrors are "narcissistic." Kohut's insights into self and selfobject relationships help us refine this truism. For as one peers at oneself in a mirror three important events take place simultaneously.

Mirrors and Selfobject Relationship

First, one sees opposite oneself a person whom others see all the time and to whom they react, with either praise, condemnation, or indifference. The mirror promises to accomplish that miracle of which Burns spoke, "To see ourselves as others see us." For a moment we can assume the position of the other person and gaze upon ourselves with more or less attention to detail and with more or less accuracy of judgment about our attractiveness to others. Happy, healthy people are consistently poor in predicting such judgments. Some well-publicized studies of self-image suggest that happy, self-confident people consistently overrated their attractiveness to others, while depressed persons were much better at predicting how other people would rate them along various scales of social desirability.

Freud had observed similar behavior a generation earlier in his great paper "Mourning and melancholia."[36] Freud notes that people who are depressed and seem melancholic tend to be very critical of themselves. A patient may berate himself or herself endlessly about his or her faults: "When in his heightened self-criticism he describes himself as petty, egoistic, dishonest, lacking in independence, one whose sole aim has been to hide the weaknesses of his own nature, it may be, so far as we know, that he has come pretty near to understanding himself."[37]

The peculiar quality of Freud's language, its rhetorical force of rolling invective, is not accidental. It matches well his general evaluation of narcissism: that it is a moral failing as well as a psychological state. And it prepares us for the denouement: "[W]e only wonder why a man has to be ill before he can be accessible to truth of this kind."[38]

By peering at ourselves in the mirror we can assess our face, examine our eyes, see into them what we are afraid others might see first, and prepare ourselves to face others.

A second, less object-related, dimension of looking into mirrors is the primitive pleasure one takes in seeing the mirror-image self, the person opposite one, mimic our every gesture. This seems to be part of the pleasure one observes in infants when they play in front of a mirror: the reflected self-image obeys exactly what one assigns it. In this sense the image responds to us as a two-dimensional selfobject: reflecting precisely what we do and obeying, therefore, our every gesture. This would seem to be part of the humor in the vaudeville stunt where one actor, dressed identically to another, pretends to be the other's mirror image. When done well one seems to see a normal mirror image assume more and more independence of the "owner," finally abusing its role as servant and so violating the unwritten law that mirror images cannot act on their own accord.

Mirroring in Japanese Puppet Theater

A beautiful illustration of this aspect of mirroring occurs in Bunraku, Japanese puppet theater. In this theater, puppet masters, dressed in black costumes with black masks, manipulate large, exquisitely carved dolls who portray human beings. A typical Bunraku play is Chikamatsu's *The Love Suicides at Sonezaki,* first performed in 1703.[39] Puppet masters are revered as supreme artists when they achieve a lifelike rendition in their puppet's actions, which mimic those of an idealized character, for example, a courtesan. This is not mere realism. The puppets are not built nor used to give an illusion of human movement (the audience sees the puppet masters move around the stage).

Supreme puppet masters use the puppet to express what a flesh-and-blood actor might not: purified action done with absolute fidelity to the law of customary action. Puppets also permit the playwright to stage bloody scenes that would not be tolerated if the protagonists were human beings. Yet the very formality of the puppet master's relationship to his puppet suggests a degree of self-selfobject control and "idealized" expression that no other stage device can offer. Japanese scholars inform us that one may distinguish up to thirteen types of address that Chikamatsu uses when referring to female characters. We may contrast the two modes of address available in some European languages (e.g., *vous* and *tu* in French) with the single mode available in American English (i.e., you).[40]

What may strike Westerners as boring artificiality is understood better as a refined examination of precisely these subtle degrees of relationship and their foundation in Japanese morality. At the same time the Japanese audience, who may know the plays by heart, responds to the puppets with unashamed affection. "At Awaji the audience apparently paid less attention to the play itself than to the puppets. The puppets they watched as a parent would watch a performing child, dwelling carefully and fondly on each gesture."[41] In Kohut's terms, the audience finds intense narcissistic pleasure in the performance of *their* puppets because the puppets respond as perfectly controlled selfobjects that mimic their masters' desires and fulfill their needs.

A third aspect of mirrors pertains to Lacan's emphasis upon the experience of wholeness versus fragmentation. In his initial formulation, Lacan grants to the mirror a positive function as an external sign that the internal self is coherent. In this sense the mirror validates the infant's deepest wish: to be complete and not fragmented. On the other side, gazing into a mirror may be the final action that precipitates profound fragmentation. For some people, like J. D. Salinger's character Zooey, looking at themselves in a mirror is particularly frightening. Zooey goes out of his way to avoid mirrors. As he applies shaving cream and prepares to shave his face, "[Zooey] looked into the mirror while he lathered, he didn't watch where his brush was moving but, instead, looked directly into his own eyes, as though his eyes were neutral territory, a no man's land in a private war against narcissism he had been fighting since he was seven or eight years old."[42]

The danger of looking at his face, which the story tells us is particularly handsome, is that of narcissistic infatuation. This suggests that Zooey is concerned about "falling into himself" as the Greek youth, Narcissus, did before drowning. Zooey's good sense permits him to find a neurotic solution to a much deeper vulnerability. To fall into himself is also to fall to pieces, into a fragmented self, the man in love with a two-dimensional image that is incapable of reciprocating the love showered upon it. A more direct example of precisely this anxiety occurs in the film *Taxi Driver*, when the main character uses a washroom mirror and exhorts himself to assume the posture of a heroic rescuer.

A similar event occurs in Ingmar Bergman's study of schizophrenia, his film *Persona*. A simple-minded nurse stares into a mirror and sees there her image merge with that of the very sick actress who is her patient. Indeed, it is now an artistic cliché to portray a character's internal confusion by catching the character's reflection in a shattered mirror. Many of the peculiar qualities of Lewis Carroll's *Through the Looking Glass*[43] derive from his incessant prosecution of the theme of mirrors as the inversion of ordinary life. Among the few uncanny moments he attributes to himself, Freud notes that he was startled to see an old man approach him in a train's hallway and recognized it as himself.[44] In mythological settings mirrors serve to distinguish the living (and vital and loving) from the dead (the frozen and incapable of love). Movie legends perpetuate the truism that vampires cannot be reflected in mirrors because they are, after all, immaterial persons. They cannot remain alive, nor can they remain dead. They are the undead, the most wretched of souls, who aim to complete themselves by absolute regression to the murderous, sucking infant who draws blood from those it loves. The vampire's absolute dependence upon its victim's blood is a sign of its absolute regression to a self-selfobject relationship that is now a matter of life and death.

In these ways one can utilize Lacan's insight about mirrors and their relationship to self-image to consider Kohut's basic theory of narcissistic development and the treatment of persons with severe narcissistic suffering. Yet there is an additional aspect of mirrors and the mirror stage that Lacan only touches upon. That aspect is the mirroring function parents play vis-á-vis their children. Ordinary language has long recognized this interpersonal mirroring in the saying that a child is the apple of its mother's eye.

David Winnicott

David Winnicott, who has been called a master psychotherapist, noted that some normal infants use certain not-me possessions in a particular pattern:

> I have introduced the terms "transitional object" and "transitional phenomena" for designation of the intermediate area of experience, between the thumb and the teddy bear, between oral eroticism and true object-relationship, between primary creative activity and projection of what has already been introduced.[45]

Winnicott does not deny that these objects or phenomena, such as babbling, may stand for the mother's breast. But he wants to stress that they are both real, external objects, and yet partly under the subjective (narcissistic) control of the infant. Winnicott's own summary of the characteristics of the transitional object is worth quoting:

1. The infant assumes rights over the object, and we agree to this assumption. Nevertheless some abrogation of omnipotence is a feature from the start.
2. The object is affectionately cuddled as well as excitedly loved and mutilated.
3. It must never change, unless changed by the infant.
4. It must survive instinctual loving, and also hating, and, if it be a feature, pure aggression.

5. Yet it must seem to the infant to give warmth, or to move, or to have texture, or to do something that seems to show it has vitality or reality of its own.

6. It comes from without from our point of view, but not so from the point of view of the baby. It does not come from within; it is not an hallucination.[46]

Paul Pruyser suggests that for Winnicott the transitional object is almost "sacred," for it permits the baby the opportunity to gain, slowly and at its own best pace, a stronger footing in the world of object relations.[47] Given that foundation, the baby can then develop basic trust in both the permanence of the world of loving others and in its own capacities to assess accurately the feelings and intentions of others toward it. With such a foundation the baby will then be able to tolerate later disappointments. In Winnicott's terms, the good-enough mother is precisely one who spontaneously "gives the infant the *illusion* that there is an external reality that corresponds to the infant's own capacity to create. In other words, there is an overlap between what the mother supplies and what the child might conceive of."[48]

To illustrate the mutual creative effort involved in the experience of good-enough mothering, Winnicott uses a simple sketch. It shows a figure representing the mother's breast (which, in turn, stands for all her giving, loving, nurturing actions) being placed in the spot where the infant has just hoped it would appear. This simple sketch describes a complex idea that has at least three dimensions to it.

The first dimension is that of the outsider, like ourselves, who sees an interaction between mother and infant (or patient and analyst): one gives, the other takes. The second dimension is that of the mother whose breasts change (for example, whose breasts are engorged with milk) and who needs to nurse, that is, needs to give in order to feel better herself (just as honest therapists need to help). The third dimension is that of the infant, who cannot generalize away from its experience to contemplate either us, the onlookers, or its mother. From the infant's perspective, its overwhelming need to nurse (and be mothered in a myriad of ways) seems to produce in its environment precisely the object it requires, namely, the breast (or any object that symbolizes the breast). Winnicott calls this last dimension the infant's shared hallucination. In his paradoxical language, the mother puts her breasts, therefore, where the baby creates them. Later, when the mother is not perfectly attuned to her infant's needs, she will fail to respond exactly as the baby wishes. Using Winnicott's language, it seems that normal parenting requires a stage of maternal preoccupation followed by a gradually decreasing level of perfect attunement. As the mother ceases to respond perfectly to her infant's demands, the infant loses hold of its illusion of union with the hallucinated breast. It then automatically scans its environment and selects from it some new object that will be under its control and yet be linked to the mother. Winnicott terms this new object the transitional object. (More rarely, it will be an activity, like murmuring to itself: he terms this transitional phenomena.)

Winnicott's own intuitive capacities and level of empathic awareness show in his phenomenologically rich language. That is, Winnicott strives to convey the texture of the baby's experience using adult language. This often leads him into writing sentences that are difficult to understand at first. He says, for example, that the transitional object comes neither from without the baby nor from within the baby. At other times Winnicott exhorts us to act a certain way toward the infant and the object. We are not to question the reality of the object:

> Of the transitional object it can be said that it is a matter of agreement between us and the baby that we will never ask the question "Did you conceive of this or was it presented to you from without?" The important point is that no decision on this point is expected. The question is not to be formulated.[49]

This passage sounds moralistic, but it is more in the nature of a therapeutic discovery. It describes the actions of an intuitive mother (again, noting that this term may identify an empathic male) or therapist who grasps that to challenge the aliveness of the particular object is analogous to challenging the child's fundamental feelings about its own aliveness.[50]

SUMMARY:
THE OCCULT AS SYNCHRONISTIC

Occult events occur to persons who have experienced a sudden loss of relationship to a person or, more rarely, ideal that has performed significant selfobject functions. The occult event itself, for example, a vision, is a massive reparative effort in which validation of the right to have needs for self-repair met is perceived in the stars themselves. The occult event seems to fit exactly one's inner needs. It seems to occur precisely when needed most and therefore seems to prove that there is an Other, force or person, who will give exactly what we need.

In this sense, occult events are synchronistic phenomena precisely as Jung understood that term. Yet, using Kohut and Winnicott, we can add to this claim and say that the Other who seems to hear our inner needs is the image of the original person who placed herself or himself precisely where our needs projected its image to be.

As we have seen, in the occult moment ordinary rules of space, time, and causality cease to rule us. We are freed of the drudgery of daily life and the emptiness of an environment that fails consistently to hear our unspoken needs. In Jung's beautiful account of the manikin we see the occult object made real, just as the transitional object comes alive in response to the child's love for it. Such an Other replicates aspects of the good-enough mother, particularly as the latter is experienced in the mirror phase of child development.

Yet for all the effort that Jung spent in creating his religious psychology and his explanations of occult events, my point of view requires us to conclude that occult moments are not an ideal route to happiness. For the person convinced of occult claims, my discussion here will seem unfair and prejudicial. Indeed, even my analysis of the selfobject functions that occult events fulfill will seem to reduce them to mere efforts at repair and not serious science.

I would not argue against this response. I would disagree that efforts at self-repair are "mere." Given Kohut's and Winnicott's profound explication of the mother-infant pair and its replication in psychotherapy, to attack "mere repair" is to attack a bona fide and important effort to rescue a self in disarray. An empathic view of the occult should draw us closer to those seeking occult solutions, not place us even further away in the camp of the cultured despisers.

Yet it is true that I have not given direct credence to occult claims. And to suggest that occult experiences are efforts at repair is to suggest that they are less than ideal solutions. I believe that I can justify these conclusions by following up Lacan's hint about the "image" and its role in the development of the mirror stage. I will suggest below that the occult mood is precisely one in which the image (or icon, text, or idea) is taken to be the paramount object of one's desire. This is in contrast to a happier instance in which one feels safe enough (that is, coherent enough and not fragmented) to focus upon actual persons, and not their representations.

To invoke Jung once more, I believe that the occult mood is a rich and complex experience of self-repair. In this mood one creates an object, like Jung's manikin, that mimics the appearance of a real person and that carries out selfobject functions. It helps the young Jung, for example, control his immense anxiety about the Jesuit. Yet these objects, like Jung's manikin, are not alive. They cannot respond to one. At best, they obey one's demands as puppets obey the puppet-master. Occult objects fail to perform the selfobject functions that the original object also failed to carry out. Jung's mother failed to control his anxiety, for example. Indeed, she seems to have added to it since she too suffered a split that made her unavailable to the infant. The little doll, which condenses Jung's feelings about himself and his father, therefore takes her place. In a similar way, occult beliefs gain significance to the degree that they give one the sense that an unseen, superior, and personalized power will respond to one's sense of fragmentation and help repair the self. In contrast to these occult moments, a more complete sense of self-regard and narcissistic unification permit one to achieve a relationship with human beings.

The occult object, like Jung's manikin, affords one a degree of emotional repair. But only another complete human being can afford us complete emotional sustenance.

6

The Occult Mood
and Its Resolution:
Occult Moments in Goethe's
Truth and Fiction

In this chapter I wish to address a question that can no longer be put off: If the occult is only partly successful as reparation, how can we demonstrate its failings without forfeiting the empathic reading we have tried to advance? For religionists this question might be better formulated as, Am I claiming that all religious experience is a variation of the occult? That is, do I mean to say that all religious experience is in response to anxieties about a fragmented self? No, I am not advancing that claim. I am saying, however, that the occult mood can appear in both religious and nonreligious contexts. The occult mood is a response to actual problems in the functioning of a person's self.

I suggest that we can rely once more on Kohut's discussion of fragmentation anxiety to give us a criterion with which we can assess occult solutions. Occult beliefs occur in response to fragmentation anxieties. They help a person avoid fragmentation because they offer the illusion of safe regression to a stage of constancy: the good-enough mothering object is there, she (or he) is not really gone, not really lost, and not really changed. Arthur Conan Doyle was especially impressed with E. A. Brackett's description of the latter's conversion to Spiritualism. Let us recall Brackett's message:

> The key that unlocks the glories of another life is pure affection, simple and confiding as that which prompts the child to throw its arms around its mother's neck. To those who pride themselves upon their intellectual attainments, this may seem to be a surrender of the exercise of what they call the higher faculties. So far from this being the case, I can truly say that until I adopted this course, sincerely and without reservation, I learned nothing about these things. Instead of clouding my reason and judgment, it opened my mind to a clearer and more intelligent perception of what was passing before me. That spirit of gentleness, of loving kindness, which more than anything else crowns with eternal beauty the teachings of the Christ, should find its full expression in our association with these beings.[1]

A child can throw its arms around its mother's neck because the mother has been there enough times to give the child the absolute conviction that she is reliable, and, by extension, the larger world of other persons is reliable too.

Brackett's occult faith is a statement that in the world beyond death this quality of mothering persists: a world of pure affection. In this sense occult beliefs all adhere to a magnificent declaration: There is no death. They proclaim that there is no actual process of change, for to change is to risk losing the very consolidation that was so hard-won and that the occult promises to maintain. As we saw repeatedly in Jung's description of synchronicity, occult faith holds that time, space, and causality itself rule only part of the world. The other part, the part of the world closest to our actual experience as coherent entities, is governed by the nonrule of synchronicity: If an event is meaningful, then our hopes about it are valid.

THE OCCULT MOOD

I have suggested that the yearning to repair a rent in a selfobject relationship constitutes the underlying need that gives rise to the occult mood. A special selfobject, the maternal figure, seems implicated in all the cases examined so far. These experiences with the mother are very early and so prior to the development of logical thinking. The actor engaged in the occult moment is not aware of the connection between need and response. Even persons of creative genius, like Augustine and Jung, look consistently *outside* themselves for the source of their mood.

Bertram Lewin, a generation before Kohut, observed a similar feature in elated moods. "In the elations, I suggest that the feeling of conviction and subjective certainty about the validity of the happy mood repeats an element in the nursing situation."[2] We have no direct reports from infants of their actual thoughts during the first years of life. But like Kohut, Lewin relies upon psychoanalytic data, gathered from work with highly regressed adult patients, to reconstruct those preverbal moods. In moments of elation adults recapture those moments most directly symbolized by the mother's breast: "The world of observation and instruction is treated as something secondhand, while the stamp of 'truth' lies . . . in the subjective experience, preideational and oral, which in the elation is the repetitive subjective experience of having been nursed."[3] Lewin's terms and overall theory are not identical to those of Kohut, but his observations coincide with Kohut's basic formulations about the maternal selfobject: She is that real, external entity whose affection permits the infant to consolidate, slowly, a coherent self.

In the occult mood one does not doubt that there is an actual, real person out there. The mother's actual existence is not questioned. She is not unreal, or a mere shadow. Rather, in occult moments she is perceived to be unavailable. We recall Mr. Z's mother, who was shut off in her own depression. The mother's actual retreat from the child and her inability to be pleased by her child casts a pall over all the child's later narcissistic pleasures. A talented physician, for example, who is the son of a depressed mother, may recognize his achievements as real and his work as important, but he feels no vitality and no sense of coherent purpose and value. The glass wall that he felt between himself and his mother now exists within himself. It permits him to recognize that he ought to be happy, but prevents him from experiencing that pleasure.

The occult mood recaptures a state of need and locates the solution to that need in the outer world. A distinguishing characteristic of all occult experience is the search outside oneself for that real (solid, actual, tangible) object which, when found, will fit perfectly one's inner needs. Given this, it is not surprising that Kohut's theorem about the need for selfobject relationships will strike those devoted to occult solutions as irrelevant to their interests and concerns. Kohut requires one to examine the actual series of events that lead up to an occult experience. As in any other instance when a person feels a sudden loss of narcissistic stability, a person caught up in the occult must be responding to a perception of failure in a crucial selfobject relationship. That is, we must suppose that the occult mood is itself the product of a causal chain. Like other moods, to be caught up in an occult event is to be a different self, often an old self, that has reemerged in a particular circumstance and now claims our allegiance.

Types of Moods: Moods as Self-states

Christopher Bollas, a contemporary psychoanalyst, has discussed the topic of moods in a series of thoughtful articles.[4] He describes the "autistic" flavor of being in a mood: "Whilst in a mood a part of the individual's total self withdraws into a generative autistic state in order that a complex internal task be allowed time and space to work itself through."[5] Bollas employs Winnicott's general orientation and terminology. I rely upon those of Kohut. I believe that we are both concerned with a feeling state, one that outsiders may term "depressive" or "grandiose" yet that, to the person "in the mood," is a vital effort to "establish fragments of former self-states."[6]

Although Bollas focuses primarily upon moods that analytic patients experience in their treatment, I believe that his conclusions are valid for the occult mood as well. In the many instances of occult experience described above, we find consistently a mood of despair over loss of the selfobject and a subsequent drive to reestablish contact with a replacement: the object of occult belief. In contrast, normal grieving includes a continuous process of recognizing, slowly, that the loved one really is lost and that one will survive that loss.

Because moods are inherently narcissistic, that is, involve the person in the mood to such an extent that other people become less important, they do not lend themselves to a traditional, altruistic value system. In other words, people in a mood are generally subjected to numerous moralisms, for example, Snap out of it! Bollas's insights about the restorative capacity of mood help clarify my argument about the occult mood. The latter cannot (and ought not) be explained away as a mere regression from object relatedness, nor as a defense against actual, current struggles in the real world of the here and now.

Rather, "moods are . . . complex self states that may establish a mnemonic environment in which the individual re-experiences and re-creates former infant-child experiences and states of being."[7] At the same time that he values this "restorative" capacity of moods, Bollas does not suggest that moods alone are sufficient to effect lasting freedom and personal growth. That greater goal emerges out of the two-person group of analyst and patient.

I believe that this is true of occult moods as well. That is, I believe that we ought to credit the occult mood with demonstrating the existence of severe narcissistic suffering. But we should not suppose that the mood itself or occult solutions are ideal responses to narcissistic deficits. I try to show why this is so in the last part of this chapter. At this point I merely record another statement from Bollas, who writes that "living through a mood is one of the idioms for the establishment of an environment."[8] I try to show that this is true of the occult mood as well. However, the environment established by occult belief is only two-dimensional. It lacks a vital sustaining quality that seems available only in actual relationships with actual persons.

Narcissistic Rage and the Attack on Selfobjects

To outsiders, the newly discovered selfobject may appear ridiculous and worthy only of derision and attack. But to attack another person's occult object or occult belief is to attack the legitimacy of that person's needs expressed in the occult mood. When Conan Doyle learned that Houdini had contradicted Mrs. Doyle's claims that she had contacted Houdini's dead mother, the great novelist was saddened and despondent. A lesser man might have become enraged and sought revenge. In both cases, the failure of the other person to value the importance one places on an occult object is tantamount to dismissing the selfobject needs it represents. As we saw above, when people feel themselves under such attack their response is narcissistic rage. One must defend one's right to feel coherent and worthy.

In spite of all these valid and important considerations, one must conclude that occult solutions are not ideal. In their worst instances, occult solutions verge on ludicrous and masochistic actions; in their best they merge into a kind of religiosity long associated with British Spiritualism and similar well-established occult traditions. In this chapter I propose to distinguish between occult solutions to narcissistic suffering and alternative solutions. I do so by considering parts of Johann Wolfgang von Goethe's great autobiographical work, *Truth and Fiction.*[9]

In this remarkable work, Goethe describes moments of despair and moments of triumph, especially during his adolescent years. During that time he struggled to consolidate his apprehensions of his own genius. This burden, added to the usual tasks of adolescence, produced moments of severe anxiety in the young man. As we can now predict, when these anxieties threatened to overwhelm him, to fragment his self, Goethe had occult experiences. In this sense, *Truth and Fiction,* like the other autobiographical accounts we have considered, serves us as an admirable case history. But the book is more than that, just as Goethe is more than a patient. For Goethe offers us not just an illustration of occult experiences in a person of genius. He also offers us a way to distinguish occult solutions to fragmentation anxiety from another kind of solution. This other solution is provided by artistic insight. To prefigure our discussion below, occult solutions to fragmentation anxiety struggle to preserve the self against change. Artistic solutions to fragmentation anxiety embrace the reality of change but find within change itself an unvarying pattern. That unvarying pattern, what Goethe calls "constancy in change," signifies the possibility of a permanent self, not fragmented by time or even death.

Goethe was not immune to fragmentation anxiety. But, at least as indicated in his autobiography, Goethe had no fear of madness, that is, complete fragmentation. Rather, the source of Goethe's anxiety was the more subtle narcissistic pressure he felt when he perceived the extent of his literary gifts. Thanks to a wealthy family and brilliant teachers, Goethe recognized early that he had within himself the makings of rare genius. In response to that pressure the young man fabricated a number of fascinating ploys to give himself time to mature as an artist. In the following I stress these factors and their relationship to the occult experiences Goethe describes throughout the early portion of his autobiography. Numerous analytic authors have discussed other, equally important, dimensions of Goethe's life.[10]

GOETHE'S OCCULT ROMANCE

Born in 1749 to a wealthy and prestigious family, Goethe eventually became Germany's greatest poet and, for many, its greatest individual. As Martin Buber remarks in his classic text, *I and Thou*, in reading Goethe one finds a fully formed "I" who confronts one with tremendous vigor and excitement.[11] Even in translation, his two-volume autobiography, *Truth and Fiction*, presents a person whose descriptions of the most ordinary objects are profoundly interesting. To measure Goethe's achievements would require a lifetime of scholarship dedicated not only to Goethe's works themselves, which amount to hundreds of volumes, but to the many people who recognized his genius even during his life.

Luckily, our task is simpler. Rather than look back at his life, as he did in his autobiography, or as most scholars do when assessing his artistic and scientific works, we may focus on a single period in Goethe's early life when he had not achieved the Olympian stature that now surrounds his name. That period is between his twenty-second and twenty-fifth year (1771–74). During this time he engaged in intense, but impossible, love affairs with many women, one of whom was affianced to another man. Following that period of intense emotional frustration, Goethe had a severe illness and then entered a period of deep fascination with the occult. During this time he met another "impossible" woman, a beautiful girl who had married a man much older and less exciting than Goethe: "The young wife of eighteen became a stepmother of five children and lived in an apartment above her husband's business. Goethe began to frequent the house; ardent scenes ensued between Tristan and Isolde, which King Mark did not relish."[12]

Since the whole story of these years is exceedingly complex, I focus on a small portion of it: Goethe's romance with Gretchen and, later, with Frederica. I suggest that each girl performed crucial selfobject functions for the young author. Each became an idealized and idealizing audience that mirrored back to Goethe a sense of his greatness and artistic gifts. In addition, each girl served as a kind of emotional bridge that linked Goethe to his adolescence, when his father planned his legal career, and to his newly won identity as a poet and writer.

Given our thesis, that loss of selfobject relationships engenders a readiness for occult experience, it is not surprising to find that Goethe had occult experiences following the loss of each relationship. I identify, as before, a causal sequence that links the establishment of an intense selfobject relationship and its collapse to a subsequent occult event. Goethe's case is particularly important because it exemplifies how a person of his stature was able to find a way back from occult solutions, in which selfobject relationships predominate, to a more complete adjustment to full and complete object relations.

Goethe's Struggles with Greatness: The Burdens of Genius

It requires no psychoanalytic speculation to demonstrate that Goethe the young man had to struggle with severe narcissistic tensions. Proof appears in his own account of his academic dissertation. In his dissertation he took upon himself the task of reworking all of Christian and Jewish belief: "I thought I had discovered that it was not our Ten Commandments which stood upon the tables; that the Israelites did not wander through the desert for forty years, but only for a short time; and thus I fancied that I could give entirely new revelations as to the character of Moses" (*Truth and Fiction*, vol. 2, p. 133).

The prospect of invalidating the basic Jewish and Christian understanding of the Pentateuch did not daunt the young man. We recall that Goethe wrote his dissertation in the late seventeenth century. We may understand that he found allies in Voltaire and other radical philosophers who challenged the intellectual hegemony of Christendom. Yet Goethe's tone in this account is not of an unbeliever attacking the whole fabric of Christian belief. Goethe does not disdain Christian beliefs. He rejected Voltaire's attacks on religion and denounced the Frenchman's intellectual substitutes. Goethe's tone is of an adamant believer discovering, hidden within the trappings of ordinary belief, deeper truths that he now needs to communicate to others who remain blind.

Looking back on his life, the sixty-year-old man who recounts his youth tells us, "Even the New Testament was not safe from inquiries: with my passion for dissection, I did not spare it . . ." (*Truth and Fiction*, vol. 2, p. 133). He adds, "In this region also, I thought I should make all sorts of discoveries. That gift of tongues imparted at Pentecost with lustre and clearness, I interpreted for myself in a somewhat abstruse manner, not adapted to procure many adherents" (p. 133). Yet the young man who labored over his new discoveries must have sensed that he was out of his depth and that his "abstruse" interpretations were grandiose in the extreme.

Like other persons of genius, Goethe struggled with the usual perplexities of youth and with the puzzle of his intellectual and artistic gifts. Like most complex actions, his grandiose dissertation performed many functions. He may well have intended to free himself from the academic life and solid Lutheran existence that would otherwise have been his. Yet we can think of many more direct ways he could have achieved that aim, none of which would require him to make so dramatic a gesture.

Goethe's own explanation seems more plausible. The Bible "first became really accessible to me" (*Truth and Fiction*, vol. 2, p. 132), he asserts, when he took upon himself the task of responding to its internal sense: "the interior, the sense, the tendency of the work" (p. 131). Goethe summarizes this method in a passage that contains his aesthetic code:

> It is everybody's duty to inquire into what is internal and peculiar in a book which particularly interests us, and at the same time, above all things, to weigh in what relation it stands to our own inner nature, and how far, by that vitality, our own is excited and rendered fruitful. On the other hand, everything external that is ineffective with respect to ourselves, or is subject to doubt, is to be consigned over to criticism. (*Truth and Fiction*, vol. 2, p. 131)

In this deeply romantic theorem Goethe locates the reader's internal response as the only valid test of the inherent inner sense of a work of art or a religious text. It is not difficult to see why ecclesial authorities found Goethe's principle inherently wrong. It violates the spirit of duty and obedience that they enforced. Using himself as an internal compass, Goethe constructed elaborate interpretations of sacred biblical texts that he acknowledged were erroneous. Yet, Goethe adds, we must recognize that his adherence to the principle of mutual affinity, in which a work speaks to our innermost feelings, "lies at the fountain of the moral as well as the literary edifice of my life" (*Truth and Fiction*, vol. 2, p. 132).

One direct implication of this creed is the assumption that we may consider placing ourselves on a level parallel to that of a text, like the Pentateuch, or a personage, like Socrates or even Jesus. To most of Goethe's professors this assumption only demonstrated the depth of his impiety (or stupidity). From the point of view elaborated in this book, Goethe's principle parallels Kohut's notion of empathy. Human beings can understand one another only when they comprehend each other's internal world.

GOETHE'S INSIGHT:
BEYOND KOHUT?

Goethe was convinced that this resonance between himself and the inner tendency of a text permitted him access to the inner meaning of the Bible's story as well as to other persons. This notion may deepen Kohut's understanding of empathic communication. Goethe points to a reciprocal element in the transaction between viewer and subject that Kohut only suggests. Goethe stresses that our own "inner nature" is made more vital by our consideration of the work of art (or another person). If we translate this aesthetic principle into clinical terms, we conclude that therapists who serve selfobject functions of others (their patients) ought also to find their own inner natures made vital and fruitful.

At first glance, this would seem to prove that Kohut and Goethe address distinct topics. Kohut's first monograph on the treatment of narcissistic conditions[13] contains numerous descriptions of the arduous difficulties therapists incur in treating narcissistically disturbed patients and the peculiar countertransference burdens that ensue. One finds little hint that serving selfobject functions of another person can be exciting and vital. One response, therefore, to my comparison of Goethe's form of empathy and Kohut's remarks on selfobject transferences would be to conclude that Goethe is actually speaking about object-level relationships in which the other responds to one as a whole and complete person.

Yet against this solution is the clear implication in Goethe's code that it is texts and traditions, like Genesis, and not merely persons, to which one may resonate and from that find joy:

> Anything which is handed down to us, especially in writing, the real point is the ground, the interior, the sense, the tendency of the work; that

here lies the original, the divine, the effective, the intact, the indestructible; and that at no time, no external operation or condition, can in any degree affect this internal primeval nature. (*Truth and Fiction*, vol. 2, p. 131)

I think that this passage describes exactly what Kohut means by an intact self. Of course, Goethe is speaking about a book, but given the absolute conviction of this passage and Goethe's own deep view of himself as the actual core of his created works, I think we can expand it to describe persons as well: In an ideal sense they too are intact, divine, and indestructible. Persons are not perfectly knowable, either to themselves or to others, but one hopes that they might be coherent within themselves; that their primeval nature, a sense of self generated out of good-enough mothering, might persist throughout a lifetime as a feeling of integrity.

In contrast to this ideal, narcissistically vulnerable persons cannot perceive themselves as integrated and complete. They cannot, Kohut has argued, because they have not enjoyed a strong enough selfobject relationship with their parents. Goethe wrote the passages quoted above when he was in his sixties, at an age when his fame was established and he had secured an internal sense of coherence after a lifetime of struggle. Like everyone else, he had moments of severe fragmentation when he could not believe and could not experience the truth of his own indestructibility. And, like everyone else in such moments, when he had lost an especially vital relationship to a person who performed selfobject functions, he was subject to occult experiences.

Occult Moments with Frederica

For many readers, the most charming passages in *Truth and Fiction* concern Goethe's relationship to a young country girl, Friederike (or Frederica). A young male friend, Weyland, knows a rural family in Sesenheim and decides that Goethe ought to meet them. The young poet is introduced to Pastor Brion and his family, which includes two girls, the younger not present when Goethe arrives. The elder daughter says, "She will come back!" and, as if by premonition, "At this instant she really entered the door, and then truly a most charming star arose in this rural heaven" (*Truth and Fiction*, vol. 2, p. 43). Goethe scholars document the revolutionary impact this new relationship had upon Goethe's poetry.

Frederica gave Goethe an audience that would mirror faithfully his deepest hopes. Frederica took up a role other women had played long before her. For example, Goethe describes one of his previous female friends:

I had no liking but for Gretchen, and no other view than to see and take in everything properly, that I might be able to repeat it with her, and explain it to her. Often when a train was going by, I described it half aloud to myself, to assure myself of all the particulars, and to be *praised by my fair one for this attention and accuracy:* the applause and acknowledgments of the others I regarded as a mere appendix. (*Truth and Fiction,* vol. 1, p. 208, emphasis mine)

I think that this passage portrays beautifully the universal need to find a selfobject who will mirror back the praise and admiration without which one cannot live. We can measure the intensity of Goethe's need for *her* (maternal) affection by the way he dismisses other people as mere appendixes. In his many descriptions of Gretchen her maternal, as opposed to her directly sexual, characteristics are paramount. When they inadvertently spent a night together, Gretchen fell asleep on Goethe's shoulder. The next morning Goethe wakes to find her "arranging her little cap: she was more lovely than ever, and, when I departed, cordially pressed my hands" (*Truth and Fiction,* vol. 1, p. 208).

As with his other female relationships, Goethe reveals undeniable erotic feelings toward Gretchen. Yet the preponderant mood seems to me narcissistic. When Goethe hears, for example, that Gretchen has referred to him as a child and she as a sister, he is deeply hurt: "I felt it intolerable that a girl, at the most only a couple of years older than me, should regard me as a child" (*Truth and Fiction,* vol. 1, p. 233).

This narcissistic wound proves intolerable: "This arrow [of affection for her] with its barbed hooks was torn out of my heart . . ." (p. 235). "I could not long work up these new thoughts without an infinite desire arising within me to see important works of art, once and away, in great number. I therefore determined to visit Dresden without delay" (p. 343).[14]

Struggles with Grandiosity: Goethe as a King

Many people count the poems Goethe composed for Frederica among the great lyrics in German literature. The fact that the aged poet regarded his time with Frederica among the few golden moments of his life, moments that echoed in his magisterial compositions, makes a comprehensive assessment of this period impossible.

We can document, however, a crucial strand within that complex set of feelings and events surrounding Goethe's relationship to the young woman. That strand is the special occult significance Goethe attributes to the comings and goings between himself and Frederica. This is already suggested in his first description: her older sister announces that she may come, and, as if by magic, Frederica appears exactly then. In other words, the young woman is summoned, like a genie or some other fantastic creature, by the proper words and sentiments.

We are prepared for this meeting because Goethe had already made it clear that he had set himself a peculiar task. On hearing of the pastor and his daughters, he had decided to dress as a poor, inconsequential "Latin rider," a young clergyman. This odd joke takes on deeper significance when Goethe explains, with some embarrassment, that he traveled incognito like Jupiter or King Henry the Fourth, who, like himself, had disguised themselves "so as to allow their own internal human nature to operate with the greater purity" (*Truth and Fiction*, vol. 2, p. 40). The narcissistic dimension of these associations is not lost on Goethe: "That a young man, without importance or name, should take it into his head to derive some pleasure from an incognito, might be construed by many as an unpardonable piece of arrogance" (p. 41).

We do not have to condemn the young man who contrived this jest to realize, at the same time, that it is a profoundly narcissistic gesture. Knowing that the pastor and his family are rural and unsophisticated, the wealthy and urbane young man pretends to assume a social position just below their own. Yet the young man, Goethe, also plays at assuming the identity of a king, Henry, and even a divinity, Jupiter. Like these grand personages, who needed to cloak their divine and semidivine powers (for kings are imbued by God as well), the young man must conceal his own grand powers. These grand powers are, I have suggested, intimations of his immense creative abilities.

Even before he met Frederica and her family, Goethe had created a self-selfobject relationship to them. He had set a stage of high drama for himself, interspersed with farce and mysteries of identification. The family he had known only by description was to play the roles he assigned to them. Given this preformed vision of the ways in which the pastor's family was to help him (to come to terms with his creative genius), we can understand why Goethe was ready to idealize Frederica. She was to be the female lead in his personal drama, while he was to be both the romantic hero and, more important, the creator who had written, acted, staged, and completed the action. Frederica and her family were like those helpless humans with whom Jupiter fell in love. Like those ancient victims of divine love, Frederica and her family had to bear the burden of greatness thrust upon them.

A Family Made to Order

An additional narcissistic element enters into the relationship between Goethe and Frederica's family. The two young men, Goethe and

Weyland, had descended upon Pastor Brion's family in order to compare it to the characters in Goldsmith's *The Vicar of Wakefield*, a novel that both men adored. Goldsmith's novel describes an idyllic vicar, Mr. Primrose, and the vicar's ideal family, especially his daughters. After Goethe has met Frederica and heard her describe "the little world in which she moved" (*Truth and Fiction*, vol. 2, p. 46), he retires with Weyland. The latter, "with self-complacency, broke out into pleasant jesting, and took great credit to himself for having surprised me with the resemblance to the Primrose family" (p. 47). Later, Weyland "had the waggery" to suggest that Goethe read portions of the novel to Pastor Brion's family. In other words, to make the comparison between the two families complete, and to demonstrate to the German family its identity with an imaginary English family, Goethe will force them to see the joke. The Brion family is to be both the butt of the jest and its audience as well. Goethe does read portions of Goldsmith's novel to the family. This demonstrates to the German family their peculiar similarities to the family described in the English novel (p. 78).

The next morning Goethe feels ridiculous in his ragged disguise and scurries away, too ashamed to be seen again by the pastor's family. Luckily, he finds a neighbor who had better clothes and borrows them, to return again to the pastor's family, this time disguised as the neighbor, George. This permits him to play another joke, first on the pastor's wife, then on both sisters, and then on everyone in succession, including the youngest boy. Tremendously pleased with himself and the impression he had made, Goethe entertains everyone by narrating part of his story, "The New Melusina." He adds, at the chapter's conclusion, "By such recitals, which cost me nothing, I made myself beloved by children, excited and delighted the youth, and drew upon myself the attention of the older persons" (*Truth and Fiction*, vol. 2, p. 60).

The centrality of this theme and its importance to Goethe's discovery of his genius is made clear by the way he begins the next chapter: "My hearers . . . were now enchanted in the highest degree by my singular narrative" (*Truth and Fiction*, vol. 2, p. 63). Because they urged him to write out the entire story, Goethe agrees to do so. In Kohut's terms, because his audience acted as supportive, fascinated, appreciative selfobjects, they helped Goethe consolidate an image of himself as a great author, not a mere jurist. Goethe adds that his story had the preternatural effect of describing an actual man and woman who lived nearby, across the Rhine: "I was much astonished, for I had thought of no couple on this or the other side of the Rhine; nay, I could not have stated how I came by the notion" (p. 64). (Jung describes a similar event in *Memories, Dreams, Reflections* when, at a dinner party, he fabricates a story that happens to describe exactly the notorious events in the life of one of his dinner partners.)[15]

Goethe does not overstate the case. Yet we cannot escape remarking that this "astonishing" incident, like so many Goethe narrates in his account of Frederica, points to a special occult power granted to him as an artist whose ideas come to him from a place he cannot name.

The young, brilliant but erratic student faced a gigantic task, which he gave to himself: to become an author who might rival the greatest English writers, including Shakespeare. This tremendous narcissistic burden weighed constantly on Goethe. "That which Herder [his great teacher] had inculcated pressed down upon me with an infinite weight. He had torn down the curtain that concealed from me the poverty of German literature . . . my own hopes and fancies respecting myself he had so spoiled, that I began to doubt my own capabilities" (*Truth and Fiction*, vol. 2, p. 65).

We see a young man of genius, pulled by thoughts of greatness and literary conquest, committed to a dull profession assigned him by his father and anxious to prove himself. Having returned to his studies in Strassburg, Goethe is morbid and sickly. By chance, as if by a voice from heaven, he is granted a sudden vacation. He immediately plans to return to Sesenheim and his Frederica, yet: "Fast as I rode, I was overtaken by the night. The way was not to be mistaken, and the moon shed her light on my impassioned project. The night was windy and awful; and I dashed on, that I might not have to wait til morning before I could see her" (*Truth and Fiction*, vol. 2, p. 67).

As we have now come to expect, given the intensity of his selfobject needs for Frederica, Goethe should report some occult event signaling the special relationship he had to the young woman. And this is exactly what we find. Since his vacation was sudden and unannounced, and since there was no way a message might have gotten to the parson's family from Strassburg, Goethe expected his late-night arrival to startle the parson's family. But this was not so: "Frederica had predicted that I should come; and who does not feel some satisfaction at the fulfillment of a foreboding, even if it be a mournful one? All presentiments, when confirmed by the event, give man a higher opinion of himself . . ." (*Truth and Fiction*, vol. 2, p. 67).

Sexual Anxieties Compared to Self Anxieties

At a manifest level Goethe's feelings for Frederica are directly and obviously sexual. They are young, excited, attractive persons strongly drawn to one another. In this sense Goethe's love poetry reflects an object-related orientation toward the young woman. Yet at another level, even before meeting her, Goethe placed Frederica in a role of selfobject. She was to be charmed, located, teased, beleaguered, and the recipient of his poetic genius. Given this dual interest in her, Goethe's odd obsessions about her become a little less mysterious. Among the oddest was his dread of kissing her. A great deal of chapter 11 of *Truth and Fiction* concerns Goethe's elaborate plans to avoid kissing Frederica in the little games that he felt obliged to play and that usually culminated in a forfeit requiring a young man to kiss his partner.

Goethe scholars as well as psychologists have examined this at length. The general contention seems to me undeniable: Goethe was tremendously concerned about sexuality, and he feared that kissing might well lead to a complete sexual experience, which he might find overwhelming. Indeed, a number of experts claim that Goethe was virginal into middle age.[16] Reik reports that many Goethe scholars hold that both Goethe and Frederica were tubercular.[17] Therefore, each would have had additional reasons to fear intense sexual involvement.

Yet alongside this object-level erotic relationship, Goethe reports a continuous series of occult events surrounding his relationship to Frederica. We have already seen that these selfobject needs existed prior to actually meeting her and her family. They continued on into the relationship. Using our occult yardstick, we can demonstrate that they persisted throughout Goethe's involvement with the young woman and, as we might expect, at its termination. (We recall that both Freud and Jung had similar occult experiences when they lost intense selfobject relationships.)

There are object-level anxieties evident in Goethe's phobia about kissing Frederica. Like other adolescents, the young man is frightened by sexuality. But there are also pre-oedipal anxieties as well. First, Goethe recalls a "curse" laid on his kissing another by a former love, Lucinda: "I saw Frederica standing opposite to her, paralysed at the sight, pale, and feeling the consequences of the curse, of which she knew nothing" (*Truth and Fiction,* vol. 2, p. 75). Yet he adds that there was a narcissistic advantage in retaining the superstition: "My lips, whether consecrated or cursed, appeared to me more important than usual; and with no little complacency was I aware of my self-denying conduct" (p. 76). In a series of exquisite passages Goethe weaves a rich description of his deep affection for Frederica (he allows her to kiss him, finally) and, at the same time, his understanding that these days of happiness would not last. Indeed, at first he says that writing to her and reading her letters were nearly as satisfying as seeing her, yet, within the same paragraph, he concludes that "this [written] intercourse" became more and more pleasant, "nay, afterward became pleasanter and dearer to me" (p. 77).

In the same vein, the sixty-year-old man writing these memoirs says, "We do not meditate on ourselves when we look in a mirror; but we feel that we exist, and allow ourselves to pass" (*Truth and Fiction*, vol. 2, p. 79). Recalling our discussion of mirrors, we should conclude that this is the sentiment of a person deeply sure of himself and not subject to fragmentation. Yet one doubts that it was true of the twenty-one-year-old student who found himself deeply in love with a girl who could not remain in his life beyond a short period of time.

As Goethe matured, took a law degree, and enlarged the scope of his literary ambition, he felt more and more clearly that he would not stay near Frederica: "I went to see her less frequently, but our correspondence became so much the more animated. Absence made me free, and my whole affection first truly bloomed by this communication in the distance" (*Truth and Fiction*, vol. 2, pp. 118–19).

A Vision on the Road to Drusenheim

In the midst of planning his departure from Frederica, Goethe planned to see her one more time. He noted, "Those were painful days, the memory of which has not remained with me" (*Truth and Fiction*, vol. 2, p. 120).

> When, seated on my horse, I held out my hand to her, there were tears in her eyes; and I felt very uneasy. I now rode along the footpath toward Drusenheim, and here one of the most singular forebodings took possession of me. I saw, not with the eyes of the body, but with those of the mind, my own figure coming toward me, on horseback, and on the same road, attired in a dress which I had never worn. (*Truth and Fiction*, vol. 2, p. 120)

As before, when he felt particularly bereft of a loving maternal (or sisterly) selfobject relationship, Goethe turned to the visual arts for solace and renewal. Immediately following his occult vision of himself (returning to the woman he had just left), he hurried to Mannheim. There he promised to let himself view the collection of classical statues, especially Laocoon and the Apollo Belvedere.

The former statue, with its gigantic father figure struggling to free the two sons engulfed by a horrible serpent, especially attracted Goethe. Applying his deep empathic sense to the group, he elaborated an interpretation of the mental state of each character. Although a colleague failed to show "any special esteem" (*Truth and Fiction*, vol. 2, p. 123) for his interpretation, he retained it and employed it in a later piece.[18]

Before leaving this discussion it may prove helpful to note yet another occult experience that Goethe describes. Like all the others we have so far examined, this too occurred after a major impairment to a selfobject relationship, followed by an actual separation. Although it is not as dramatic as the vision on the road to Drusenheim, it illustrates directly my central theorem.

Following a quarrel with his sister, who had devoted herself to him, Goethe arranges a long excursion into the country, "free as to my resolution, but oppressed as to my feelings—in a condition when the presence of silently living nature is so beneficial to us" (*Truth and Fiction*, vol. 2, p. 182). Walking by himself, seeking some response to his deepest wish, he happens upon an occult solution: "From the depth of my soul, arose, as it were, an absolute command, according to which, without delay, I was to fling this knife into the river. If I saw it fall, my wish to become an artist would be fulfilled; but if the sinking of the knife was concealed . . . I was to abandon the wish and the endeavour" (p. 182).

Although he tosses the knife immediately upon conceiving this test, he does so in a way that precludes any direct confirmation: he sees the splash, but not the knife enter the water. He adds, "For the moment, at least, the external world was spoiled for me: I abandoned myself to my imaginations and feelings . . ." (*Truth and Fiction*, vol. 2, p. 183). I think that this is a beautiful description of a sequence that begins with the loss of his sister (and the selfobject functions she fulfilled for him), followed by narcissistic vulnerability, followed by a half-hearted occult solution that is designed to reduce that narcissistic tension, followed by a period of depression. The great poet of nature here finds the "external" world unattractive, that is, it does not manifest loving maternal interests in his fate and feelings. To save himself he must withdraw to a more ideal world.

THE OCCULT MOOD:
THE PAST RECOVERED

In the occult mood, images and thoughts of times past are more important than the accurate perception of current actual relationships. As Goethe said of his relationship to Gretchen, and later to Frederica, he could enjoy thinking about these women and savoring their images within his imagination, but he could not abide their presence. The occult mood occurs in response to fragmentation anxiety. It has the central task of restoring a sense of coherence and stability to the self. To this task images, especially paintings and photographs, appear particularly well suited. For images, like the statuary to which Goethe felt drawn, do not vary. They do not alter in front of one's eyes. Images are direct, unchanging, and fixed. Images are therefore unalterable portraits of the loved one (the selfobject) who is unavailable and lost.

In the midst of his great struggles against his own psychosis, following the break with Freud, Jung found himself drawn to painting and sculpting, even at times playing with blocks. In all these activities he secured for himself stable and coherent representations of a nonfragmented self. Jung's later formulations of his archetype theory and his enthusiasm for guided affective imagery as a therapeutic mode retain this early affection for images (or symbols). In many ways Jung views the aims of psychotherapy to comprise the examination and classification of the internal images (as in dreams) that emerge to consciousness out of the personal and collective layers of the unconscious.

Given this orientation we can see why Jungian theorists also find it necessary to bring to their patients' awareness "archetypal" images found in the histories of art and religion. In each case, occult theorists give to images in all forms a weight that far transcends mere aesthetic pleasures. The great images of the smiling Buddha, Christ on the cross, and the Yin-Yang symbol from Taoism yield, according to occult teaching, increased security and serenity for those who view them. When Jung finds that a patient's dreams contain more and more clearly identifiable symbols of an unbroken circle (a mandala), he believes these are direct signs of psychic balance. Since psychic balance is the aim of therapy, the presence of these magic circles signifies that the end of treatment has been reached—cure. (In his first great Jungian text, *Symbols of Transformation*,[19] Jung found it necessary to use hundreds of illustrations to validate his claims.)

There is, however, a second kind of stability. As I suggested above, one can look for stability either in a fixed portrait of the lost selfobject (its image), or one can find stability within the processes that govern one's relationships to others, including those who perform selfobject roles for us.

Two Kinds of Stability: Pattern in Change

We have assumed that the search for a stable self is universal. The basic need to feel coherent and unfragmented requires each of us to find some way to feel that our world is predictable so that our selves will remain unshattered. Occult beliefs and teachings offer one form of stability. Occult teachers claim that the iron rule of causality is suspended: we are free, in the occult mood, of the constraints imposed on us by natural laws of force and reaction, cause and effect. In a similar way, occult teachers claim that space does not really separate us from loved ones, for space can be crossed in an instant of telepathic communication. The oceans of distance that separate one person from another can dry up, instantaneously, when occult powers are invoked. So too, the ordinary flow of time, with its inexorable pull away from the present, can be stopped and reversed. Occult teachers contradict the usual belief that time flows in only one direction. In the occult mood we are reunited with long-dead persons; we meld past time and present time together; we reclaim as living and real loved ones who left us long ago. The occult mood is also a mood in which the future is wrestled out of limbo and brought to the present. Occult teachers tell us that there are moments when, through special gifts, one can know the future, see its operations, and sometimes control it. In all these ways occult teachings are schemes to create a static world. In that static world nothing actually comes into existence and nothing passes from existence. In the occult world the laws of space, time, and causality that seem to govern human life are suspended.

To persons outside of occult teachings, the shape of occult experiences is predictable. This principle (or assumption) has led us to examine occult events in Augustine, Freud, and Goethe, persons separated by time, nationality, and character. In each of their stories we find a pattern of loss followed by occult attempts to repair that loss.

In contrast to the occult mood, one may feel safe enough to search for stability amidst change. In contrast to the occult principle of synchronicity, which denies causal thinking, one may seek to locate patterns between cause and effect, that is, to locate what deficits give rise to which effects. To do that, to find an underlying pattern of stable change, one must be willing to tolerate a prolonged search.

This was the feature of Kohut's work that I felt made it most applicable to an inquiry into occult experience. Kohut has permitted us to identify causal sequences, that is, to find what seems to be a pattern that unites the ancients and the moderns, the great and the ordinary among us. I have identified this pattern as the need to find occult solutions to the loss of selfobject relationships. The interpretations of this pattern offered in this book may prove to be erroneous or limited. Yet the search for pattern is a search for stability, too. In this sense Kohut's propositions about selfobject needs ought to be as satisfying, at some level, as the occult beliefs that we have investigated. The nature of Kohut's scientific claims differs from those of the occultists, but our hopes to find a stable patterned world that we can understand do not differ.

The Persistence of the Self

In our discussion of fragmentation anxiety the issue never was, Am I real? but Will I persist? The difference between these two questions is crucial. The first question can be answered easily: Yes, you do exist.

The second cannot be answered with perfect certainty. The question, Will I persist?, in all its articulate and inarticulate variations, can only be addressed to another loving, caring person in whose hands we must trust ourselves. That other person is precisely the one who must perform those psychological functions (selfobject functions) that permit us to bridge our current experience of self with an anticipated future experience.

We return again to the problem of time. We have seen that following acute moments of fragmentation anxiety an occult experience ensues. In this occult experience time as an ongoing sequence of events is overcome. Jung's profound concerns with synchronicity, developed from his own struggles against fragmentation, show vividly how a psychological doctrine can partly overcome the terror of diachronic experience. Synchronicity declares that the temporal sequence of events is of no consequence. Causal explanations require one to know which action occurred first: for causes always precede effects. But synchronicity is an acausal principle: it states that the sequence of events, their temporal relationship to one another, is of no concern. Rather, what links one event to another is the meaningfulness we can discover between the two events. These strands of meaning are direct links in a chain forged by the observer. That chain of discovered meanings serves to bind together a self that threatens to dissolve into unimaginable terror.

The issue of the persistence of the self has a long philosophical history. The great French philosopher René Descartes declared in his famous meditation on the permanence of the self, *Cogito ergo sum* ("I think, therefore I am"). Harry Guntrip calls this meditation the perfect schizoid formula. Guntrip means that Descartes's formula expresses directly the disturbing thought that one cannot prove that one exists. If one assumes a radical, skeptical stance and demands a logical demonstration that one's experience of self is valid, one cannot simply point out that the majority of persons believe that they are actual beings, surviving in time. As Descartes notes, they might all be wrong. As Jung says in *Memories, Dreams, Reflections,* in some moods one may wonder if we are all not cast members of someone else's dream. When that dreamer awakes we might fade away, like a dream forgotten in the morning.

To counter this skeptical conclusion and prevent the fragmentation anxiety associated with it, Descartes argues that although one may doubt that one is an actual, physical being, living independently of others, one cannot doubt that one doubts. In the very act of doubting one expresses doubt. I can doubt that I have extension in space and time; I cannot doubt that I doubt. This undoubtable fact, that at least I exist as a thinking being, gives us a foundation for supposing that our ordinary (nonfragmented) experience of self is authentic. Descartes generalizes this dictum to argue that since I think, there must be a thinking object, and that is myself. (Like all metaphysical claims, even this modest assertion has been challenged. Strictly speaking, Descartes can only conclude: since I doubt, there is doubting. But that does not prove that the doubting belongs, necessarily, to the thing called "I.")

Descartes's demonstration does not quiet all our possible fears. He may have proved that during the moment one doubts one is, at least, existing as a doubter, but what about afterward? What guarantees that we will persist over time as a coherent entity? When we sleep or fall unconscious or let our minds wander (or free-associate), what thing or force will hold us together? Kohut and other contemporary analysts have answered this question: good-enough mothering. With an adequate foundation in self-selfobject relationship to the mothering person, we learn to feel coherent in ourselves and to find new selfobject relationships when we need them. In a word: selfobjects are those other, real persons who are empathic enough to sense these needs and meet them adequately. Meeting them adequately means that the mother (that is, the mothering person) grasps the child's (and adult's) needs to feel that his or her existence as a person is more or less guaranteed by the actions of the other person. In metaphysical terms the good-enough mother inculcates a sense that "one cannot fall out of the world."

Resting in the Everlasting Arms

Human beings do not exist as independent agencies, as insulated actors who have no vital need to be in relationship with others. To have no others available to oneself is to fall into the terrors of fragmentation. Good parents, good friends, and good therapists find ways to dissolve the barriers that separate one person from another, one self from another self.

To illustrate how a good mother can accomplish this, Kohut turns to one of his favorite examples: the little piggy game. In this game, a parent examines in sequence each toe or finger of the child, playfully tugging on it, naming it, and then turning to the next part. In a real sense, to focus upon these *parts* of the child's body, rather than upon the *whole* of the child, is a mild form of fragmentation. In fact, in some versions of the game, the "last little piggy" is lost, taken away, and it cries "wee, wee" all the way home.

> The psychological precondition for the success of this game is given by the fact that a cohesive self has already been established, but that its cohesion is new and therefore still insecure. . . . One secret of the success of this

game is the mother's empathic grasp of the degree of the child's ability to tolerate this threat to his newly formed cohesion. In focusing on each of his toes, one by one, she takes the small toddler's barely established cohesive body-self apart—yet, watching his tense face (which, however, after many repetitions simultaneously expresses glee at the anticipated joyful resolution), she does not allow the threat to become too great, and at just the right moment she will embrace the whole child and the fragmentation is again undone.[20]

The absolute horror that dismemberment arouses in all people would seem to be another instance of fragmentation anxiety. We note that "castration anxiety," one of the central anxieties Freud said animated neurotic defenses, is also a profound symbol of fragmentation: a crucial defining body part is cut off and so the whole body-self destroyed. The European response to the New World, following the first reports of cannibalism among the American Indians, focused primarily upon the dismemberment of the body. In many vivid and wildly romanticized woodcuts one sees statuesque nude women and heroic nude males cavorting with human limbs.[21] In this case, the white European culture found the other culture to be a perfect screen on which to project its deepest anxieties. The woodcuts that depicted these highly imaginary scenes were shocking, uncanny, and very popular.

In Kohut's example, the mother is empathic precisely because she senses the limits of her child's capacity to tolerate the game. The game, like some aspects of analytic therapy, permits the child to experience a modicum of fragmentation, but, just as importantly, demonstrates that someone will be there. In contrast, and as Winnicott argues in a distinct context, infants, children, and adults will tolerate a lack of maternal (selfobject) response for only so long. Once that temporal limit is passed, the game has ceased and trauma has begun.

A three-and-one-half-year-old, for example, was persuaded to nap with her mother. She did so on the understanding that the mother would be there when she woke up. She slept, woke up, and found the mother standing in the room. She burst into uncontrollable sobbing and was not comforted until the mother apologized for not being beside her. Some patients who are especially prone to fragmentation find the end of the analytic hour difficult in a similar way: having entered into a self-selfobject relationship with the good-enough analyst, the sudden end of the hour evokes both rage (How could you do this to me?) and depression (How long will I be without you?). In retrospect one supposes that the little girl permitted herself to sleep, which is to suffer a moment of fragmentation, on the assumption that her mother would be there waiting on the other side, as it were, when she awoke.

When she woke and found herself "abandoned," she experienced a moment of fragmentation and anger: How dare she fail me that way?

GOETHE AND THE CONSOLIDATION OF SELF

All people are limited in their capacity to tolerate fragmentation anxiety. We each have a point beyond which we retreat from object relations and seek narcissistic sustenance (sometimes in alcohol, sometimes in sexual actions, sometimes in occult experience). When that point is reached and there is no adequate selfobject response, one must repair oneself. In Jung, this took the form of delving into his own fragmented experience and searching there for stable underlying paradigms—what he termed the archetypes. In Goethe, self-repair took the form of temporary occult experiences, followed by a deep fascination with nature, and that, in turn, followed by artistic labor.

As usual, Goethe anticipates these psychological issues when he describes, in exquisite detail, the processes by which he composed his first sensational novel, *The Sufferings of Young Werther*, in 1774, when he was twenty-four. After describing his criticisms of English "graveyard" poetry, and the numerous melancholy poses that young men of his time assumed, Goethe says he had long contemplated suicide. But his suicide had to be of noble sort. It would not do to use a mere gun on himself. Goethe rather required himself to plunge a "handsome, well-polished dagger" into his heart (*Truth and Fiction*, vol. 2, p. 214). At one point, Goethe raised such a dagger to his chest, but could not force himself to push it through his skin and into his chest. Since he could not do this, he "resolved to live. But, to be able to do this with cheerfulness, I was obliged to solve a poetical problem, by which all that I had felt, thought, and fancied upon this important point should be reduced to words" (p. 214).

In the terms developed in this book, Goethe's poetic problems centered on consolidating his many talents, separating himself from yet another painful love affair with an impossible woman, and reversing the moments of fragmentation that preceded his attempts at suicide. The accuracy of this last judgment is illustrated, I think, in the imagery Goethe uses to describe the moment in which his plans for *The Sufferings of Young Werther* fell into place: Goethe heard that Carl Wilhelm Jerusalem, a young man he knew slightly, had killed himself following two narcissistic blows: he had been humiliated by a superior officer, and a friend's wife had rejected his ardent affections.[22] Goethe recognized in Jerusalem's actions his own impulses. Yet Goethe avoided Jerusalem's fate:

> [A]t this moment the plan of "Werther" was formed, and the whole shot together from all sides, and became a solid mass, just as water in a vessel, which stands upon the point of freezing, is converted into hard ice by the most gentle shake. (*Truth and Fiction*, vol. 2, p. 214)

I think that this is a beautiful metaphor for the process of rapid consolidation of a self that has overcome fragmentation (or what Goethe sometimes terms "halfness" [*Truth and Fiction*, vol. 2, p. 215]). In another context, the metaphor of self as frozen water might seem ominous; here, though, it evokes the power of the moment when a transition of state occurs, from liquid to solid in an instant, in the twinkling of an eye. Jerusalem's suicide (which could not have been a gentle shake to him) affected Goethe deeply because it gave him an immediate creative solution:

> To hold fast this singular prize, to render present to myself, and to carry out in all its parts, a work of such importance and various contents, was the more material to me, as I had again fallen into a painful situation, which left me even less hope than those which had preceded it, and foreboded only sadness, if not vexation. (*Truth and Fiction*, vol. 2, pp. 214–15)

Having finished the short book in some four weeks, as if in a trance, Goethe felt "as if after a general confession, once more happy and free, and justified in beginning a new life" (*Truth and Fiction*, vol. 2, p. 217).

It might appear that writing *Werther* was itself a sufficient achievement for Goethe and its reception by others less important. If so, my general argument that even artistic geniuses require actual selfobjects would be suspect. It would also support a notion of art as a lonely struggle of oneself against oneself, as if one might compose poetry and yet desire no readers. But Goethe himself does not support this picture of creativity. Having sweated out the novel in a remarkably short time, Goethe reads it to a colleague, Merck. But Goethe's novel fails to move him: "Without luring from him any sign of admiration I adopted a more pathetic strain" (*Truth and Fiction*, vol. 2, p. 218). But even this fails to shake from Merck sufficient praise and admiration. Goethe says Merck's failure to praise him made Goethe quite beside himself: "Had a fire been at hand, I should have at once thrown in the work" (p. 218). We learn later that Merck had been in terrible psychological straits and had not actually heard the novel as Goethe read it aloud. Keeping directly to the issue at hand, Goethe adds that he had a clean copy made and, precisely on the day his sister married, received a letter from an editor requesting a manuscript: "Such a coincidence I looked upon as a favourable omen" (p. 219).

Again, when he felt narcissistically vulnerable because his colleague seemed less interested than he had hoped, and because his devoted sister was less available to him than before, Goethe looks for a bit of occult validation. He finds it in the coincidence that having lost a sister he gained an editor, that is, someone who appreciated his creative works and who would praise him.

SUMMARY:
BURDENS OF CREATIVITY

Even very creative artists, like Goethe, and creative thinkers, like Augustine, require the presence of actual persons to sustain their narcissistic achievements. I suggested that this was especially important to Augustine when he composed his *Confessions:* his reader's response was crucial to maintaining his newly forged sense of a saved self. In a similar way, Freud needed followers and Jung needed to find his inner experiences validated in traditional teachings of Eastern religions. In each case the other (as audience, as disciple, as fellow mystic) affirmed the validity of these particular routes toward self-coherence.

Which is better? Which route is the more adaptive or higher level? These are fair questions—an ideal book would answer them; I do not. I am not, however, proposing complete agnosticism with regard to the question of validity and value. To the degree that occult teachings direct one's attention away from others, that is, actual human beings, and toward *images* of human beings (or other spiritual beings), they are less adequate.

To invoke an old distinction from logic, occult teachings often claim that the map of the territory is equivalent to the territory itself.[23] In this sense occult teachings are intellectualistic; they elaborate portraits of lost selfobjects, but usually mistake those portraits for the actual, lost persons. In this sense occult teachings are similar to idolatry: they elaborate exquisite pictures of what one needs but provide no route to the objects themselves.

7
*Alternative Solutions
to Fragmentation
Anxiety*

In this final chapter I summarize my previous discussion and draw two conclusions. First, because selfobject needs are universal and unending, everyone is liable to occult experiencing. The shape of that experience is determined by numerous factors, but its intensity is determined by the fragmentation anxiety aroused: the more anxiety, the greater the intensity of the occult event.

Second, there are alternative solutions to the problem of overcoming fragmentation anxiety. These solutions are offered by religious thought, aesthetic and intellectual doctrines, and literature. Augustine was able to secure himself against fragmentation anxiety by using, in part, his audience as imagined selfobjects whose response to his confession helped him reconstitute himself. This is true, surely, of other authors as well. When Goethe struggled with his own suicidal impulses he suffered moments of severe fragmentation. He overcame these deficits by writing his famous novel *The Sufferings of Young Werther,* and projecting into its hero his own extreme moods. In that novel we find Goethe's darker moods made flesh, examined by the author, and, finally, rejected. When the novel was published, many young men identified themselves completely with young Werther. They too felt caught in an impossible love affair, and they chose Werther's solution to end their agonies: suicide. These unfortunate young men should have identified themselves with Goethe, who saved himself by composing the novel and killing its hero.

Occult beliefs and actions center upon representations of persons or personal spirits, but not upon actual three-dimensional objects. In the two stories of occult experience we considered in the Introduction, for example, each actor in those dramas focused upon images or ideas about spiritual beings, not upon solid beings themselves. These representations of other people are fixed and therefore stable. They are concrete representations of a self that is not fragmented. Such representations help preserve a stable, coherent self because they reveal the existence of selfobjects located exactly where one needs them. In this way occult beliefs help prevent fragmentation anxiety because they demonstrate the existence of "personal" powers that will not permit us to fall into terror. Occult beliefs do so by promising us that nothing really changes, that death is an illusion, and that we can retrieve what seems lost.

In contrast to the occult response to fragmentation anxiety, artistic and scientific work may help one discover within change itself a principle of constancy. I do not mean this to be a paradoxical statement. Unlike occult solutions to fragmentation anxiety, some forms of aesthetic doctrines and other intellectual systems affirm the centrality of pattern in human experience. Patterns of birth, adolescence, maturation, and death are as constant, in their way, as the static world portrayed in occult teachings.

To affirm *this* level of constancy one need not deny the actual existence of change, loss, mourning, and restitution. Some artistic achievements, like Goethe's *The Sufferings of Young Werther*,[1] remain important to our generation because they demonstrate to us the truth that adolescent terrors are not new and that there is a pattern, a meaning, even to these episodes of fragmentation. Other forms of art seem to offer similar demonstrations of pattern within change. It would be interesting to consider how painting, for example, affects us and how it counters fragmentation anxiety; however, I consider three great classes of solutions: (1) those offered by religious beliefs, (2) those offered by aesthetic and intellectual doctrines, like Marxism, and (3) those offered through literary experience.

I have said that occult experience is a response to fragmentation anxiety and that occult beliefs are attempts to prevent fragmentation anxiety from reoccurring. Everyone, at some time or another, feels vulnerable to fragmentation. Yet not everyone has occult experience, nor does everyone take up occult beliefs. There are, in other words, other solutions to the problem of fragmentation. I have focused primarily on one: that offered by the occult. I have also described artistic solutions to fragmentation anxiety: we saw this especially in the lives of Verdi and Goethe. It appears, also, in sections of Carl Gustav Jung's autobiographical account, *Memories, Dreams, Reflections*,[2] when he describes his struggles to discover if he were primarily an artist or a scientist.

Occult experience occurs in response to the feeling that one is falling apart, fragmenting into separate pieces that cannot be put back together again. This threat to the coherence of the self arises because one has lost access to another person whose principal task was to help maintain one's boundaries. These selfobject tasks are as important for the survival of the self as are eating and drinking. As Kohut says in numerous passages, the other person's role as selfobject is to give us the "psychological oxygen" without which we cannot live. Using this metaphor, we can see why the threat to the loss of the selfobject is so disturbing: without the selfobject one will suffocate and die. I find that occult experience is one way people retrieve the lost connections between themselves and their selfobjects.

RELIGIOUS SOLUTIONS
TO FRAGMENTATION ANXIETY

There are other ways to retrieve a sense of relatedness to others and to the great powers that dominate human life but that are hidden, that are occult. The way toward reunification of self and other that has enjoyed the greatest respect and continues to dominate the West is offered by religion. The great world religions, like Judaism or Christianity, offer a view of the self and its relationships that is intrinsically one of relationship. These relationships exist in each dimension of human encounter: between self and others, between self and nature, and between self and God.[3] In their theological traditions and within their folk traditions, even in our time, Judaism and Christianity portray the ultimate force that rules human beings as a personal one. This personal force, God, will sustain us through all tribulations, losses, and suffering if we are in relationship to God. This is true even if we cannot see God, even if the divine is not tangible. Paul says that we can still hope for eventual reunion:

> We know that the whole creation has been groaning in travail until now; and not only the creation, but we ourselves, who have the first fruits of the Spirit, groan inwardly as we wait for adoption as sons, the redemption of our bodies. For in this hope we are saved. Now hope that is seen is not hope. For who hopes for what he sees? But if we hope for what we do not see, we wait for it with patience. (Romans 8:22–25)

There is no challenge, no task, and no situation of despair that God has not seen and solved through God's love. God's love is not merely the love of a parent for a child, or a friend for a friend. According to traditional teachings, God's love is that of a part of the self for the whole self. God acts as both an esteemed parent who responds to God's creatures, God's children, with love and discipline; and God acts as a selfobject who, in our time of collapse, will not fail us. Given these immensely deep views of God one might wonder why religion has not preempted entirely occult teachings.

One answer to this question is the historical observation that traditional religions have lost the battle in their struggles against the claims of scientists and philosophers who rejected the teachings of the church. The rise of occultism in the West is linked to the decrease in the intellectual status attributed to religious thought. Arthur Conan Doyle, for example, was heir to a critical and scientific tradition that contradicted Christian teachings about the soul and its fate. By the middle of the nineteenth century in Europe and America the most esteemed intellectual task was science and people's faith rested in scientists, not theologians.

In response to the overwhelming intellectual victory granted to science and scientists over religion and religionists, occult experts identified themselves with the scientists. Occult terminology and treatises almost always mimic the forms of scientific communication dominant in the period. We saw, for example, that Carl Jung, the founder of analytical psychology, and an American psychoanalyst, Jule Eisenbud, both claimed that their occult principles were actually newly discovered laws within the domain of psychology. The ironic aspect of occult teachings is that although their format may be scientific, with tables, charts, and photographs that purport to document the alleged events, their content is religious. In many occult treatises, for example, those by the American mystic Edgar Cayce, one finds claims about reincarnation, life after death, and salvation, which are traditional religious ideas, transformed into empirical claims.

This deep yearning to appear scientific animates many occult descriptions of other realms, like that of Atlantis or Mars, and other modes of being, like heaven. In his *History of Spiritualism*,[4] Conan Doyle recounts numerous descriptions of heaven sent to us through mediums and other occult modes of communication, like spirit writing. In these accounts, as in other accounts of occult realms, are detailed descriptions of the "higher sciences" available to denizens of those realms. Indeed, earthly scientists who cross over to life in heaven are guaranteed access to laboratories and facilities that are well equipped to help them continue their research efforts in their new home.

Jung said explicitly that he wished to find a way to retrieve, through his psychology, the essential truths of the twelfth-century alchemists he studied. These essential truths (or wishes) are all evident in the alchemical treatises of that period: the search for immortality, for an elixir of youth, and for the divine center within the self that is identical to the godhead.

AESTHETIC SOLUTIONS:
THE SEARCH FOR PATTERN

Artists like Goethe also respond to fragmentation anxiety. They make no promises about an afterlife, yet they too demand some sense of permanence about themselves. They gain it in their idealized efforts: the work of art. Goethe, whom we have seen in his most chaotic moments, reflected upon the narcissistic need to rescue a sense of self without recourse to occult beliefs. He made this concern the central theme of his poem "Constancy in Change."[5]

The poem begins with reference to an ancient anxiety expressed in the *carpe diem* poems of antiquity. Time passes quickly, everyone dies; therefore, seize the day and make the best of it. In the first five stanzas Goethe describes how our bodies change from youthful vigor to middle-age lassitude to old age. Against these profound narcissistic injuries, in which our bodily self falls apart, we have no physical defense.

All are gone; this substitution
Has your name and nothing more.
Like a wave it lifts and passes,
Back to atoms on the shore.

Goethe's aesthetic answer to this form of anxiety is to find the existence of a pattern within change and to document that pattern within the pattern of his poetry. That documentation, his art, is given to him by a mothering figure, the Muse to whom Homer sang. It will last forever:

See in each beginning, ending,
Double aspects of the One;
Here, amid the stampeding objects,
Be among the first to run,
Thankful to a muse whose favor
Grants to you one unchanging thing:
What the heart can hold to ponder;
What the spirit shapes to sing.

(Trans. J. F. Nims, 1983).

While I think Nims's is a fine poetic translation and the most moving of the many available, it does not convey entirely the force of the

German term translated as "unchanging." That term, *Unvergängliches*, means something like the absolutely imperishable. It is opposed to the transitory, the ephemeral, all those earthly things that pass away and perish, which are *vergänglich*. Goethe's term refers to that part of the self that is absolutely unlike the transitory structures, our bodies and our ordinary consciousness, that all pass away.

This might appear to be a religious idea. One might believe that Goethe (and perhaps Kohut) both advance a solution to fragmentation anxiety identical to that discovered by the great world religions some three or four thousand years ago: the doctrine of soul. There is some merit in this point of view. Human beings have suffered fragmentation anxiety for as long as they have conceptualized their own death. The immortal soul is imperishable. It will last forever in a state of glory. The doctrine of soul overcomes and conquers the threat of personal annihilation.

Goethe's solution to the problem of fragmentation is not the same as the doctrine of soul and its immortality. That doctrine asserts that beneath the surface of change and loss is an immortal substance, the soul, which does not change. Goethe suggests that within the processes of change itself, and within our consciousness of those events, we may find an enduring pattern, a form. Because we are alive and conscious of that fact, we can perceive that permanence of form precisely as we perceive the processes of change that compose each moment. The arts and other creative achievements of the human spirit provide us viewpoints from which we may perceive these forms.

Are these forms wholly independent of us? Are the arts subtle forms of science that permit us to find truths that have lain there waiting for us? No. We note a simple but significant fact: Goethe makes these claims about the permanent features of life within a highly formal, rigorous structure called poetry. One vital dimension of the continuity he describes in "Constancy in Change" is, in fact, guaranteed only by the poem's structures or forms. Like other products of the human spirit (*Geist*), poetry helps us create the forms and objects we need to discover. This facet of human creativity suggests that what we need most is not simply out there waiting for us to call it into existence. The poem, novel, or insight that links us to others and helps us preserve a sense of self is created by human beings who share the same needs for permanence. Like the good-enough mother and the numerous ways in which she attends to us, human cultural achievements are co-created. We find in them what we need because we have, in part, created them out of those needs. Goethe's poem "Constancy in Change" expresses a solution to the issue of fragmentation anxiety that is neither religious nor occult. As we have seen, even as a young man Goethe rejected traditional religious authorities and traditional religious teachings. Goethe felt that his artistic genius elevated him to a status from which he could assess folk religion and reject it. In its place, Goethe substituted the intellectual achievements of his poetry, his novels, scientific work, and his great biography, *Truth and Fiction.*

MOURNING AND RESTITUTION
IN JOHN KEATS

John Keats's Boyhood

Suffering the loss of loved persons does not guarantee artistic success. But in Keats's life, cut short and devastated by tragedy, personal loss dominated his experience and his poetry. When Keats was eight and a half (in April 1804), his father was thrown from a horse, cracked his skull, and died. His family was almost destitute, since his father's small holdings were tied up in court battles. His mother remarried two months later. In March 1805, his maternal grandfather died. This left the family in additional difficulty since the will was exceedingly obscure. Four years later, his mother was ill at Christmas and died in March 1810, of consumption (tuberculosis).[6]

At fourteen John became the family protector. His grandmother appointed two trustees to oversee the accumulated family monies and to help raise John, his two brothers, and his sister. One trustee died; the other, Richard Abbey (whom most lovers of Keats have come to hate), decided that the boys should earn their keep and learn a trade. He apprenticed John out as a surgeon's assistant. Keats was an excellent student and did well at his work.

Three years later, in 1814, while a medical student, John wrote his first known verses. His grandmother's death that December meant that his young sister had to leave her brothers and live with Abbey, who prevented John from seeing her as easily and as often as both wished. When Keats was twenty-three, his adored brother, George, married and left for America. His brother, Tom, began to show signs of consumption. John nursed him, held him in his arms as he died, and buried him in December 1818. In the meantime, John had become involved with Fanny Brawne, and late in 1819 they became engaged. Within three months he himself began to show signs of consumption. He offered to break off his engagement with Fanny, but was refused. But by the middle of that year, 1820, when he was twenty-five, Keats was gravely ill. He had written most of the poetry he would ever compose. His doctors believed that he could not last through another English winter. They ordered him to Italy, where he arrived in the late fall. There, four months later, in February, he died.

Keats and Memory

Given a life filled with so much sorrow, it is not surprising that we find someone of Keats's intelligence pondering the nature of death and the suddenness with which pleasure is replaced by pain. Memory is the culprit. Our deepest suffering lies in memory. Yet memory is also our sole source of pleasure; it safeguards our fondest wishes and, at the same time, our fondest recollections. Memory is secure, it is ours, and cannot rust or be destroyed by moths, as Keats says in one of his letters. Life can surprise us, but memory is stable and unchanging. Hence there is a moment, a sacred point of transition, in which an actual sensed pleasure is transformed into its memory. Keats celebrates this moment of reconciliation between desire and loss in many poems. It is memorialized in his phrase "to gild the lapses of time."

The links between Keats's traumatic boyhood and his art are many. We cannot doubt that his sufferings shaped his art and life. But those sufferings, which were severe and continuous, are not as rare as his genius, which is not as rare as his poetic achievement. We can say that Keats's life and even his pain were typical, but his courage and his poetry are singular.

Having lost father, mother, and beloved brother, and himself imperiled with consumption, Keats wished to escape to an earlier state of infantile existence where such trauma could not touch him. This is most obvious with regard to his mother, whom he adored in life, nursed on her deathbed, and revered in death. Keats recalled the deathbed scene numerous times, in his private letters and his poems, some of which are precise descriptions of the initial stages of pulmonary tuberculosis.

Keats was fascinated by death, but not as the destruction of life. He described it as an uncanny sleep, mysterious in its origins and mysterious in its outcome.[7] I believe that Keats moved from a passive identification of sleep and poetry and death, each promising a relief from the painfulness of mourning, to an active confrontation of that pain. Consequently, his evaluation of poetry changed. This is most evident in his unfinished and unpublished cantos, *The Fall of Hyperion*, which we consider below. In his earliest poetry Keats hoped to recapture a "gilded moment"; in his later poems he documented why that wish could not be fulfilled.

Keats and the Restoration of
the Lost Object

In his earliest poems, for example, in his imitations of Spenser, Keats is unconvincing. He strains to evoke fierce portraits of manliness and power, but his imagery betrays him:

Lo! I must tell a tale of chivalry:
For large white plumes are dancing in mine eye.

For while I muse, the lance points slantingly
Athwart the morning air: some lady sweet,
Who cannot feel for cold in her tender feet,
From the worn top of some old battlement
Hails it with tears, her stout defender sent.
(Specimen of an Induction to a Poem, spring 1816)

In other poems from this period Keats writes about the fluttering, stirring, nestling movements of breezes, about soft sounds, fading music, silence, and the sad, sweet, flowing tears of vaguely pictured young ladies. While these are conventional poeticisms, in Keats they are alive. He is acutely sensitive to such transitional moments.

Your accents bland
Still sounded in my ears, when I no more
Could hear your footsteps touch the gravelly floor.
Sometimes I lost them, and then found them again;
You changed the footpath for the grassy plain.
(To Charles Cowden Clark, 122–26)

This is a beautiful message of love. Keats stalks the transitional moment. He recalls the end of a conversation and listens attentively to the sounds of his friend's departure. He can distinguish the path from the grassy plain by the subtle alteration in the sound of the footsteps.

We find a similar theme in *How Many Bards Gild the Lapses of Time?* and *On First Looking into Chapman's Homer.* "Gilding the lapses of time" expresses Keats's aim well: to preserve, through his art, those lost moments of lapsed time in which pleasure was turned into memory. Keats's fascination with drinking, sipping, tasting, and feeling and with female breasts are associated with lapses. It connotes maternal laps and the lapping of infants and small animals. These, in turn, are linked to experiences of satisfaction, swooning, hazy visions, and other transitional moments between sleep and waking. In these early poems Keats assigns himself a task: to secure these moments against the dissolution of time, just as the swan attempts to nestle its "diamond water" against the inevitable force of gravity.

Poets are special creatures who brood over the lapses of time and produce, from that concourse, the progeny of poetry: progeny that are immortal,

A thing of beauty is a joy forever
Its loveliness increases; it will never
Pass into nothingness.

(*Endymion*, 1–2, April 1817)

Keats counters the danger of regressing too far, too quickly, into idiosyncratic pleasures—into the lap of the idealized mother—by appealing to the male god, Apollo. He, the god of poetry, represents a mythical ideal of masculinity. Hence Keats asks:

What is more gentle than a wind in summer?
What is more soothing than the pretty hummer
That stays one moment in an open flower,
And buzzes cheerily from bower to bower?

He answers himself eighteen lines later, "Poesy, O Poesy! for thee I hold my pen." His invocation is also a prayer—should Apollo oblige him:

Then the events of this wide world I'd seize
Like a strong giant, and my spirit tease
Till at its shoulders it should proudly see
Wings to find out an immortality.

(*Sleep and Poetry*, 81–84, 1816)

Without the benefit of this fatherly, divine love, the poet cannot read what is written in nature. The gilded moments will dissolve, flit onwards:

The visions are all fled—the car is fled
Into the light of heaven, and in their stead
A sense of real things comes doubly strong,
And, like a muddy stream, would bear along
My soul to nothingness . . .

(155–59)

This urge toward a regressive identification with the mythic god, and the fear of "real things," appear again in Keats's lament, "How many bards gild the lapses of time," and in his more famous sonnet, *On First Looking into Chapman's Homer.* In the sonnet, Keats celebrates the momentary pleasure of *first* reading Chapman. The poem's central images are of finding oneself amazed, dumbfounded, and so stilled by the awesomeness of the scene, like Cortez's men who are "*silent* upon a peak in Darien."

This central theme reappears in the odes of 1819. Again and again Keats evokes images of the cessation of desire; neither its fulfillment nor its denial, only its permanent stasis. It is the growth of love, not its completion, that fascinates him:

> They lay calm-breathing on the bedded grass;
>   Their arms embraced, and their pinions too;
>   Their lips touch'd not, but had not bade adieu,
> As if disjoined by soft-handed slumber.
>
> (Ode to Psyche, 15–18)

> Adieu! adieu! thy plaintive anthem fades
>   Past the near meadows, over the still stream,
>   Up the hill-side; and now 'tis buried deep
>   In the next valley-glades:
> Was it a vision, or a waking dream?
> Fled is that music:—Do I wake or sleep?
>
> (Ode to a Nightingale, 75–80)

The central argument of *Ode on a Grecian Urn* is that happiest are those who have not seen the consummation of their love. And the greatness of art, the potter's and the poet's, is that they too can preserve such moments in their representations of "evergreen felicity."

Keats's Mature Poetry

In contrast to his earlier pursuit of the gilded moment, Keats sounds a new theme in his later poems: that moment of upswelling power in which an object is rocked gently. A fine example occurs in *Sleep and Poetry*:

> . . . as when ocean
> Heaves calmly its broad swelling smoothness o'er
> Its rocky marge, and balances once more,
> The patient weeds; that now unshent by foam
> Feel all about their undulating home.
>
> (376–80)

"Shent" is an ancient English word meaning disgraced or ruined. It is derived from the root *skande*, which means to be put to shame or confusion. Keats uses it to describe the seaweeds' "feelings" of upheaval when they are rocked by the wave. While this is gross personification, it is effective. Keats's celebrated empathy is here magnified by referring to their undulating home. This makes concrete and beautiful the conventional insight that emotional suffering is a kind of upheaval. This stanza occurs in the midst of Keats's account of naked nymphs who dry "cherishingly" Diana's timorous limbs. In *Endymion* Diana was a demon-lover who threatened the voyeuristic male; here her power and the poet's fascination are suggested by the image of the sea's immense power. His earlier lines stated his hopes for a gilded moment; these lines exemplify them. Their slowness and lassitude complement Keats's subject. Indeed, we cannot read and understand them without slowing down our own imaginative capacities. We can verify this if we recall how quickly an actual wave sweeps into the shore and subsides.

This stanza gains in power to the degree that it controls our response. It works like the hypnotist who insinuates himself into his subject's life by naming what the latter does. Once the subject recognizes that she is indeed breathing deeply and assents to the hypnotist's claims that it is his doing, the trance is accomplished. The essence of the trance is that an autonomous process, like breathing or private sensations of our body's status, is experienced as if it were now under the control of another. The occult aspect of hypnosis consists in turning what is an active capacity into something we suddenly experience as if it were outside our control. Keats's fascination with this kind of experience is evident in his numerous references to altered states of consciousness, from opium dreams to drunkenness to fever.[8]

This would not make Keats a unique poet. It would not account for his work, which is immortal, while the numerous paeans and harangues of sixties drug gurus, for example, have evaporated. Keats's achievement was to create artifacts that represent that (regressive) wish and, at the same time, represent an assessment of the constraints of reality upon it. His poems reveal emotional antinomies; they do not attempt to solve them.

To Gild Time Is to Freeze Time

The wish to gild time has its dark side, too. Keats revealed it in *The Eve of St. Agnes.*

> Having returned to her bedroom, a young maid, Madeline, undresses:
> Her rich attire creeps rustling to her knees:
> Half hidden like a mermaid in sea-weed,
> Pensive awhile she dreams, awake, and sees,
> In fancy, fair St. Agnes in her bed.
>
> (230–33)

The synesthesia of these lines is famous. But the posture in which Keats places his heroine is also noteworthy: because she is frozen in a state between sleep and wakefulness Madeline can hope to see what is not there; that is, she can hope to create a real thing out of her insubstantial wishes. She is dreaming while awake, a definition of an altered state of consciousness, if not psychosis.

Keats repeats this portrait in other poems where he describes women whose faces are contorted with grief, looking at but not seeing their surroundings. We cannot forget that he had seen such grief in his mother, then experienced it himself at her death, and then at his brother's death. For the child, the fact of death is doubly mysterious. Death takes away a loved and strong person and drives the remaining parent away—into a private and frightening world of suffering. It is said that Keats did not mourn the deaths of his family members in the usual way. I think he was terrified of repeating the suffering he had experienced so keenly; he knew that mourning is an intensely narcissistic and painful labor. The survivor's ego is caught up in the immense task of undoing and setting to rest each of the affectionate bonds with which it was tied to the deceased.

Hence mourning is a form of psychopathology. It is little remarked upon, as Freud notes in "Mourning and Melancholia," because it is so common.[9] As psychopathology, it is the inverse of public institutions, including death rituals that constrain mourning by shaping appropriate forms of bereavement. Mourning is exquisite and unrepresentable pain. Like all pain, it causes the ego to collapse upon itself: "The poet's soul is concentrated in his toothache." For the child caught up in a family where mourning is cut short, as was Keats's mourning when his mother remarried only two months after the death of her first husband, we suspect that grief unspoken or unspeakable will retain uncanny fascination. Keats was in this state for most of his adult life. We see this illustrated in his fragment, *The Fall of Hyperion*, where he describes his fascination with the attire of the priestess who mourns the fallen king, Saturn.

NATURAL SIGNS OF
INTERNAL DESPAIR: UPHEAVAL

Before considering *The Fall of Hyperion*, we note how many of Keats's most moving lines evoke both the happy and frightening qualities of upheaval. The much-loved fifth verse of *Ode to a Nightingale* works like the earlier lines about the "unshent" seaweed. In the fifth verse of this ode Keats portrays a complex but momentary sensation: mixed scents that strike one in a garden. Because the poet-narrator is sitting in the garden in the evening, he can identify the flowers around him only by the scents drifting up to him. The flowers and other plants are at his feet: he cannot see them. Hence he has to guess their individual identities as their odors *rise* to the level of his nose:

I cannot see what flowers are at my feet,
Nor what soft incense hangs upon the boughs,
But, in the embalmed darkness, guess each sweet
Wherewith the seasonable month endows
The grass, the thicket, and the fruit-tree wild.

(41–45)

The "embalmed darkness" suggests a state of death, in which there is no light. Yet the scents that rise to the poet's face are endowed by nature, that is, they are given to human beings on a rising current of warm air. This theme of the wafting, giving, and uplifting forces of nature reappears in other great poems of this period of Keats's career, including *Ode on Melancholy* and *Ode on Indolence*. This theme also occurs in the third stanza of another great poem, *To Autumn:*

Then in wailful choir the small gnats mourn
    Among the river sallows, borne aloft
    Or sinking as the light wind lives or dies;
And full-grown lambs loud bleat from hilly bourn.

(27–30)

It is not difficult to see how this image of swelling and uplifting power is rooted in the poet's imaginative reconstruction of the experience of suckling. The pillowed breast, the sweet milk given in the warmth and happy cooing of the nursing mother, whose touch and smells coincide with the satisfaction of the infant's hunger, are all elements of paradise. Yet the difference between Keats's original efforts to recapture that regressive mood, to be taken ". . . like a child at suckling time" (*Endymion*, Book III, 456), and this portrait of insects rising on the wind is immense.

Keats can describe the insects' experience because he comprehends empathically their complete dependence upon the wind that carries them. For only a very light creature can be borne aloft that way. At the same time and within the same poem Keats reinvokes our human experience of feeling uplifted by our emotions. We are borne aloft in a similar manner by a similar force. In other words, this stanza is directly about the gnats being borne aloft, and it is also about our human fate.

In his earlier images Keats desired to return to this moment of fantasized bliss. Like an avid hypnotic subject, he could not wait to be held by a superior power, to fall into its arms and have his every need satisfied, just as the infant falls into its mother's arms, sure of safety and the rich pleasures of eating, sucking, and smelling its mother's body. It does not surprise us, therefore, to learn that when asked to recite *Endymion* to his idol, Wordsworth, Keats chanted it, pacing the room in long rhythmic strides. The poem acted, in part, as a device for instituting a regressed state of consciousness and so avoiding the imminent suffering around him.

All this changes in *To Autumn.* Keats does not chant the verses to this famous poem. He does not attempt to induce a dreamy, altered state of enchantment and hallucination. The simple beauty of his description of the gnats, who mourn something, is that they do indeed rise and fall as the wind "lives or dies." That motion echoes and resembles the infantile experience, but it is not mere dreaming. Keats's lines represent the wish to rest upon the mother. The poem recognizes that this wish cannot be granted; poetry can invoke the memory of the lost mother, but it cannot resurrect her. Keats's earlier poems aim at hallucinatory revival, exactly as Freud said of dreams in general. This poem, *To Autumn,* aims to depict potentials for beauty in our common human world.

Many of Keats's early poems are about his internal life and conflicts, especially his struggles to reconstitute himself, to avoid fragmentation in the face of his great losses: the deaths of father, brother, and mother and his own imminent death by consumption. But *To Autumn,* a much later poem, is about autumn, a beautiful season, full of particular qualities and, as many commentators have noted, full of its own music, the distinctive sound of the lamb, the gnats, and the wind. I believe that Keats recognized the difference between his early poems, which aim to induce an altered state of consciousness in which dreams dominate, and his later poems, which aim to describe the wish for regression but also its impossibility. He considers this issue directly in a very late poem, *The Fall of Hyperion: A Dream.*

THE FALL OF HYPERION:
THE TASK OF POETRY

Keats had begun a poem on the tragedy of Hyperion, a Greek deity whom he linked to both Apollo and Prometheus, in the fall of 1818. He revived the few stanzas in 1819, hoping to make it into an epic worthy of comparison to Milton's masterpieces, *Paradise Lost* and *Paradise Regained.*

The poem's action takes place in an arcadian glade. The poet drinks a magic potion that makes him swoon, almost die, and then confront a mysterious goddess, whose name, Moneta, means memory. Moneta attacks the poet-dreamer for being what Keats feared he was: a mere dreaming thing. "A fever of thyself. Think of the Earth; / What bliss even in hope is there for thee?" (169–70). Keats's hero responds in courtroom style:

> If it please,
> Majestic shadow, tell me: sure not all

These melodies sung into the world's ear
Are useless: sure a poet is a sage,
A humanist, physician to all men.

(186–90)

To this the prophetess replies with great derision and force, "Are thou not of the dreamer tribe?"

W. Jackson Bate says that Moneta's challenge is a Christian one, parallel to an admonition to follow Christ, who took upon himself the burdens of the world's sins.[10] This is plausible, but we stress the fact that Keats's story is only a parallel to the Christian story. Keats explicitly rejects traditional Christianity. At the same time he defends poetry as a form of empathic love:

Every sole man hath days of joy and pain,
Whether his labours be sublime or low—
The pain alone; the joy alone; distinct:
Only the dreamer venoms all his days.

(172–75)

I wish to emphasize the way Keats describes Moneta's passionate rebuke:

What am I then? Thou spakest of my tribe:
What tribe?—The tall shade veiled in drooping white
Then spake, so much more earnest, that the breath
Moved the thin linen folds that drooping hung
About a golden censer from the hand
Pendant. "Art thou not of the dreamer tribe?"

(193–98)

Keats repeats these phrases twenty lines later:

Then the tall shade, in drooping linens veiled,
Spake out, so much more earnest, that her breath
Stirred the thin folds of gauze that drooping hung
About a golden censer from her hand
Pendant.

(216–20)

Why would Keats repeat this image and in so awkward a fashion? His editor and friend, Woodhouse, had suggested editing both verses, erasing most or all of the second. Yet Jack Stillinger says that Keats did not want to delete either, nor to revise them, and that Woodhouse's penciled remarks are critical conjectures.[11] This increases the mystery, for it means Keats chose to retain these awkward lines.

We know from daily life and from the theory of dream interpretation that when an apparently trivial item is repeated it has a special, often unconscious, meaning. In addition, the idiosyncratic items of one's daily life are the most personal and most revealing. Freud said that he could publish his patients' deepest fears and anxieties and describe their perversions with no danger of revealing their identities, but to mention a few of their superficial characteristics would make them known.

There are grounds, then, for arguing that these repeated lines are of particular importance for Keats. Aileen Ward pointed this out when she noted that the image of the "shrouded mother" is the ultimate one in Keats's thought.[12] Ward says that it is the image of his mother shrouded in her coffin. But the poem's image is of a woman shrouded in white who mourns the fall of her beloved master and king, Saturn. The veils uplifted by the woman's passionate breath are mourning garb as well as burial garb. Moneta's role in the poem is to complete a sacrifice to the memory of the fallen king and to admonish the young man whose miserable dreaming is unimportant and a mere fever. We think of Hamlet, whom the ghost admonishes and who lacerates himself for failing to act and choosing the art of theater over direct action, just as Keats had chosen a career of artistic dreaming.

Moneta is memory and an agent of revenge. She attacks the good conscience of the living, who, because they survived while the ideal godlike man was killed, incur a double burden of guilt. The most worthy die while the least worthy, those who loved imperfectly, survive. The labor of mourning is the ego's effort to free itself from the numerous memories it retains of the lost object. Recall that Keats did not mourn the death of either his mother or his brother. The failure to mourn results in either an excessive defense against feeling or regressive attempts to restore the original relationship. Keats refused to take the first route. In his initial poems he tantalized himself by seeking moments of hallucinatory fulfillment in which he was united with the "million-pleasured breast."

The Fall of Hyperion is an act of mourning through the medium of the epic poem. It is most powerful in the lines that evoke the terror and awe of Moneta's robes. (When we see Saturn himself we are disappointed, and even more let down by the demigod Hyperion.)

But yet I had a terror of her robes,
And chiefly of the veils, that from her brow
Hung pale, and curtained her mysteries
That made my heart too small to hold its blood.
This saw that Goddess, and with sacred hand
Parted the veils.

(251–56)

Keats struggles to convey the idea of mourning transformed by the nobility of its subject:

. . . Then saw I a wan face,
Not pined by human sorrows, but bright-blanched
By an immortal sickness which kills not;
It works a constant change, which happy death
Can put no end to; deathwards progressing
To no death was that visage; it had passed
The lily and the snow; and beyond these
I must not think now, though I saw that face—

(256–63)

Greater than human sorrow is the destruction, the *fall* of the father-god, Saturn, whose fate prefigures the destruction of the son-god, Hyperion. Keats draws upon his tragic knowledge of the onset and progress of consumption when he describes Moneta's pallor. Yet if we believe Keats, his theme is more than solitary loss; it is the universal loss of infantile hopes. Those hopes are not for immortality alone. They are for the "god-like" existence of receiving and giving "warm love." When Saturn speaks, it is to mourn his loss of the capacity to love his planet:

Moan, brethren, moan; for we are swallowed up
And buried from all godlike exercise
Of influence benign on planets pale,
And peaceful sway above man's harvesting,
And all those acts which Deity supreme
Doth ease its heart of love in.

(412–17)

Unlike the Greek and Roman deities, who when overthrown promised bloody vengeance, Keats's Saturn falls into melancholy. He mourns the loss of his relationship to the earth and its human creatures. Bate has suggested that this has distinct echoes of the Christian deity, who suffered for others. It also represents a child's ideal portrait of a father who cannot love the child—not because the child is unworthy, but because forces beyond human control have intervened. Hence the poem says that there has been disaster, but it is not death, "There is no death in all the universe" (423), for, as Keats says in a great line, "Clouds still with shadowy moisture haunt the earth, / Still suck their fill of light from sun and moon" (420–21).

Hyperion was to bring an end to this bitter state of unrequited mourning. Keats appears to have envisioned this, yet when we see Hyperion we are less optimistic: "He paces through the pleasant hours of ease / With strides colossal, on from hall to hall" (38–39). Keats wrote twenty more lines and then abandoned the poem, which was not published in his lifetime. The poem is a fragment, and who can say what a man of Keats's ability could have fashioned from it? Keats returns to the theme of a gentle, but overwhelming, power in one of the poem's naturalistic observations:

> "Saturn, sleep on, while at thy feet I weep"
> As when, upon a tranced summer night,
> Forests, branch-charmed by the earnest stars,
> Dream, and so dream all night, without a noise,
> Save from one gradual solitary gust,
> Swelling upon the silence; dying off;
> As if the ebbing air had but one wave—
> So came these words, and went.
>
> (371–78)

This solitary gust of air, like the gentle wind that buoys up the swarm of gnats, or like the sea water that unshents the weeds, is a natural analogue of *spiritus*, that is, the divine *pneuma* that animates all living things. This uplifting power is not the "Holy Spirit" of traditional Christian belief. But neither is *pneuma* simply the body's mechanical respiration. Keats means it to convey the feeling, the actual quality of our common human world. He associates that quality with the benign forces of the universe. The gusts of wind that lift up the gnats are features of the natural world around us—as are the sun, the earth, and the patient moon. Like these immense features of the landscape, the ebb and flow of *spiritus* may be interpreted first this way, and then another, just as some religions hold that the moon is masculine, while the majority believe that it is feminine.

Pneuma is an aspect of the real world. We may not be able to list exhaustively its meanings, but that does not prevent us from being warmed by its beauty. Part of the poet's task is to discover truths about the world and to convey them back to us, truths that are beautiful and deathless. This is a social task; part of the poet's responsibility as a member of culture and, as Keats says, a fellow creature.

The Confrontation with Memory

In *The Fall of Hyperion* Keats confronts memory itself. He does not avoid suffering the pain he knows that it, in the guise of Moneta, will bring. He does not avoid criticizing his own tendency to exploit the pull toward regression and pretty pieces of paganism, as Wordsworth termed *Endymion.* Keats counters mere prettiness with the moral imperative of poetry: poets ought to feel "the giant agony of the world" (157). They can do this by examining their internal world and eternal longings to avoid the pain of loss and the pain of mourning, both of

which depend upon the examination of memory. This is why Keats has
the poet-hero confront Moneta. Having wanted to flee in terror from
Moneta's robes and the pallor of her face, the poet stays, for there is a
benign light in her eyes:

> . . . As I had found
> A grain of gold upon a mountain's side,
> And twinged with avarice strained out my eyes
> To search its sullen entrails rich with ore,
> So at the view of sad Moneta's brow
> I ached to see what things the hollow brain
> Behind enwombed; what high tragedy
> In the dark secret chambers of her skull
> Was acting . . .
>
>   (271–79)

Keats had trained as a surgeon in the days when operations consisted
in sawing off body parts as quickly as possible, there being neither anes-
thesia nor antisepsis. By all accounts he was good at his work. These
lines suggest that he was equally unafraid to reveal his infantile fantasies. The poet's urge to know the mother's body, to tear from her
womb the hidden secrets, is akin to the child's oral craving. Both are
exacerbated by the mother's withdrawal from the child as she falls into
the schizoidlike reveries of deep mourning. Moneta is both memory and
mother earth, the ultimate source of strength and wealth, just as her
breasts are the ultimate refuge and solace to which the poet is drawn.
After he fell Saturn had rested upon the ground, ". . . listening to the
Earth, / His antient [sic] mother, for some comfort yet" (325–26).

KEATS AND THE REPAIR OF
A FRAGMENTED SELF

Keats is a favorite poet of depth psychologists because he exemplifies
the power and indestructibility of infantile hopes. Alongside mawkish
verses about the million-pleasured breast are his unembarrassed descriptions of longing for an absent father. Both Moneta and Saturn are
as awesome as all parents are to infants who must navigate in a world
of giant figures. Keats's fascination with mourning and his violent, then
passive response to fierce women are typical of the young child who
blames one parent for the death of the other.

Alongside these exhortations and childish verses are Keats's subtle
and beautiful evocations of the presence of an actual good. Wallace
Stevens,[13] another great romantic, said that the task of poetry was to
find in the external world semblances of internal feelings. I think this is

true. At least, it helps us explain why Keats's repetitious description of the uplifting power of wind, water, and other natural forces is so important to him (and to ourselves). All these are semblances of the original good object, the mother's million-pleasured breast. But the odes are not hallucinatory. The natural analogues of *pneuma* are authentic features of the external world. They are qualities that appear in the relationship between human animals and their environment. They are affordances upon which we gain some moments of actual pleasure.

Stevens does not say why some poetic images are more powerful than others. Psychoanalytic experience may help us. Those images, those semblances of feeling that replicate qualities of the original good and now lost object will be more powerful and more moving than those that do not. We see this truth illustrated in Keats's sonnet *Bright Star*. Keats returns to the problem of retaining the love of a woman, probably his fiancée, Fanny Brawne. Like Moneta, the female object is attractive and repellent. She is both the North Star and Venus, the evening star; she is aloof and icy, but nevertheless benign. The double reference—to the cold and distant star that signals the North Pole and to the warm and southerly planet that signifies passion and sexuality— is well suited to the poem's central anxiety. Is the universe benign and loving or hostile and cold? For the child, this is a crucial question: Is there a place for me in the world of others, or will I perish out of hunger and longing?

> Bright Star! would I were steadfast as thou art—
>   Not in lone splendour hung aloft the night
> And watching, with eternal lids apart,
>   Like nature's patient, sleepless Eremite,
> The moving waters at their priestlike task
>   Of pure ablution round earth's human shores,
> Or gazing on the new soft-fallen mask
>   Of snow upon the mountains and the moors—
> No—yet still steadfast, still unchangeable,
>   Pillowed upon my fair love's ripening breast,
> To feel for ever its soft swell and fall,
>   Awake for ever in a sweet unrest,
> Still, still to hear her tender-taken breath,
> And so live ever—or else swoon to death.

The bright star is both sleepless (as are all depressed and mournful persons) and yet loving. It oversees an ancient and patient ritual of ablution—it blesses the waters circling the globe. Each of these images maintains the emotional tension that we know Keats the man suffered. Balancing the archaic wish to meld into the mourning parent, to join her and so abandon the struggle against depression, is the emphatic no of the ninth line. As we have seen already, what counterbalances that urge is the discovery of a semblance of it in the body and person of another. Like the gnats borne aloft by the wind, the tree branches borne upward by a single gust of warm air, and the mingled scent of flowers that rises up to tell him their identities, these last lines evoke a transcendent dimension of *pneuma:* "To feel forever its soft swell and fall."

Keats is fond of the word "still"; it appears here three times and numerous times in other poems. To still is to quiet and to comfort, as a mother stills a child. It is also an admonition. The mother, her music, and her breath are still, they have not faded away. Just as Keats had stilled himself to hear the footsteps of his departed friend, these lines are insistent demands for unbroken comfort. The first draft of the eleventh line reads, "To touch forever, its warm sink and swell." That warmth counterbalances the cold, deathlike mask of snow, which in color and feeling is like Moneta's face.

Poetry as a Route to Consolidation of the Self

Counterbalancing this regressive urge toward hallucinatory wish fulfillment is Keats's intellectual capacity. His profound need for reunion with the lost mother (as object and selfobject) might have taken an occult direction in someone less talented. His good fortune was to discover his profound capacity to articulate these object and selfobject needs. In the terms developed above, Keats seems to have consolidated himself in the way that Augustine did: by finding in his audience the admiration and listening he required.

Keats's biographers make it clear that toward the end of his brief career, Keats realized the depth of his genius. He also realized that he was dying of the same disease that had claimed his brother and mother. He did not deny that this wretched fate enraged him. A fine instance of rage and self-consolidation occurs in a fragment, one of the last pieces Keats wrote:

> This living hand, now warm and capable
> Of earnest grasping, would, if it were cold
> And in the icy silence of the tomb,
> So haunt thy days and chill thy dreaming nights
> That thou would wish thine own heart dry of blood
> So in my veins red life might stream again,
> And thou be conscience-calmed—see here it is—
> I hold it towards you.

Keats had considered this theme before in his attempted epic, *The Fall of Hyperion.* He links it directly to the issue of fantasy and its permanence and his continuation as a poet after his death, that is, to the problem of death anxiety and its alleviation through selfobjects:

> . . . Who alive can say,
> "Thou art no Poet—mayst not tell thy dreams"?
> Since every man whose soul is not a clod
> Hath visions, and would speak, if he had loved,
> And been well nurtured in his mother tongue.
> Whether the dream now purposed to rehearse
> Be Poet's or Fanatic's will be known
> When this warm scribe my hand is in the grave.
>
> (11–18)

The mother tongue is English. Yet it is also his mother's richly endowed image once warm and devoted, then lost in a state of depressive mourning, then herself finally cold and fixed in rigor mortis. Keats says directly that he too recognizes that some dreams are mere fanaticisms, while others may become poems—that is, more than dreams. His warm hand, that is, his creativity as an author, is the one thing that will survive him. Indeed, it may carry out his will—punishing those he hates, comforting those he loves.

Even in his first effort to tell the story of Hyperion, Keats had considered the special power he invested in his writing. The first lines of *Hyperion: A Fragment* describe Saturn, a god defeated and alone, sunk into melancholy. Even the streams running near him are silent:

> . . . Upon the sodden ground
> His old right-hand lay nerveless, listless, dead,
> Unsceptred; and his realmless eyes were closed;
> While his bowed head seemed listening to the Earth,
> His ancient mother, for some comfort yet.
>
> (17–21)

The sick god and the sick poet both bow down and seek comfort from the mother who has hurt them in the worst possible way—abandoned them to a melancholy mood between sleep and death.[14]

Keats's poems are confrontations with memory. Many of them, especially his early efforts, are regressive attempts to avoid current suffering by imagining a happier, idyllic time. In these chantlike evocations hallucinatory wish-fulfillment is the dominant goal, and memory is avoided. These are not the goals of his later poems, which evoke and make evident the authentic beauty of our natural and human worlds. Keats's observations are permanent discoveries. They are public goods.

OCCULT REFLECTIONS
IN JOHN UPDIKE'S
THE WITCHES OF EASTWICK

Another solution to the problem of fragmentation is that made available through artistic expression. This route is especially evident in literature, where the intellectual debate between traditional religious
teachings and modern antireligious ideas can be made clear. To illustrate some features of this aesthetic route I consider a passage from
a contemporary American novel, *The Witches of Eastwick* by John
Updike. In this novel, Updike reflects upon a world in which the devil
is a pathetic con artist and boneheaded inventor and the devil's former
opponents, the church and her ministers, collapse into faddish political
movements.

In the last portion of the book Updike describes the thoughts of a
young woman who knows she will die of cancer within the year. She
examines the sky on a July morning:

> *For the last time,* thought Jenny Van Horne, *the exact blue of such a July
> day falls into my eyes. My lids lift, my corneas admit the light, my lenses
> focus it, my retinas and optic nerve report it to the brain. Tomorrow the
> Earth's poles will tilt a day more toward August and autumn, and a
> slightly different tincture of light and vapor will be distilled.* All year,
> without knowing it, she had been saying good-bye to each season, each
> subseason and turn of weather, each graduated moment of fall's blaze and
> shedding, of winter's freeze, of daylight gaining on the hardening ice,
> and of that vernal moment when the snowdrops and croci are warmed
> into bloom out of matted brown grass in that intimate area on the sun-
> ward side of stone walls, as when lovers cup their breath against the
> beloved's neck; she had been saying good-bye, for the seasons would not
> wheel around again for her. Days one spends so freely in haste and preoc-
> cupation, in adolescent self-concern and in childhood's joyous boredom,
> *there really is an end to them, a closing of the sky like the shutter of a vast
> camera.* These thoughts made Jenny giddy where she sat.[15]

Updike gives these thoughts to Jenny as she sits in a church pew listening to a young preacher who realized too late that there were actual
evils within Eastwick that the church had overlooked in its fascination
with issues like the war in Southeast Asia. Later, this young preacher,
Brenda, asks a layman, Darryl Van Horne, to preach to her congrega-
tion. He accepts and preaches a sermon about the horrors of God's
creation. This layman, who is Jenny's husband, attacks the traditional
view of God as loving and benign by enumerating the variety and style
of parasitic worms that inflict humankind. Only a horrible creator, Van

Horne asserts, could bring into being gigantic worms that feed inside our stomach and eventually devour us from within. Quite directly, then, Updike contrasts the religious world view that had dominated the church with an antireligious view evident in Van Horne's sermon. Van Horne himself, the novel tells us, is probably an agent of the Devil, or the Devil himself who has found in the old city of Eastwick, Rhode Island, three women who are willing to be his servants.

Jenny is literally dying by fragmentation; she is eaten away from the inside by a cancerous growth (induced in part by the three witches who hated her for marrying Van Horne). The first portion of her meditation describes a process of fragmentation. By enumerating the mechanics of sight, from the first registration upon the retina to the ending processes in her brain, Jenny treats her body as if it were already fragmented, as if it were made up of bits and pieces of machinery that function well at the moment but will soon fail.

Yet Jenny's meditation as a whole, with its precise and detailed account of natural beauty, is not fragmented. Unlike occult stories of fantastic adventures in never-never land, Updike's reflection on Jenny's experience is plausible and therefore moving. For Jenny is mourning, one by one, the simple pleasures that make up ordinary life. We sense that perhaps for the first time she really sees the intense blue of the July sky for itself. She recognizes and salutes this marvelous color; she also says good-bye to it. This saying good-bye, this mourning, is a kind of labor or work in which one savors the bittersweet feelings attached to each object associated with the lost loved one.[16]

The final metaphor in Jenny's meditation recapitulates Jenny's original thoughts about her eyes and the processes of vision. Updike's image of the sky as itself a vast camera is another melancholy image of heaven reduced to a machine that looks at us. Heaven is no longer the home of a caring God. When she dies, Jenny will close her eyes and no longer see the graduated moments of change that make up the flow of time. However, in response to this thought Jenny has a premonition (an occult form of knowledge) that *"behind that shutter must be an eye, the eye of a Great Being."*[17] Yet the novel also says that the sky itself, once the abode of a loving God who neither slumbered nor slept, that is, whose eyes were never closed, is empty. In traditional religious teachings, in an age when religion had not lost out to science, Jenny would know that she cannot fall out of God's love. She would believe that nothing occurred in her life that was not seen by a loving, observing Deity. If Jenny had lived and died in an earlier age, when the devil was a real figure to the New England mind, she would know that death was not the ending of her existence, but the beginning of a new relationship with her Creator.

The great Jewish psalms proclaim again and again that there is no final separation from God. There is no final task of reconciliation between human and human, and human and God, which God cannot accomplish. There is no self so fragmented that it cannot be repaired by retrieving a lost relationship to God. If human beings remain open to God's love they will be secure.

But, as Updike makes clear throughout this novel and others like it, persons living in the modern age, in which mechanisms seem to have replaced relationships, have little access to these traditional beliefs. Even though Jenny conjures up the idea of a Great Being behind the camera lens, she cannot sustain her belief in God's existence. Brenda's sermon is accurate: Jenny is the victim of witchcraft, yet Jenny cannot be saved by Brenda's tentative faith. Jenny returns to her meditations on nature and the work of mourning: *"I will never see icicles dripping from the eaves again,* Jenny thought, *or a sugar maple catching fire."*[18]

Like the rest of us, Jenny cannot see the actuality of evil in her life. The church's great task, to carry us over the chasm of death, remains unfulfilled. We are lost. Even if the physical church remains and even if church leaders struggle to become relevant to contemporary issues, the essence of the faith, its proclamation of imperishable union with God, is dissolved. Updike's novels, in this sense, are themselves richly composed lamentations on the loss of God's presence. Updike's novels are part of the collective process of mourning that began in the nineteenth century when rationalist thinkers declared that God had died and we were alone on the open sea.

SUMMARY:
COMPETING SOLUTIONS

We have considered a number of solutions to the problem of fragmentation anxiety. In the first six chapters of this book we examined the occult solution. In this last chapter we have considered alternative solutions: those offered by religion, aesthetic theories, and literature. Each of these nonoccult solutions has its value and its costs. Religion offers by far the greatest resources in the struggle against fragmentation. Yet it is difficult for modern persons to appropriate its great wealth. Aesthetics, in the form of a theory of life like that offered in Goethe's poetry, appeals directly to one's intellectual yearnings. Aesthetic doctrines are not religious doctrines. Aesthetics provides a sense of tradition, and it offers a sense of unchanging pattern, namely, the stable processes of change itself.

Yet aesthetic theories and doctrines are bloodless and dry. To affirm Goethe's insights about the patterns within change in his poem "Constancy in Change" requires one to think about one's life and to abstract from it a pattern. This pattern will remain even as we die and dissolve. Other intellectual doctrines, like Marxism or Freudianism, also serve to replace traditional religious authorities. These doctrines also require one to find abstract patterns within the processes of change itself. For the Marxist that pattern will emerge in the full light only at the end of history when the great natural processes that make up human evolution have completed their work. For the Freudian the patterns that make up an individual's history will emerge finally in the end of therapy. In those patients courageous enough to accept them, these insights will be sufficient to secure ordinary unhappiness.

The literary solution differs from the aesthetic solution. Keats and Updike do not advance aesthetic doctrines. These artists do not propose theoretical answers to the problems of living, nor to the basic issue of fragmentation anxiety. Rather, Keats and Updike offer their works, one a body of poems, the other poetry and novels, as responses valid in themselves. Jenny Van Horne's meditation on her death is not an abstract idea. It is a moving and plausible narration of a modern woman's internal world. To go back to our earlier discussion of empathy, the literary response to fragmentation anxiety is perhaps the one that reflects best our internal experience. Jenny's suffering is undeniable and her fantasies about the sky closing its eyes upon her echo our contemporary loneliness.

Which of these solutions is better than the others? Which is ultimately the most sustaining? These are questions I ask but leave unanswered.

Freud References

Unless otherwise noted, all Freud references are to volumes in *The Standard Edition of the Complete Psychological Works of Sigmund Freud,* 24 volumes (London: Hogarth Press and The Institute for Psycho-Analysis). I use the *Standard Edition* date and notations for volume and initial page number.

(1891b) *On Aphasia.* London and New York, 1953.
(1893c) Some points for a comparative study of organic and hysterical motor paralyses. *Standard Edition,* 1, 157.
(1895d) *Studies on Hysteria. Standard Edition,* 2.
(1900a) *The Interpretation of Dreams.* London and New York, 1955; *Standard Edition,* 4–5.
(1901b) *The Psychopathology of Everyday Life.* London, 1966; *Standard Edition,* 6.
(1905c) *Jokes and Their Relation to the Unconscious. Standard Edition,* 8.
(1905d) *Three Essays on the Theory of Sexuality. Standard Edition,* 7, 125.
(1905e) Fragment of an analysis of a case of hysteria. *Standard Edition,* 7, 3.
(1907a) *Delusions and Dreams in Jensen's "Gradiva." Standard Edition,* 9, 273.

(1907b) Obsessive actions and religious practices. *Standard Edition*, 9, 3.

(1908a) Hysterical phantasies and their relation to bisexuality. *Standard Edition*, 9, 157.

(1908b) Character and anal erotism. *Standard Edition*, 9, 169.

(1908d) "Civilized" sexual morality and modern nervous illness. *Standard Edition*, 9, 179.

(1909b) Analysis of a phobia in a five-year-old boy. *Standard Edition*, 10, 3.

(1909d) Notes upon a case of obsessional neurosis. *Standard Edition*, 10, 155.

(1910a) Five lectures on psycho-analysis. *Standard Edition*, 11, 3.

(1910c) *Leonardo da Vinci and a Memory of His Childhood. Standard Edition*, 11, 59.

(1912–13) *Totem and Taboo. Standard Edition*, 13, 1.

(1912b) The dynamics of transference. *Standard Edition*, 12, 99.

(1913f) The theme of the three caskets. *Standard Edition*, 12, 291.

(1913i) The disposition to obsessional neurosis. *Standard Edition*, 12, 313.

(1914b) The Moses of Michelangelo. *Standard Edition*, 13, 211.

(1914c) On narcissism: an introduction. *Standard Edition*, 14, 60.

(1914d) On the history of the psycho-analytic movement. *Standard Edition*, 14, 3.

(1914g) Remembering, repeating, and working-through. *Standard Edition*, 12, 147.

(1915a) Observations on transference love. *Standard Edition*, 12, 159.

(1915e) The unconscious. *Standard Edition*, 14, 161.

(1916–17) *Introductory Lectures on Psycho-Analysis*, rev. ed. *Standard Edition*, 15–16.

(1917b) A childhood recollection from *Dichtung und Warheit. Standard Edition*, 17, 147.

(1917c) On transformations of instinct as exemplified in anal erotism. *Standard Edition*, 17, 127.

(1917d) A metapsychological supplement to the theory of dreams. *Standard Edition*, 14, 219.

(1917e) Mourning and melancholia. *Standard Edition*, 14, 239.

(1918b) From the history of an infantile neurosis. *Standard Edition*, 17, 3.

(1919g) Preface to Reik's *Ritual: Psycho-Analytic Studies. Standard Edition*, 17, 259.

(1919h) The "uncanny." *Standard Edition*, 17, 219.

(1920a) *Beyond the Pleasure Principle. Standard Edition*, 18, 3.

(1920g) *Beyond the Pleasure Principle. Standard Edition*, 18, 7.

(1921c) *Group Psychology and the Analysis of the Ego. Standard Edition*, 18, 69.

(1922a) Dreams and telepathy. *Standard Edition*, 18, 197.

(1923a) Two encyclopaedia articles. *Standard Edition*, 18, 235.

(1923b) *The Ego and the Id.* London, 1962. *Standard Edition*, 19, 3.

(1924c) The economic problem of masochism. *Standard Edition*, 19, 157.

(1925h) Negation. *Standard Edition*, 19, 235.

(1925i) Some additional notes on dream-interpretation as a whole. *Standard Edition*, 19, 125.

(1925j) Some psychical consequences of the anatomical distinction between the sexes. *Standard Edition*, 19, 243.

(1926d) *Inhibitions, Symptoms and Anxiety. Standard Edition*, 20, 77.

(1927c) *The Future of an Illusion. Standard Edition*, 21, 3.

(1930a) *Civilization and Its Discontents. Standard Edition*, 21, 59.

(1932a) The acquisition and control of fire. *Standard Edition*, 22, 185.

(1933a) *New Introductory Lectures on Psycho-Analysis.* London, 1971; *Standard Edition*, 22, 3.

(1936a) A disturbance of memory on the Acropolis. *Standard Edition*, 22, 239.

(1939a) *Moses and Monotheism. Standard Edition*, 23, 3.

(1940a) *An Outline of Psycho-Analysis. Standard Edition*, 23, 141.

(1941c) A premonitory dream fulfilled. *Standard Edition*, 5, 623.

(1941d) Psychoanalysis and telepathy. *Standard Edition*, 18, 177.

(1950a) *The Origins of Psycho-Analysis.* London and New York, 1954. Partly, including "A Project for a Scientific Psychology," in *Standard Edition*, 1, 175.

(1954) *The Origins of Psychoanalysis.* Ed. M. Bonaparte, A. Freud, E. Kris. New York: Basic Books.

Notes

PREFACE

1. See *Cahiers du Cinema*, "John Ford's *Young Mr. Lincoln*," *Screen* 13 (1972): 2–15. See also *Movies and Methods*, ed. Bill Nichols (Berkeley: University of California Press, 1976); and Ted Gallagher, *John Ford: The Man and His Films* (Berkeley: University of California Press, 1986).

INTRODUCTION: THREE STORIES OF
THE OCCULT

1. All definitions are taken from "Occult," in *The Oxford English Dictionary* (Oxford: Clarendon Press, 1933), 7:45–46.

2. Is the occult a kind of religious experience? Are all religious experiences, to the degree that they involve a human being making claims about a transcendental presence, occult? If one had a clear understanding of what the term *religion* referred to, and if one felt that definition was unassailable, then one might suggest that this essay on the occult was actually a psychology of religion. But I have discovered no such definition of religion and therefore do not claim that this study is a comprehensive psychology of religion. There are many types of psychology, ranging from social psychology to neuropsychology to behavioral studies to dynamic psychologies.

Within each of these types of psychology are various subdisciplines. Within dynamic psychologies one finds Jungian "analytic" psychology, psychoanalysis, and many others. Within contemporary psychoanalysis one finds Classical Theory, Object Relations Theory, Ego Psychology, and Selfpsychology, and probably others as well. Articulate and thoughtful members of each of these schools have elaborated rich theoretical terms that one could apply to the range of behavior called "religious experience." A comprehensive psychology of religion seems to me to be an impossibility at this time.

3. R. Laurence Moore's study, *In Search of White Crows: Spiritualism, Parapsychology, and American Culture* (New York: Oxford University Press, 1977), is a comprehensive contemporary study of occult beliefs in an American context. His is primarily a historical approach. His notes and references to published and nonpublished sources are extremely useful. In addition, his reviews of sociological explanations for the rise of occult beliefs are judicious. An earlier philosophic consideration of occult claims and the epistemologies upon which they are erected is Antony Flew's study, *A New Approach to Psychical Research* (London: Watts & Co., 1953). Flew approaches claims for telekinetic powers, for example, strictly as a prescientific set of claims which ought to be understood and investigated as a set of rival hypotheses similar to those advanced in ordinary psychological theories. Flew's book is additionally useful, for he reviews, as does Moore, the history of modern occult beliefs and practices as codified in the English and American branches of learned societies dedicated to psychical research.

Similar to Flew's examination of the logic of occult beliefs is John Cohen's book, *Behaviour in Uncertainty and Its Social Implications* (New York: Basic Books, 1964). Cohen reasons through the various ways in which human beings struggle to quantify, or at least rationalize, their actions in situations where the evidence for and against a set of claims is ambiguous. While he does not concern himself directly with occult claims, Cohen's general approach helps explain why eminent scientists, as well as ordinary mortals, might choose to believe claims about the afterlife, for example, that are extremely unlikely. Cohen's chapter 10, on divination practices, is fascinating. In addition to the usual astrological claims, palmreading, crystal gazing, and such techniques for telling the future, Cohen describes *sciomancy,* divination by reading shadows, *molybdomancy,* by interpreting the sound of molten lead dropped into water, and *ovomancy,* by examining the germ of an egg, and others. See also F. C. Cohn, "Time and the Ego," *Psychoanalytic Quarterly* 26 (1957): 168–89.

T. H. Leahey and G. E. Leahey review contemporary occult practices and schools of thought as they impinge upon what many people would consider scientific psychology. They contrast this kind of science, what one might term the mainstream of academic psychology, from "pseudosciences" on a variety of grounds, the principal one being that the pseudosciences, like Scientology, attempt to answer ultimate questions; that is, questions that normally come under the domain of religion; see T. H. Leahey and G. E. Leahey, *Psychology's Occult Doubles: Psychology and the Problem of Pseudoscience* (Chicago: Nelson-Hall, 1983), 237–45. Another standard text is J. Webb's *The Occult Establishment* (La Salle, Ill.: Open Court, 1976), as well as his *The Occult Underground* (La

Salle, Ill.: Open Court, 1974). Both are excellent studies of the social dimensions of occult beliefs and occult groups.

Many occult groups and parapsychological organizations as well produce journals on a regular or semiregular basis. Among the best established and often cited are the older serials. See, for example, *Proceedings of the Society for Psychical Research* (London, 1883–) and a similar periodical, *Journal of the American Society for Psychical Research,* begun in 1906. Interest in the occult has not abated. For a list of more than one hundred contemporary journals dedicated to issues in the occult, see *Ulrich's International Periodicals Directory, 1985* (New York: Bowker, 1985).

Freud maintained a lifelong concern with occult claims. He wrote about them and their relationship to psychoanalysis throughout his life. (See below, chap. 3 and notes.) Jung was continuously involved with occult issues, beginning with his doctoral dissertation on a young woman who claimed to be a spiritual medium. (See below, chaps. 3 and 4 and notes.) Later psychoanalysts failed to share Freud's concerns with the occult. Those who did, like Jules Eisenbud, did not convince their colleagues of its vital place in psychoanalytic practice. See Jule Eisenbud, "The Use of the Telepathy Hypothesis in Psychotherapy," in *Specialized Techniques in Psychotherapy,* ed. G. Bychowski and L. Despert (New York: Basic Books, 1952); idem, "Behavioral Correspondences to Normally Predictable Future Events," *Psychoanalytic Quarterly* 23 (1954): 205–33, 355–89; idem, "On the Use of the Psi Hypothesis in Psycho-analysis," *International Journal of Psycho-Analysis* 36 (1955): 370–74. Eisenbud's efforts to raise the psi hypothesis, that of an extraordinary mental energy that enables one to predict future events, among other things, met with sharp debate. A portion of that debate is reported in G. Devereux, ed., *Psychoanalysis and the Occult* (New York: International Universities Press, 1953).

The core concept in psychoanalytic clinical work is "transference." Basic references on the concept of transference include: Freud's brief but fundamental essays, "Fragment of an analysis of a case of hysteria" [Dora] (Freud, 1950e); "The dynamics of transference" (Freud, 1912b); "Remembering, repeating, and working-through" (Freud, 1914g); "Observations on transference love" (Freud, 1915a); and *Inhibitions, Symptoms and Anxiety* (Freud, 1926d). Given its central place in the clinical theory, every major advance in psychoanalytic technique and psychoanalytic theory has reconsidered the meaning of the phenomenon called transference. For example, Kohut formulated his new ideas about narcissism, which we investigate below, in terms of the new concept "narcissistic transference"; Heinz Kohut, *The Analysis of the Self* (New York: International Universities Press, 1971). Important texts on the meaning and place of transference include P. Greenacre, "The role of transference: universal phenomenon and hardest part of the analysis," *Journal of the American Psychoanalytic Association* 2 (1972): 671–84. H. Blum, ed., *Psychoanalytic Explorations in Technique: Discourse on the Theory of Therapy* (New York: International Universities Press, 1980) contains nineteen essays by major psychoanalytic authors, and is an excellent resource.

4. Arthur Conan Doyle, *The History of Spiritualism* (New York: George H. Doran, 1926), 2:134.

5. Ibid., 2:145–46.

6. Antony Flew, *A New Approach to Psychical Research* (London: Watts & Co., 1953), 42.

7. Conan Doyle, *History of Spiritualism,* 2:93.

8. Charles Higham, *The Adventures of Conan Doyle* (New York: W.W. Norton, 1976), 289.

9. Conan Doyle, *History of Spiritualism,* 2:94.

1. OCCULT EXPERIENCE IN
EVERYDAY LIFE

1. Freud, 1919, p. 248.

2. Ernest Jones, *The Life and Work of Sigmund Freud* (New York: Basic Books, 1957), 3:381.

3. Ibid., 383, emphasis added.

4. Freud, 1914c.

5. Heinz Kohut, "The Two Analyses of Mr. Z," *International Journal of Psychoanalysis* 60 (1979): 3–27.

6. Ibid., 4–5.

7. Ibid., 5.

8. Ibid., 8.

9. See esp. Heinz Kohut, "Forms and Transformations of Narcissism," *Journal of the American Psychoanalytic Association* 14 (1966): 243–73; idem, *The Analysis of the Self* (New York: International Universities Press, 1971).

10. Kohut, "Two Analyses of Mr. Z," 14.

11. Ibid., 15.

12. Ibid., 16.

13. Ibid., 15.

14. Ibid., 17.

15. Ibid.

16. Ibid.

17. Ibid., 16.

18. Ibid., 17 n. 2.

19. Kohut, "Forms and Transformations of Narcissism."

20. Heinz Kohut, "Introspection, Empathy, and Psychoanalysis," *Journal of the American Psychoanalytic Association* 7 (1959): 459–83. Reprinted in idem, *Search for the Self* (New York: International Universities Press, 1978), 205–32.

21. Ibid., 231.

22. Ibid., 211.

23. Ibid.

24. Ibid., 205.

25. Thomas Hardy, *Jude the Obscure* (1895), 171.

26. Kohut, *Analysis of the Self,* 90–91.

27. W. Kelly, in a personal communication, 1985.

28. Kohut, *Analysis of the Self,* 231.

29. Heinz Kohut, *How Does Analysis Cure?* (Chicago: University of Chicago Press, 1984).

30. Virginia Demos, "Empathy and Affect: Reflections on Infant Experience," in J. Lichtenberg, M. Bornstein, and D. Silver, eds., *Empathy II* (Hillsdale, N.J.: Analytic Press, 1984), pp. 9–34.

31. Kohut, *Analysis of the Self.*

2. INSIDE THE OCCULT EXPERIENCE

1. Freud, 1917, p. 233.
2. Freud, 1917, p. 232.
3. Charles Darwin, *On the Origin of Species*, 6th ed. (New York: Macmillan Co., 1962), 94, emphasis in original.
4. Freud, 1895, p. 295.
5. Freud, 1900.
6. G. Kittel, ed., *Theological Dictionary of the New Testament* (Grand Rapids: Wm. B. Eerdmans, 1964), 2:305.
7. Freud, 1923b, p. 51.
8. Freud, 1900a.
9. Freud, 1927.
10. On ritual, see Freud, 1907; on uncanny experience, see Freud, 1919; and on Moses, see Freud, 1939.
11. Freud, 1933.
12. Jule Eisenbud, "On the Use of the Psi Hypothesis in Psycho-Analysis," *International Journal of Psycho-Analysis* 36 (1955): 373.
13. Ibid., 371.
14. Ibid., emphasis added.
15. Ibid., 371–72.
16. Ernest Wolf, "Selfobject Relations Disorders," in M. R. Zales, ed., *Character Pathology: Theory and Treatment* (New York: Brunner/Mazel, 1984), 23–38.
17. Ibid.
18. Eisenbud, "On the Use of the Psi Hypothesis," 372.
19. Ibid.
20. Ibid., 370.
21. Ibid., 372.

3. OCCULT MOMENTS IN THE LIFE
OF SAINT AUGUSTINE

1. William James, *The Varieties of Religious Experience* (New York: Collier Books, 1902), 138, emphasis in original.
2. Ibid., 139.
3. L. Kaplan, *Bibliography of American Autobiography* (Madison: University of Wisconsin Press, 1961).
4. Henri F. Ellenberger, *The Discovery of the Unconscious* (New York: Basic Books, 1970).
5. Eugene TeSelle, *Augustine the Theologian* (New York: Herder & Herder, 1970), 191.

6. Augustine, *The Confessions,* trans. R. S. Pine-Coffin (London: Penguin Books, 1961). Quotations in chap. 3 are from this edition, which is cited as *Confessions.*

7. V. Tausk, "On the Origin of the 'Influencing Machine' in Schizophrenia," *Psychoanalytic Quarterly* 2 (1919): 519–56.

8. Heinz Kohut, "Introspection, Empathy and Psychoanalysis," *Journal of the American Psychoanalytic Association* 7 (1959): 459–83.

9. See Heinz Kohut, *The Restoration of the Self* (New York: International Universities Press, 1977); and idem, *How Does Analysis Cure?* (Chicago: University of Chicago Press, 1984).

10. Heinz Kohut, "Thoughts on Narcissism and Narcissistic Rage," *The Psychoanalytic Study of the Child* 27 (1972): 360–400.

11. John Wisdom, "Testing an Interpretation within a Session," *International Journal of Psycho-Analysis* 48 (1967): 44–52.

12. Kohut, *Restoration of the Self,* 91.

13. See J. Loder, who uses a similar five-step model to describe what he terms "convictional experience," *The Transforming Moment: Understanding Convictional Experience* (San Francisco: Harper & Row, 1981). In contrast, see J. Moussaief Masson, *The Oceanic Feeling: The Origins of Religious Sentiment in Ancient India* (Boston: Keuwer, 1980).

14. Ludwig Wittgenstein, *Philosophical Investigations,* trans. G. E. M. Anscombe (New York: Macmillan Co., 1953).

15. James, *Varieties of Religious Experience.*

16. Erik Erikson, *Childhood and Society* (New York: W.W. Norton, 1950).

17. Heinz Kohut and Ernest Wolf, "The Disorders of the Self and Their Treatment: An Outline," *International Journal of Psycho-Analysis* 59 (1978): 414.

18. Heinz Kohut, "Forms and Transformations of Narcissism," *Journal of the American Psychoanalytic Association* 14 (1966): 243–73.

19. J. Fowler, *Stages of Faith* (San Francisco: Harper & Row, 1981).

20. Kohut and Wolf, "Disorders of the Self," 414.

21. Erik Erikson, *Young Man Luther* (New York: W.W. Norton, 1958).

22. Ludwig Wittgenstein, *Philosophical Investigations,* 3d ed., trans. G. E. M. Anscombe (New York: Macmillan Co., 1958), 1–3.

23. Freud, 1915e.

24. See S. Post and J. Miller, "Apprehensions of Empathy," in *Empathy I,* ed. J. Lichtenberg, M. Bornstein, and D. Silver (Hillsdale, N.J.: Analytic Press, 1984), 217–35. "In keeping with nineteenth-century thought, Freud also maintained discreet fascination with the uncanny and allied topics" (p. 224).

25. Freud, 1920a; Freud, 1923.

26. Freud, 1920.

27. Kohut, *How Does Analysis Cure?,* 25, emphasis added.

4. FREUD, JUNG, AND THE RETURN
OF THE OCCULT

1. See H. Trevor-Roper, *The Crisis of the Seventeenth Century* (New York: Harper & Row, 1967).

2. William James, *The Varieties of Religious Experience* (New York: Collier Books, 1902).

3. Henry Miller, *Reflections* (Santa Barbara, Calif.: Capra Press, 1981), 30–31.

4. A. Porter, "Giuseppe Verdi," in *The New Grove Dictionary of Music and Musicians,* ed. Stanley Slade (London: Macmillan & Co., 1980), 19:637.

5. Ibid., 637.

6. Ibid.

7. Freud, 1933a.

8. Freud, 1933a, p. 159.

9. Freud, 1933a, p. 160.

10. Freud, 1927c; Freud, 1939a.

11. Freud, 1933a, p. 160.

12. Freud, 1921c. See also G. Zilboorg, *Freud and Religion* (Westminster, Md.: Neuman Press, 1958); and W. W. Meissner, *Psychoanalysis and Religious Experience* (New Haven: Yale University Press, 1984), chap. 2.

13. Volney P. Gay, "Against Wholeness: The Ego's Complicity in Religion," *Journal of the American Academy of Religion* 47:539–55.

14. Ernest Jones, *The Life and Work of Sigmund Freud,* 3 vols. (New York: Basic Books, 1953–57).

15. See the chap. entitled "Occultism" in ibid., vol. 3.

16. Freud's writings upon the occult extend from his early comments (1901b), through his middle period (1919h), and into the last epoch of his work. Like his fascination for religion, Freud's interest in the occult never waned. Nor did it evaporate upon the completion of his self-analysis. Indeed, toward the end of his life Freud seems to have dropped his official reserve toward occult claims. He does not align psychoanalysis with occult disciplines. But he does not rule out the possibility that their theories might be valid. See, i.e., his papers on telepathy (1941d, 1922a) and on dreams and the occult (1925i, 1933a, [lecture XXX], 1941c). See also Strachey's discussion of these papers in Freud, *Standard Edition,* 18:175–76, 196.

17. Jones, *Life and Work,* 3:385.

18. See ibid., 3:378; and Freud, 1901b.

19. Jones, *Life and Work,* 3:379.

20. Ibid., 3:380.

21. Ibid., 1:99.

22. Augustine, *The Confessions,* trans. R. S. Pine-Coffin (London: Penguin Books, 1961), 197–98.

23. Jones, *Life and Work,* 1:139.

24. Ibid., 1:110.

25. Ibid., 1:110–11.

26. Ibid., 1:108.

27. See ibid., vol. 3; and Freud, 1901b.

28. Jones, *Life and Work,* 1:106, emphasis added.

29. Freud, 1901b, p. 261.

30. Freud, 1901b, p. 260.

31. Jones, *Life and Work,* 3:386.

32. Jung's basic concepts of individuation, synchronicity, and teleology are all linked to experiences that fall under a general heading of occult events. Jung asserts that mature, fully individuated persons will show an abundance of occult experiences, e.g., in which a person about whom they are thinking intensely suddenly appears. These synchronistic occurrences are to be expected and cherished by those who have gained insight into their own psychological depths. A fully individuated person will enjoy perceiving how inner events, like dreams and wishes, find correlates in outer events, like the discovery of a bird about which one has dreamed. Freud held to the opposite opinion. As persons mature they have fewer and fewer such experiences, (1919h).

33. Freud, 1919h.

34. Volney P. Gay, *Reading Jung: Science, Psychology and Religion* (Chico, Calif.: Scholars Press, 1984).

35. Carl Gustav Jung, *Memories, Dreams, Reflections* (New York: Random House, 1961). Quotations in chap. 4 are from this edition, which is cited as *MDR*.

36. W. Kelly, personal communication, 1985.

37. A. Goldberg, ed., *The Psychology of the Self: A Casebook* (New York: International Universities Press, 1978), 329.

38. Ibid., 304.

39. P. Homans, *Jung in Context: Modernity and the Making of a Psychology* (Chicago: University of Chicago Press, 1979), refers briefly to this dream and its central place in Jung's self-understanding. In fact, the general argument of Homans's volume parallels that set forth here. He too utilizes Kohut's formulations to analyze narcissistic aspects of Jung's character. We differ substantially in our emphasis. Homans uses *MDR* to locate Jung within a stream of modern thought. He focuses primarily upon the development of Jung's works, arranges them into four distinct phases, and is not concerned directly with Jung's lifelong fascination with the occult. John M. Gedo also discusses this dream in his major piece on the Freud-Jung correspondence. Gedo argues persuasively that each man required the other, first as profound friends, and then as profound enemies, "Magna est vis veritatis tuae et praevalebit," in *The Annual of Psychoanalysis* (Chicago: Chicago Institute for Psychoanalysis, 1979), 7:53–82. For additional discussion, see also Max Schur, *Freud: Living and Dying* (New York: International Universities Press, 1972); H. W. Loewald, "Transference and Countertransference: The Roots of Psychoanalysis," *Psychoanalytic Quarterly* 46 (1977): 514–27; and David W. Winnicott, review of *Memories, Dreams, Reflections* by Carl Gustav Jung, *International Journal of Psycho-Analysis* 45 (1964): 450–55.

40. Goldberg, ed., *Psychology of the Self: A Casebook*.

41. Ibid., 29.

42. Ibid., 31.

43. Ibid.

44. Ibid., 31–32.

45. Henri F. Ellenberger, *The Discovery of the Unconscious* (New York: Basic Books, 1970); Homans, *Jung in Context;* and Gedo, "Magna est vis veritatis tuae et praevalebit," have amplified these connections. See also Gay, *Reading Jung*, introduction.

5. JUNG'S OCCULT PSYCHOLOGY:
A SYNCHRONISTIC MOMENT

1. See Carl Gustav Jung, *Memories, Dreams, Reflections* (New York: Random House, 1961); idem, *Freud and Psychoanalysis*, vol. 4 of *The Collected Works of C. G. Jung* (Princeton: Princeton University Press, 1961); and Freud, 1914d, and others of Freud's works from that period.

2. Carl Gustav Jung, *Symbols of Transformation* (1912; New York: Moffat Yard & Co., 1916), originally translated as *Psychology of the Unconscious*, revised 1952.

3. Freud, 1914c.

4. Hans Loewald, "Transference and Countertransference: The Roots of Psychoanalysis," *Psychoanalytic Quarterly* 46 (1977): 516.

5. Ibid., 517.

6. W. McGuire, ed., *The Freud/Jung Letters: The Correspondence Between Sigmund Freud and C. G. Jung*, trans. R. Mannheim and R. F. C. Hull (Princeton: Princeton University Press, 1974). This book is cited as *Letters* in chap. 5.

7. Freud, 1907a.

8. Jung, *Memories, Dreams, Reflections*. This is cited as *MDR* in chap. 5.

9. See Augustine, *City of God* xviii.36; see also R. H. Charles, *The Apocrypha and Pseudepigrapha of the Old Testament* (Oxford: Oxford University Press, 1913), 32.

10. Max Schur, *Freud: Living and Dying* (New York: International Universities Press, 1972).

11. Ibid., 64–66.

12. Freud, 1950a (1895).

13. Schur, *Freud: Living and Dying*, 105.

14. Freud, 1936a; Ernest Jones, *The Life and Work of Sigmund Freud*, (New York: Basic Books, 1957), vol. 3.

15. Schur, *Freud: Living and Dying*, 225–30.

16. Freud, 1936a.

17. Schur, *Freud: Living and Dying*, 229.

18. Freud, 1936a, p. 243.

19. Freud, 1913f; 1930a; 1933a.

20. Jung, *Symbols of Transformation*.

21. *Hamlet*, act 5, scene 2, line 347.

22. Henri F. Ellenberger employs the concept of creative illness in his analysis of both Freud and Jung in his *The Discovery of the Unconscious* (New York: Basic Books, 1970).

23. Carl Gustav Jung, "On Synchronicity," in *The Portable Jung*, ed. Joseph Campbell (New York: Viking Press, 1952), 505, emphasis in original.

24. Ibid., 510.

25. Heinz Kohut, *How Does Analysis Cure?* (Chicago: University of Chicago Press, 1984).

26. Heinz Kohut, *The Analysis of the Self* (New York: International Universities Press, 1971), chap. 1.

27. Jung, "On Synchronicity," 511.

28. Ibid., 511–12.

29. Ibid., 513–14.

30. Ibid., 517–18.

31. A. Jaffe, *From the Life and Work of C. G. Jung* (New York: Harper & Row, 1971), 34.

32. Jacques Lacan, "Le Stade du Miroir comme formateur de la fonction du je," in *Ecrits* (1949; Paris: Editions du Seuil, 1966). See J. P. Muller and W. J. Richardson, *Lacan and Language: A Reader's Guide to Ecrits* (New York: International Universities Press, 1982), 26–41, for an excellent outline of Lacan's argument as formulated in the written text of 1949. This is the text that David W. Winnicott quotes in his comments on mirroring in his famous paper on transitional objects, "Transitional Objects and Transitional Phenomena," *International Journal of Psycho-Analysis* 34 (1953): 89–97. See also J. Mehlman, ed., *The French Freud*, Yale French Studies 48 (New Haven: Yale University Press, 1972); E. Bär, *Semiotic Approaches to Psychotherapy* (Bloomington: Indiana University Press, 1975); and Jacques Lacan, *Speech and Language in Psychoanalysis*, trans. A. Wilden (Baltimore: Johns Hopkins University Press, 1968).

33. Freud, 1923b.

34. Muller and Richardson, *Lacan and Language*, 30.

35. Ibid., 31–32.

36. Freud, 1917e.

37. Freud, 1917e, p. 246.

38. Freud, 1917e, p. 246.

39. D. Keene, *Four Major Plays of Chikamatsu* (New York: Columbia University Press, 1961).

40. Ibid., 29 n. 31.

41. Junichiro Tanizaki, *Some Prefer Nettles*, trans. E. G. Seidensticker (Tokyo: Tuttle, 1955), 107.

42. J. D. Salinger, *Franny and Zooey* (Boston: Little, Brown & Co., 1955), 92.

43. Lewis Carroll, *Through the Looking Glass, and What Alice Found There* (London: Macmillan & Co., 1871).

44. Freud, 1919h.

45. Winnicott, "Transitional Objects and Transitional Phenomena," 89.

46. Ibid., 91.

47. Paul Pruyser, *Between Belief and Unbelief* (New York: Harper & Row, 1974), 111.

48. Winnicott, "Transitional Objects and Transitional Phenomena," 95, emphasis in original.

49. Ibid., 95, emphasis in original.

50. Erik Erikson's conception of "mutuality" as explained in his *Childhood and Society*, 2d ed. (New York: W.W. Norton, 1963), is pertinent to Winnicott's notion. Both conceptions delineate a shared area of human experiencing in which fundamental patterns of ego development are laid down. Both assert that the nursing pair is paradigmatic of later love relationships. Failure in either dimension produces ego impairment and even more serious problems, e.g., Winnicott's analysis of his schizoid patients typically involves an assessment of their early

failure to establish successful relationships to transitional objects (see David W. Winnicott, *Playing and Reality* [London: Tavistock Publications, 1971], chap. 6).

Transitional objects may be libidinized and so subject to the array of neurotic distortions. But they need not be. Winnicott distinguishes normal development with such objects and the etiology of fetishism. Winnicott's early championing of an essentially nonlibidinal theory of ego development makes him a forerunner of Kohut, among other contemporary theorists. In his major contributions to the theory of narcissism (see Kohut, *Analysis of the Self;* and idem, *The Restoration of the Self* [New York: International Universities Press, 1977]), Kohut notes that what he calls the idealized parental imago (*Analysis of the Self,* 32–33) is continuous with transitional objects. Like Winnicott, Kohut holds that one can (must) conceive of the development of self-feelings (narcissistic stages) apart from—though not in opposition to—libidinal development.

It would not be accurate to say that Winnicott's notion of the transitional object parallels exactly Kohut's basic theorem about self and selfobject relationships. Each man developed his point of view from within a specific intellectual milieu and with reference to a particular patient population. Kohut began his career as an exponent and teacher of classical ego psychology with little reference to the so-called English school of Melanie Klein and W. R. D. Fairbairn. He worked primarily with high-level adult patients. Winnicott began as a pediatrician, then studied with many major figures in the English school, and treated very sick children as well as very sick adults.

In addition, their two concepts, transitional object and selfobject, are distinct. Most important is that Winnicott refers to an actual *thing* that the child invests with importance, e.g., the favorite comforter. In contrast, Kohut refers to a human relationship between *persons,* in which we invest the other with a fundamental task of doing for us what we cannot do for ourselves. These tasks, what Kohut termed selfobject functions, include the maintenance of self-esteem, the regulation of inner tensions, and similar crucial tasks of self-repair.

6. THE OCCULT MOOD AND
ITS RESOLUTION

1. Arthur Conan Doyle, *The History of Spiritualism* (New York: George H. Doran, 1926), 2:94.

2. Bertram D. Lewin, *The Psychoanalysis of Elation* (New York: W.W. Norton, 1950), 181.

3. Ibid.

4. See Christopher Bollas, "Character: The Language of the Self," *International Journal of Psychoanalytic Psychotherapy* 3 (1974): 398–418; idem, "The Transformational Object," *International Journal of Psycho-Analysis* 60 (1979): 97–107; idem, "On the Relation to the Self as an Object," *International Journal of Psycho-Analysis* 63 (1982): 347–59; idem, "Expressive Uses of Countertransference," *Contemporary Psychoanalysis* 19 (1983): 1–34; idem, "Moods and the Conservative Process," *International Journal of Psycho-Analysis* 65 (1984): 203–12.

5. Bollas, "Moods and the Conservative Process," 203.

6. Ibid.

7. Ibid., 204.

8. Ibid.

9. Johann Wolfgang von Goethe, *Truth and Fiction*, trans. John Oxenford, Weimar edition, n.d. Quotations in chap. 6 are from this edition, which is cited as *Truth and Fiction*. The German title is *Dichtung und Warheit*, which can be rendered into English as either *Fiction and Truth* or *Poetry and Truth*.

10. See Freud, 1917b; T. Reik, *Fragment of a Great Confession: A Psychoanalytic Autobiography* (New York: Farrar, Straus & Giroux, 1949); and Kurt Eissler, "Tentative Notes on the Psychology of Genius," in *Goethe: A Psychoanalytic Study*, 2 vols. (Detroit: Wayne State University Press, 1963).

11. Martin Buber, *I and Thou*, trans. W. Kaufmann (1957; New York: Charles Scribner's Sons, 1970).

12. Johann Wolfgang von Goethe, *The Sufferings of Young Werther*, trans. Harry Steinhauer (1774; New York: W.W. Norton, 1970), 102–3.

13. Heinz Kohut, *The Analysis of the Self* (New York: International Universities Press, 1971).

14. Regarding the visit to Dresden and the importance of art itself, see *Truth and Fiction*, 1:234ff.: "One must be a young man to render present to one's self the effect Lessing's 'Laocoon' produced upon us, by transporting us out of the region of scanty perceptions into the open fields of thought." The entire passage constitutes Goethe's romantic manifesto and response to dreary (Christian) visions of life: "The ancients had recognized death as the brother of sleep . . ." (1:343).

15. Carl Gustav Jung, *Memories, Dreams, Reflections* (New York: Random House, 1961).

16. See Eissler, "Tentative Notes on the Psychology of Genius"; see also O. Rank, *The Don Juan Legend*, ed. and trans. David G. Winter (1924; Princeton: Princeton University Press, 1975).

17. Reik, *Fragment of a Great Confession*.

18. Freud attempted a similar feat in his interpretation of Michelangelo's statue of Moses (see Freud, 1914b).

19. Carl Gustav Jung, *Symbols of Transformation*, originally translated as *Psychology of the Unconscious*, rev. 1952 (New York: Moffat Yard & Co., 1916).

20. Heinz Kohut, *The Search for the Self*, 2 vols. (New York: International Universities Press, 1978), 744–45.

21. M. Palencia-Roth, "Cannibalism and the New Man of Latin America in the 15th and 16th Century European Imagination," *Comparative Civilization Review* 12 (1985): 1–27.

22. Goethe, *Sufferings of Young Werther*, 101–3.

23. J. Z. Smith, *The Map Is Not the Territory: Studies in the History of Religion* (Leiden: E.J. Brill, 1978).

7. ALTERNATIVE SOLUTIONS TO
FRAGMENTATION ANXIETY

1. Johann Wolfgang von Goethe, *The Sufferings of Young Werther*, trans. Harry Steinhauer (1774; New York: W.W. Norton, 1970).

2. Carl Gustav Jung, *Memories, Dreams, Reflections* (New York: Random House, 1961).

3. Martin Buber, *I and Thou*, trans. W. Kaufmann (1957; New York: George H. Doran, 1926).

4. Arthur Conan Doyle, *The History of Spiritualism* (New York: George H. Doran, 1926).

5. I am grateful to Hans A. Thorner, "On Repetition: Its Relationship to the Depressive Position," *International Journal of Psycho-Analysis* 66 (1985): 231–36, for mentioning this poem. Thorner, in turn, refers to E. Blum, "Betrachtungen über das Problem der Wiederholung," *Confina Psychiatrica* 7 (1964): 197–215. R. Gray, *Poems of Goethe* (Cambridge: Cambridge University Press, 1966), suggests that the last verse is directly about the self, "a secure recess of indestructible selfhood" (p. 183). See also M. Swales, ed., *Goethe: Selected Poems* (London: Oxford University Press, 1975), 153–55; and C. Eastman, *Goethe's Poems* (New York: F.S. Crofts, 1941), 205–6.

6. Among major works on Keats are Charles Clarke and Mary Cowden Clarke, *Recollections of Writers* (1878); C. Aiken, "John Keats," *The Dial*, June 1925; James Ralston Caldwell, *John Keats' Fancy: The Effect of Keats on the Psychology of His Day* (Ithaca, N.Y.: Cornell University Press, 1945); Lionel Trilling, *The Selected Letters of John Keats* (New York: Farrar, Straus & Young, 1951); Kenneth Muir et al., *Keats: A Reassessment* (Liverpool: University Press of Liverpool, 1958); Aileen Ward, *John Keats: The Making of a Poet* (New York: Viking Press, 1963); Harold Bloom, *The Visionary Company: A Reading of English Romantic Poetry* (New York: Doubleday Anchor Books, 1963); Walter Jackson Bate, *John Keats* (Cambridge: Harvard University Press, 1964); Walter Jackson Bate, ed., *Keats: A Collection of Critical Essays* (Englewood Cliffs, N.J.: Prentice-Hall, 1964); and Ian Jack, *Keats and the Mirror of Art* (Oxford: Clarendon Press, 1967). One cannot explain supreme artistic achievements as the product of regression alone. Water does not run uphill; randomness does not generate pattern, and complex aesthetic and intellectual puzzles cannot solve themselves. Psychoanalytic criticism of Keats has overlooked this important truth. It has illuminated the conflictual sources of his suffering but has not shown how his poetry overcame them.

7. For from sleep one may awaken; just as from death one may wake into a dream from which one cannot escape, as Hamlet said. L. N. Jeffrey, "A Freudian Reading of Keats's *Ode to Psyche*," *Psychoanalytic Review* 55 (1968): 289–306, emphasizes how Keats linked mysterious women with death itself. This is clear in Keats's visionary poems, *La Belle Dame Sans Merci, The Eve of St. Agnes, Ode to Psyche,* and *Bright Star,* as well as in many portions of the long poems. The critic and psychologist Andrew Brink has elaborated on this theme: Keats's extreme anxiety over his engagement to Fanny Brawne may have precipitated his rapid decline to tuberculosis. Keats's sonnet *Bright Star* has occasioned many fine and thoughtful readings; for a review see John Barnard, ed., *John Keats: The Complete Poems* (London: Penguin Books, 1973), 685–86, from which all citations of Keats's poetry in this chapter are taken. See also Brink's comments in his *Loss and Symbolic Repair: A Psychological Study of Some English Poets* (Hamilton, Ont.: Cromlech Press, 1977), 157–58.

8. See W. B. Ober, "Drowsed with the Fume of Poppies: Opium and John Keats," *Bulletin of the New York Academy of Medicine* 44 (1968): 862–80.

9. Freud, 1917e.

10. Bate, *John Keats*, 600.

11. Jack Stillinger, ed., *The Poems of John Keats* (Cambridge: Harvard University Press, 1978), 672 n.

12. Ward, *John Keats: The Making of a Poet*, 340.

13. Wallace Stevens, *The Necessary Angel* (New York: Alfred A. Knopf, 1951), 34–35.

14. See James Hamilton, "Object Loss, Dreaming and Creativity," *Psychoanalytic Study of the Child* 24 (1969): 488–531; Jeffrey, "Freudian Reading of Keats's *Ode to Psyche*"; and Brink, *Loss and Symbolic Repair*.

15. John Updike, *The Witches of Eastwick* (New York: Fawcett, 1984), 302.

16. Freud, 1917e.

17. Updike, *Witches of Eastwick*, 303, emphasis in original.

18. Ibid.

Index